THE TRAGIC PROTEST

ZYGMUNT ADAMCZEWSKI

THE TRAGIC PROTEST

THE HAGUE

MARTINUS NIJHOFF

1963

I wish to acknowledge here my debt of gratitude which can not be repaid:

To Montana State University, where this work has evolved from notes gathered for lectures I gave there under the title: "Philosophy in Literature"; and where it was generously supported by research grants for the purpose of preparing the manuscript –

To the following copyright holders who gave me the privilege of quoting:

Aeschylus' *Prometheus Bound* translated by G. Murray – George Allen & Unwin Ltd;

Sophocles' *Oedipus the King* translated by T. H. Banks – Oxford University Press;

Goethe's *Faust* translated by L. Macneice – Oxford University Press and Faber & Faber;

Ibsen's *An Enemy of the People* – Walter J. Black;

Miller's *Death of a Salesman* – The Viking Press;

Sartre's *The Flies* translated by S. Gilbert – Alfred A. Knopf Inc. and Hamish Hamilton Ltd;

Vercors' *The Insurgents* translated by R. Barisse – Harcourt, Brace & World Inc;

Camus' *The Fall* translated by J. O'Brien – Hamish Hamilton Ltd;

Beauvoir's *Les Bouches Inutiles* – Librairie Gallimard;

Dostoyevsky's *The Possessed* translated by C. Garnett – W. Heinemann Ltd and The Macmillan Co, N.Y.

To all those who awakened and modeled my reflections on the tragic theatre in existence, who impressed these – some from unknowing distance but some in personal ties – and without whom the present exploration could not have been attained: W. Tatarkiewicz, Theodor Erismann, H. Windischer, A. Lesky, C. E. M. Joad, R. L. Saw, James Gutmann, John Wild, Charles Morris, Henry Bugbee, also John Gielgud, Hans Hotter, Paul Muni and Jerzy Nowiak –

To the great man to whom this book is properly dedicated because from him I have – insofar as I have – learned to think:

MARTIN HEIDEGGER

Table of Contents

CHAPTER I

The Tragic - Introduction

From the chorus of god-drunken satyrs celebrating nature's mystic revival in the green Hellenic spring-time – to the thick blackness of arresting headlines stamped by the midnight presses: this is the long transformation of the word "tragic" through the history of the Western world. No wonder then that if someone proposes to deal with what is tragic, there is hardly any initial orientation about the trail his ideas are to follow. Will it be historical pursuit of formal growth of a genre in the literary arts? Or a nontemporal analysis of some few specific canons to rule all art? Will it be, quite differently, a psychology of misfortune, of common thirst for sensation, of the malaise in the present times? Or a flight toward some immutable values purchased only in suffering? Such treatments there have been in the hands of philosophers, historians, critics, linguists, journalists. Will "tragic" yield to an approach which does not try to emulate any of these? What way of access could this be and of what import?

On the following pages an attempt will be made to steer a definite course between two equally inviting strands, one being the territory of tragic art, the other the tragic provinces of life. That such a course should be possible, is clearly attested by the conception underlying everyday usage of the word "tragic." In this usage there may be a tie, more than derivatory, to the stage or to literature; but there need not be. And this usage surely corresponds to something, if word is any more than noise. What is a man's intent, when the word "tragic" appears on his lips? Is it no more than a reference to spectacles he may see, read about, experience, or is it of some inner concern, too? Such a question, if it can be properly put, definitely transcends the field of linguistic analysis of meaning of a particular word. It is not the semantics of the word "tragic" but rather what it may open a view of, that will be unveiled here, if the attempt succeeds.

There is a deeper justification of the proposed sense of exploration. That is embedded in a primitive condition of the human mind, naive and unspoiled yet by the grooves of criterion setters. It is easily forgotten in the usual, only too adult adjustment, and may be invoked through fairy tales which serious people spare no time for. That stage of mind is one where the awesome question of reality is neither raised nor settled. Can it be true that man so lightly outgrows his childish faith in dragons, nymphs, and magicians, thereafter knowing that these are not real? Can it be true that dragon-slaying, nymph-adoration, magical conquests, are no constituents of an adjusted, mature person's life? Can it be true that all people, after a certain age, know perfectly well what is real and what is not, that those who try and often fail to pin down this distinction are just yielding to aberration? Or is it not more likely that ordinary assumption of criteria for reality results not from reasoned conviction but from tired inadequacy, that it is undertaken provisionally and with limited scope, that it is promptly discarded not only in lunacy, not only in nightly desires, but wherever daily pursuits seem not to thrive on it? If this be so, then this primitive conscious vision lies close at hand; where one need not ask if what is there for him is there for anybody else, where one's courage draws on one's own illusions, where what may be seen as well as what is seen is up to one's choice. This kind of mental expression is open, even if surreptitiously, to the most hard-boiled character, since it is due to what is more indubitably present in all humanity than soul, will, or reason: imagination. It is to this imaginative consciousness that appeal must be made, when fact and fiction are to be harnessed together, not because a distinction between them is wanting, but because it is not wanted. And that is precisely the case when entities of creative art are to be treated as though they belonged to real life or when life is to trust the mirror of art without reservation. That is the case in the exploration of what is tragic.

It may seem to follow that "tragic" is not a category of rational order but only a mold of human imagination. This in a way is true, but in what way precisely, that cannot be said at this stage. Even the strength of "only" would be now tending toward misinterpretation, not to speak of more obscure matters. These may come into light later, but not before some lamps are lit. With introductory words anticipations only may be gathered or discarded.

One of the latter is aesthetic, in the popular sense of the word. That is, what has been said already says that no anticipations of aesthetic theory are in place here. When research stays on the level of primitive imagination, prior to the distinction between real and unreal, to merge art with life, it cannot serve as guideline for thoughts on what is distinctive within art. No canons of composition can be forthcoming, even the very concept of composition, implying a composer, must remain inadmissible; since, unlike the one of tragic art, the composer of tragic life will be here in question. No analysis of form need be expected, and when a form of vision is described, it will not be what artistic critics are used to dissect. Purely aesthetic instruments, such as plot, contrast, harmony, proper pitch, likeness, recognition, completeness, will be of no use and no relevance at all. And it hardly need be mentioned that the age-fortified classification of artistic kinds remains strictly out of bounds.

Here is perhaps the proper place to introduce a stylistic apology. It is clear to everyone with a neat sense of seemliness in language that the use of unattached adjectives is very awkward in English. No one reading these paragraphs can be blamed for fidgeting when molested again and again with "the tragic" instead of "tragedy." The excuse has perhaps transpired in the preceding passage. It may not yet be apparent what the pages to follow will be about, but it should be more than apparent that they will not be about tragedy, understood as a literary composition, capable of performance in a theatre, preferably in language embellished by versification, and comprising a beginning, a middle, and an end. On later pages perhaps the word "tragedy" will turn up; but if so, this term will not be the noun from which the adjective "tragic" derives, but rather it will be a noun obtained from, and depending for its sense on, that adjective the sense of which is still to be elucidated. Thus no relief for a linguistic purist can be promised until the operations on "tragic" are joined with those involving the noun it is to qualify. That noun will be "protest."

If the word "tragic" is not to be associated with a spectacle, not to be used as an aesthetic conception of form, then a very irritating problem can be avoided. It is the problem which scores of serious questioners have left unresolved, the problem concerning the source of tragic beauty. What is it that men enjoy in viewing a tragic spectacle? How is such enjoyment possible and in what terms could it be justified? In a great many cases the commitment to such questions suggests a feeling of guilt, a moral perplexity on the part of the questioner who misleadingly pretends to be asking about a purely aesthetic value. But even where this search for absolution from guilt is not satisfied, another absolution has already taken place: that of the viewer from the viewed. What is tragic is then to be found only among the objects exposed to the supposedly separate subject who does not partake in it. What is tragic is then not his, though he may claim possession of its beauty; it remains but a spectacle. This aesthetic absolution of man from the tragic may indeed be what prevents him from its deeper understanding. To resolve the tragic essence may be possible not for the man who absolves himself from it as enjoyment and environment but rather for someone whose existence is involved, surrounded, and penetrated by it. To the existence of such men imaginative access will be attempted here.

Not only does the view of a mere spectacle bar thorough penetration into its being tragic, it also lightly entices toward conceptual misdirection. This is due to the colloquial near-equivalence of some allied conceptions. In very many contexts, aesthetic, journalistic, conversational, where the word "tragic" occurs, the word "dramatic" could be used instead, this in turn could be replaced by "eventful," and that perhaps even by "exciting." That ordinary discourse of ordinary people pliantly fuses some kin of ideas, is neither objectionable nor avoidable. But kinship is far from identity. The exploration of the tragic must not be burdened by extraneous and haphazard fusions of meaning. Some preventive disentanglement is required, and it should also serve to eliminate other feasible misconceptions about the lines of approach to follow.

In their historical roots lodged in the soil of Greek artistic creation, the tragic and the dramatic are certainly related. Tragic poetry actually constitutes only a species of the dramatic genus whose other species is comic. Thus even a very superficial glance makes clear that what is dramatic need not be tragic, as long as mere spectacle is in question. Divorced from this original aesthetic application the concepts still carry that divergence. Yet out of the theatre the logical subordination no longer holds. If it did, one could not think of anything tragic which is not dramatic. Can that be done or not? To answer that, less superficial considerations must be introduced.

What is dramatic in present human life and thought remains more close and faithful to its artistic roots than what is tragic; or, to put it differently, the word roots of the tragic go deeper into the matter of existence while those of the dramatic remain in the more shallow layers of form. Dramatic political announcements are made, dramatic developments occur in scientific or economic affairs, there are dramatic moments in sports, dramatic effects in interior decoration, dramatic clashes of personalities. Of what significance is the dramatic in all those situations? Its import can be brought without remainder into the expression: it is like a drama. In other words, the force, the tension, the surprise referred to in such contexts are imitatively compared to force, tension, surprise effected in a satisfactory theatrical spectacle. Why is there any forceful impact on sensibility? What factors build up the tension? How enjoyable or unenjoyable is the surprise? Such persistent material questions do not have to be answered nor asked. It is only the form of experience, in life as well as in art, that qualifies it as dramatic. And life is here the copyist, providing only the reflected shine of effects that genuinely belong to art. In such a transference of dramatic effects into life no one seriously questions the applicability of the concept: using the term is here no presumption. What is the corresponding situation in regard to the tragic? One may be tempted to think that this term is also legitimately used to express the feeling of life's being like a tragedy. But where is it used thus? One speaks of tragic misfortunes, sufferings, intentions, describing the experiences of certain persons, and naturally in such descriptions a resemblance is pointed out to what may be expectably found in a tragic spectacle. Yet there is a difference. When the term "tragic" is genuinely proper in life, to think of artificial imitation, of contrivance, of formal theatrical effects, is absurd and brutal. Here there is no reflected shine from artistic creation. Life is never just "like" a tragedy; it is either, as well as art may be, tragic, or else a pretense at tragedy. Hence the propriety of application of the term must be subject to much more care than is the case with the term "dramatic." It cannot be questioned that "tragic" is often used loosely and frivolously; the point is that such uses can be questioned and exposed as fraud. And to decide that, one needs no comparisons with the theatre. On the other hand, one does need support of dramatic art experienced to discover that life is also dramatic. The relation of likeness which has a univocal direction in the dramatic, originating from the stage, is ambivalent for the tragic. And this is the reason why the legitimacy of use of dramatic conceptions outside the realm of art depends mainly on formal aesthetic criteria, while on the contrary human life cannot be tragic due to form only. The question of what makes for the tragic content of existence in this instance or that is never irrelevant.

If, unlike the source of the dramatic, the source of the tragic is not found in that art which coined both words, from whence can it be traced? This very understandable query again clearly anticipates the progress of the present enquiry into what is tragic. The preceding contrast was intended for the time being only to provide some sense for the distinction of what may be tragic without being dramatic. This can now be supplied. Contents of everyday life of humanity become tragic owing to the presence of that trait in existence – still nameless – which also inspired Greek poets in their creation of tragedy, but which is independent of that creation and thus need not be dramatic. To illustrate this abstract formulation a little more specifically: forceful, surprising impact of tension was stressed earlier as the formal effect of what is dramatic in life. It is not hard imaginatively to produce situations of man which could be found tragic but which would lack such effect entirely. Are empty monotony, enfeebling failure, foreseen disintegration, not conceivable as tragic? Yet they are in opposition to those dramatic effects of surprise, force, tension, and would hardly fit as proper formal ingredients for what is to grip thoroughly a first night audience. What, if anything, makes them tragic, is not an aesthetic criterion of drama. This fact strengthens the sense of approaching what is tragic on a level below the distinction between "solid" reality and "mere" artistic composition.

Their relation to art by no means exhausts the contrast between the tragic and the dramatic. This can be seen further by observing the point of contact between "dramatic" and "eventful." If in certain contexts these terms are interchangeable it is because, strictly speaking, only events can be dramatic. When reference is made to a dramatic character or picture, the license of such linguistic spread rests upon the possibility of understanding such a character as responsible for certain overt activities, or such a picture as evoking certain consecutive experiences. It is these activities or experiences that may be dramatic, and they are events. Does this suggest a complete equivalence of scope between "dramatic" and "eventful"? Yes and no. The answer hinges upon an ambiguity of the word "eventful." It can be taken as, for one thing, containing or composed of events. In this sense the lives of all men without exception are equally eventful; yet no one would say they are equally dramatic. The other sense is more elusive. Events happen to everybody: in a very exact comparison the whirlwind of an adventurer and the plodding pilgrimage of a humdrum homebody equally wander inmidst of spatiotemporal changes, concords and conflicts, apparitions and abolitions. And yet, days on which literally something happens all the time many people would not gladly find eventful. What is their further demand? What do they miss? Vaguely they could name the absent as something "exciting." But this could be a very vacuous and mutable reference. If life which is full of events is yet not eventful, is it not proper to conclude that what is there missed is not the presence and quantity of events but their quality and pattern? In other words, not that things happen – this wish must always be satisfied – but how things happen? If they produce no forceful impact, if there is never a surprise waiting, if inner resources are not aroused into tension, then life is not eventful. And that means it is not like a drama.

But what is the weight of the exclusion implied in saying that only events, if not all events, are dramatic? There is after all the world-view which, more or less disguised, predominates today, according to which there is nothing but events, processes, occurrences of space and time. If this is right, then to say that only these can be dramatic would be a senseless redundancy. To combat this complex world-view generally is in this place impossible. Perhaps a breach into its fortified safety can be effected by concentrating on the limitations of the concept of events. The English word "event" descends from Latin origins and tells in Anglo-Saxon terms as much as "that which comes out" or "outcome." This root by no means indicates self-dependence or self-completeness, since questions arise: comes out of where? outcome of what? The world constructed of sheer exits without entries or that to which any entry or exit appertains reminds one of the grin without the cat. However, etymology is not a complete theory of meaning, and so it may be said that this root of the word "event" is no more than accidental. But what more is in the concept? To avoid the appearance of overstressing one particular word of one particular language, it may be asked what word other peoples use to think of the same concept. The French "événement" will not help much because of its identical origin. But the German "Ereignis" adds light, saying roughly "that which may be appropriated"; and the Polish "wyda-rzenie" suggests even more: "the outflow of gifts or endowments." It can hardly be the long arm of coincidence stretching over the Romance, Germanic, and Slavic modes of speaking of events, es-pecially since the suggestions are not identical as though all deriving from one root. Yet they are alike. There is a common thinking way leading to that out of which events come into awareness, that which harbors them before they are appropriated by man, that which endows his life with gifts. The reference must be kept indeterminate, since even to say "something" may already be saying too much. But if speech is not entirely arbitrary, if it stems from some primordial and immediate sense of existence, then it can be safely said that what is thought in the concept of events is not all there is, that it must be thought in correlation and not as an all-filling sufficient category. What the notion of events must be correlated with as their source remains as yet entirely dark. A less obscure consideration resulting from the preceding observations concerns what may be called the recipients of events. Are men events? When analyzed by methods of science, physics, biology, psychology even, and when consistently regarded as no more than what such scientific dissection may show of them, the answer is likely to be positive. Each man is then reduced to a set of results of examinations, observations, experiments: a series of events. And here the previous situation reappears. Are not these results again only outcomes related to what comes out in them? Will one not expect that there is always more in the human being beyond what already shows itself in scientific observations? More and more to be drawn upon in future ones? Every science avowedly, ostentatiously sets its own limits for the sake of method and the events which it then can register must lie within those limits; and what of that which lies beyond that limitation? To disregard such residues would be to claim for science an impossible divine completeness. Moreover, this scientific treatment, however complete, concerns by hypothesis only men observed. But they are not what the question was raised about. It asked about men as recipients of events, and so men observing. If the above difficulties arise in the way of regarding men observed as no more than events, it must be so much more hazardous to extend this thesis to men as observers of events. Science is as notoriously helpless here as to yield the field to poetry. What pertains to his own existence as he lives it each man is willing to hold more poetically than scientifically, relying less on mathematics than on imagination.

About the human being then this conclusion is not entirely baseless: that there is more in him or of him than shows in events. To sharpen this point, it is advisable to think of character. Even observed from outside, character is more properly understood as that which issues in certain events as symptoms, clues toward analysis, behavioral manifestations, rather than merely as their sum total. But when thought of not from outside but as his own, no man will readily admit his character to be no more than the public ensemble of events which can be appropriated in observation by others. Such an admission would annihilate all that he properly owns, would suspend him over an abyss of nothingness – if not hurl himself down there.

It is time to take up the thread of pursuit of the tragic. Actually it has never been left far behind. The seemingly random excursions after other ideas have been controlled in the aim of deepening the gulf between the tragic and the dramatic. Their contrast can now be viewed far from the criteria of artistic composition and form, on the ground itself of human existence. The term "dramatic" has a legitimate family resemblance to "eventful," since one whole line of its descendance goes there. This line was pursued now. The art of the drama is understood as creation or mimesis of events to which it owes its imaginative pattern. But beyond or underneath the sphere of events over which the arch of potential dramatic power is spanned, there is a domain less accessible, harder to name, more elusive to precision method, and in this domain man has his own stake. From there wells up the tragic.

Some events are tragic. To this is due the other-sided kinship of the word "dramatic." Tragic events can be sudden, striking, overwhelming, adapted to the dramatic pattern. But these features would not suffice to qualify any event as genuinely tragic. Here indeed is room for pretense and hypocrisy, for loose and bombastic speech. Under a critical eye it turns out that no event is tragic just as an event. Death may be a relief, injury may be self-induced, natural cataclysm thrilling, torture enjoyed, ruin and devastation according to plan, broken love a pretext for vengeance, exile emancipation. There is no warrant for finding events tragic without disclosing who or what is involved in them. The tragic essence is not openly displayed in the sphere of events. What makes an event tragic must be sought from where it is no more than an outcome.

Common speech is witness that not only events are tragic, that "tragic" is well linked with a person, a choice, a vision or truth. And these are tragic not by license or metaphor, as is the case with "dramatic." More is significant: they can be tragic without reference to a specific series of events. Whoever accepts this fact, needs no further demonstration of the independent source of the tragic beyond the sphere of events; and who has a doubt about it, will have to weigh it in the scales of examples to follow.

How much has this explication accomplished? At best it has brought into relief the sense of examining the tragic not on the aesthetic surface, not in the formal dimensions of drama, not even in the sphere of public events. It may have justified some such pseudo-socratic statement as that the goal of this rightly understood exploration lies not in what is composed as tragedy, nor in what appears as tragic, nor in what tragically happens, but in WHAT IS TRAGIC.

But this result does not shine any clearer than as an eliminative negation. Some positive lighting is overdue.

If it is right to say that man observing is not exhausted in the events he observes and that certain events can acquire tragic color for him because of what he is as an observer, then I have reason to assume the possibility of a TRAGIC VISION of the world. The ambiguous word "vision" must be here understood as comprising not what is seen – since this could be no more than events – but how it is seen; a mode of observing rather than the observed field. What happens then to the observer happens tragically, if the observer sees it to be tragic. This possibility of tragic vision is introduced, it may be noted, in contrast to the impossibility of dramatic vision. The latter is impossible in the sense contemplated here, if the dramatic belongs wholly to the sphere of events, if it is a pattern of what is seen, perhaps even an arranged pattern, but not a way of seeing. To put it otherwise, there is no such thing as dramatic truth, but only truth presented or appearing dramatically. On the other hand, truth which is distinctly and genuinely tragic, truth in which content and not just form is tragic, truth which is displayed only to those whose vision is tragic, is a prospect not to be dismissed. What the content of such tragic truth may be, will have to be examined.

This prospect, however, must be entertained within its limitations. The impression can now arise as though the tragic could provide some specific intelligence to be regarded as pure theory, even containing the germ of a separate science, the science of the tragic. The words readily betray absurdity. Why? Because pure theory, especially solidified into science, is an abstraction concerned with the observed and not the observing, aiming at truth and consciously disregarding whose truth it may be. This abstraction bifurcating man's life into theoretical and practical would be completely unwarranted here. Nothing has been asserted here about the independence of theory of the observed from practical activity of the observing. On the contrary, both events as seen and vision as the act of seeing are to be taken in correlation with there being someone to see. No matter what the advantage or disadvantage, tragic vision may not be cut off into pure observation, if the tragic human being is not to be abstracted into a pure observer. And if he were, nothing tragic would ever happen to him.

Is there not a significant difference between what happens and what happens to you? From the angle of scientific theory there is none, since you are only X, Y, or Z, you only happen to be; what happens is reported by any one amongst many people who happen to see it. But for you who are for yourself neither a scientist nor a scientific event, the difference is there. For one thing, if something happens to you, you see it. Yet this is only a fraction of your involvement in it. You are yourself, before, and while, and after it happens: you are more than an element in what happens. Despite that, you are by no means indifferent to what happens. You after are no longer just what you were before, you bear a new stamp within. And this not merely in the sense of symptomatic causal aftereffects, as when you suffer periodic headaches in consequence of war concussion; of these, none need be in evidence. Still, though not obviously affected, you are forever the man to whom this happened, even if you make yourself forget it; especially then, if psychology is to be trusted. Can you say: it just happened to happen to me? Often you try, dissociating yourself from any intimacy with what happened. Sometimes you cannot, sometimes you must recognize that some happenings could not happen to every X, Y, and Z, while they do happen to you. You partake of them, they belong to you. In this intimacy is your role a purely passive one of a recipient? You are impressed and stamped by the events which happen to you; do you not put your impress and stamp upon them? Could they intimately belong to you if you did not? As on a former occasion, look at the model of unspoiled childish experience. A peculiarly interesting trifle, a skill self-acquired, a discovery made; these are claimed by a child as "mine," guarded and envied, before it has any conception of what possession signifies in the adult world, with what values and joys it is tied – witness such childish boasts and claims with regard to hurts, misadventures, material losses, even family bereavements. Is there no such tendency toward appropriation of happenings in the mature human being? From what other root derive pursuits of glory even distorted into herostratism, economic necessities of competition and regulation of legal property, even all jealous longings for privacy on which society has been built? It would seem impossible to describe a human being not appropriating what happens to him, not claiming events in his existence as his own. Such claims need not be open, often their precious nature consists in silence; nor need they be devoid of selection and extend indiscriminately over the whole lifetime. But the tendency, the reaching out, the grasping with or without merit and sometimes ruthless though seemingly virtuous – this is a human heritage. Whoever you are, what you live in, through, and amongst, you want to call your own, you try to mold to your demands, you strain through your receptivity, you see by your own vision. What happens to you is thus yours by right of capture; and this as much in pain and defeat as in world triumph. As you live, you are indeed much more, or less, than a contemplative observer. But this does not yet touch the question of how some things must happen just to you.

The vision of the human being, in some instances possibly tragic, can thus never without distortion be treated as purely theoretical. To see events is to make them one's own. To observe what happens while one exists is to blaze a trail around and to be branded ineradicably in one's own fire. There is a word in the ordinary English language which in its familiarity obscures precisely such suggestions contained in its Greek roots. "Character" means originally a distinctive stamp, impress or brand, and also that which does the stamping, impressing or branding. I wish to use the preceding considerations precisely to evoke afresh this Hellenic flavor of what is taken today for granted. They are variations on this obvious theme that to be human is to have a character. The tragic vision now becomes an issue of the TRAGIC CHARACTER in men. It was suggested earlier that what is tragic will not be most successfully opened in terms of an outside alien spectacle but rather as a penetrating involvement. Now it may be a little clearer how inevitable that involvement is, if there is to be any human tragic character.

The ambivalence of the notion of character with regard to passivity and activity, its brand and its branding, points to another problem which is particularly drastic in reference to the tragic character. It is the problem of determined necessity which in aesthetic discussions of tragedy usually assumes the expression of tragic inevitability. With regard to just form and composition in art it may seem relatively simple. What impresses the spectator as somehow inevitable in a tragic play is, after all, only a matter of what its persons are made to do and say by the author in advancement of his plot. All the author has to do is to express convincingly the idea that such and no other adventures and actions properly must or should happen to people who would speak such words and make such gestures. And yet – this word: "properly" may give a pause to thought. Is it no more than the propriety of aesthetic criteria divorced from what is outside of art? Would the strength of such purely artificial and limited propriety be sufficiently impressive? Hardly. The borderline between fiction and fact, art and life must be again obliterated if the spectators are to be not only aesthetically titillated but really gripped in the sense of something properly inevitable. "Properly" must be derived not from norms of propriety but from needs of property. That means a reference to what is owned and owed, what belongs, what is intimately appropriated. And if appropriation is nothing but character in human existence, no wonder then that what properly happens, thus appearing inevitable, issues from character. It is not even a coincidence that in the watered down sense these words have in the idiom of the theatre the opposite of what is inevitable is said to be "out of character."

The aesthetic demand for inevitability from character in a tragedy does not resolve but passes onto the issues of life the problem mentioned: of determined necessity. It is not enough to say that each man's character appropriates and makes inevitable what is to happen to him and not to someone else. What must be asked further is: what makes character, what makes it such and no other, what makes it tragic? To this enquiry there are two alternative avenues of approach. One, in the Western world much more articulate, at least outwardly, is the faith of fate. It is the acceptance of destiny imposed from without, of being made by other hands, of subjection to what cannot be otherwise. It offers through history many shades and varieties, from a stoic submission to a more or less personified Moira, through a Christian beatific surrender to the absolute will of the omnipotent spirit, to a modern reliance on the universal order of scientific determinism. The other trend, just as persistent if less outspoken and rationalized, is the faith of freedom. It is the possibility of determination from one's own core of being, belief in making oneself in an exclusively human way, and more than just belief, the driving, striving struggle for its veri-fication in works beyond words. With the rational conception of order being indispensably one and the same for all in the world at large, the self-determining faith could not but appear in kinship with disorder, often as adversary to reason, thus non-logical, and if logic be the power of words, then unspoken. Yet it has never been sterilized out of existence.

These two movements of the human mind, which have been engaged in so many encounters, sometimes disjunctive as fire and water, sometimes commingled as the hot and the wet, have certainly common roots and aims. They move from man's reflection on his own being, its whence, where, and whither; they search for answers which would be final. They are both concerned with the wonder of anyone who thinks: why must this be there for me? In entirely different fashions they touch the problem of necessity which is the origin of man in one case, of which man is the origin in the other. That events are inevitable sometimes, and sometimes tragically so, for some characters, is neither proof nor denial of their determination, where only a single mode of determining is thought of. But perhaps there is a deep root notion from which both courses of human events may derive, both where man is determined and where he determines. To this notion I give the name of choice.

In most colloquial and many contemplative uses the word "choice" is restricted to acts of the mind, if not clearly supported or dictated by rational deliberations, then at least involving some organized consciousness such as the human kind. Yet there is the possibility, even the need, of thinking about choice with a more basic reference which if one could not sustain, one should not be able to understand conscious rational choices at all. The basic thought of choice refers to that which underlies every finite existent, which makes it this rather than that or that or that, which outlines the one from the many, which above all lets it be or not be. All creation, all transformation, as well as all destruction, rests in a choice. It may be naturally objected that this is anthropomorphic thinking, that knowledge of how the mind of man acts is here transferred illegitimately to regions which are neither of man nor even of the mind, as far as is known. Is this actually so? For one thing the knowledge invoked here is somewhat dubious. What do you know of how man's mind chooses? What thinker has defined it precisely, what writer has described it convincingly, what scientist has had laboratory success with it? On the other hand, can it be denied? What has been denied is only that choice for man could be not determined from outside and from before. To deny choice as such would be to see life as no more than make-believe, not to mention a conflict with fairly general convictions. What makes it impossible for anyone to dismiss choice entirely is the need to analyze life in terms of what led to a particular choice and also what resulted from it. Not only history but also physics would be rendered incoherent. And yet to be exact I must say that man knows even in his own life the circumstances, conditions and consequences of choice rather than choice itself. Thus what is transferred in thinking of choice in not exclusively human terms is not knowledge but some simplifying primitive belief. And then, is the direction of this transfer evident? Does not the human element lodge in precisely those circumstances, conditions and consequences of choice, which can be studied, rather than in choice itself? If this were so, there is nothing to prevent thinking of choice from starting not with man but with what makes man, one of many things, be. Such thinking can subsequently transfer the notion of choice into the human sphere and enquire what makes the popular, human dimension of choice, what makes a man a man, what makes this man not any other, what makes man choose thus rather than otherwise. Such basic thinking may also do justice to the mystifying fact just mentioned, that men have nothing like knowledge of choice even in their own life. This may be accounted for in the dark idea that human knowledge has to deal with only what is possibly in existence while choice is what all in existence presupposes already.

How is this notion related to what was previously discussed, the problem of necessary determination? The two approaches which were contraposed can now be said to be concerned with two separate aspects of choice in the life of man. The belief in universal destiny and order penetrating into whatever you feel and do and see concerns you in so far as you are chosen. The belief in your own power of creating, making yourself in your own way concerns you in so far as you choose. Whenever from choice there is any determining, there is something determined. The strife of the two movements mentioned is not about choice as the root of determination, it is about their opposed contentions, in one case that you as a man are always determined, in the other case that you are always determining. A clear decision between them is out of the question when mystery covers the notion of choice. When this notion is taken radically as underlying all in existence, it must exceed the human context of this strife with its restriction to the mind of man. Because if it be true that you are only chosen, not only you are chosen; and if it be true that it is you who choose, you do not choose all there is. In simpler words, choice would cease to be a term of human psychology and could be spoken of in connection with mating dogs and blossoming flowers as well as with tossed coins, falling stones and exploding suns. Naturally it would be an unwarranted jump to ascribe the power of choice to them; but then it may be equally a jump to vest that power in a man's mind.

Now it is possible to rephrase the problem in that phase of it which is of immediate concern. The result is this: what is inevitable is so because it is chosen. This expression is not intended to decide between the opposing contentions about man. Its mention of choice preserves the needed contingency. But it is intended to supply meaning, although an ambiguous meaning, to that inevitability which is tragic. What happens inevitably in your life depends on choice. It is left open, however, whether the choice has been made for you or left in your own hands. It is still true that what happens to you is a matter of your character, that what is yours is yours by appropriation, that what you may thus properly have is for you inevitable. All this, however, can now be interpreted as saying either; this must be there for you, because it is so chosen; or alternatively: this must be there for you because you do not choose otherwise. Your character which is your destiny is a matter of choice; is the choice yours? This is the big question left open now, but not abandoned.

Here is then the outlined trail of pursuit of the tragic. If it is correct to maintain that events by themselves are not genuinely tragic, the search of tragic essence must delve into the question how events are seen and received by man. This introduces a tragic vision. If it is correct to say that existing man is never just a theoretical observer, the vision must be deepened by an enquiry into what is proper to a man who sees life tragically. This introduces a tragic character. If it is correct to say that character inevitably determines the course and pressure and color of life, just as inevitably arises the problem of determining a character to be tragic. This introduces a TRAGIC CHOICE. If it is correct to think of choice basically as that from which any existence must issue, the enquiry into the tragic strikes against the foundations of all thought. This means that the source of man's tragic possibilities is his own disposition in the world he dwells in, his proper way to be, his ethos.

~

After the weighty, winding disquisitions of the preceding pages, it will be well to interpose a few preparatory and simpler notes on that concept which is to serve as guideline in the illumination of what is tragic. It is the concept of protest. Certainly premature would be an effort to display the tie which is to bind it to the conception of the tragic. The contents protested will be lit in the light of individual illustrations. What must be elaborated now, however, is the significance of the very concept. What is a "protest?" In most Western languages this word appears in similar shape, descended from the Latin origin. It means there an open witness for something or someone. What follows then immediately is that he who protests must bear witness seeing in his own way, standing directly connected with what is protested. This leads further. The protest is not simply an observation registered neutrally as though by a machine. It is at least to an extent an involvement, an interest, a degree of being affected. It must induce in the witness a public declaration, or an overt sign, or at least an inward response: some gesture of his own which, whether communicated or not, remains in his existence. A protest does not happen to happen to you, your character puts it forward. It is chosen.

This interpretation of protest is only too apparently led along the lines developed in the preceding discussion. Actually the main object here for the moment is that the concept of a protest should not be taken too lightly as signifying no more than a verbal expression like many others, nor should it be assigned semantically to some specific scientific vocabulary, as of jurisprudence, psychology, or social science. It may well belong to prescientific and presemantic origins.

There is, however, in the common understanding of the word "protest" another undeniable element which seems to be etymologically later. That is the special meaning of protest as witness of dissent. Dissent is: feeling not in accord, withdrawal, perhaps clash. Thus today a protest can easily be taken as a negative, critical, opposing gesture or attitude, even to the dimensions of rebellion. Two questions may be suggested by this linguistic phenomenon.

For one thing, it may be wondered how it is possible that on the one hand he who protests is participating, involved, affected, and on the other hand he is understood as withdrawing, opposing, affected not in accord. The obvious answer here is that what he is feeling and involved about, and what he is dissenting and withdrawing from, are two different things. This answer may be a little too obvious. The wonder may reappear later.

Another question which may be prompted by the dual meaning of "protest" is this. Is it just a coincidence that where there is originally an open witness or declaration of something, it eventually becomes a witness or declaration against? Is this not paralleled by the fact that when someone is spoken of, in literature, politics, even science, as "having something to say", more often than not what is meant is that he has something to criticize, to oppose, to abolish or reform? This can be superficially dismissed as merely a symptom of the restlessness and malcontency of the human species. But perhaps there is some ground for this. Perhaps the human medium for peace, enjoyment, acceptance, is silence, while the efforts of expression, artistic, verbal, organic, are due to discord, withdrawal, and rebellion. It could then be speculated that speech starting with cries in the crib and ending with mutters of the moribund is for man the medium of protest; that protest in the simpler, non-dissenting sense would be a loose luxury, unless there is always in life litigation, demand of defense, compulsion to clash; that this is how this word changes meaning along with words as such, which from a straightforward "use for" are swept into "use against." Such a train of thought would carry a long way toward the view that protest is not only rooted in a man's way to dwell in the world, his vision, character, and choice, but more specifically in that vision, character, and choice, which is tragic.

No more is needed in this introduction on the subject of protest, since its various shades, aims, and outcomes will be brought into light in the following chapters. These few words and what they point to may remove the impression of arbitrary contraposition of words in the phrase: THE TRAGIC PROTEST.

~

Where the advancing pursuit of the tragic may extend, has been intimated. But in what manner is this advance to be undertaken, what will it be on the lookout for, from what bases can it start? Hints only have been given to these elementary points; and now they must be explained.

To obtain access to the tragic essence one must not absolve himself from it as may happen in contemplation of a spectacle but rather penetrate into existence which is tragic. But whose existence is that? In one strict sense the only existence in which one may be involved is one's own. From this it would follow that to know what is tragic one must live through it. And if what is for him tragic is thus proper to him, it can never be appropriated publicly. Here then the chance of obtaining common knowledge of the tragic must vanish altogether. Still, is there not a secondary sense in which a man can penetrate and be involved in the existence of others? Such are the beliefs about intimacy of sympathy and love, possibly also of hatred and struggle. What makes possible such intimate ties between men is an intentional effort of imagination. What makes their presence publicly available is communication through language, but not language as such, colloquial, depersonalized, prosaic, rather language made private, fashioned anew, suggesting a unique transference of experience only with those intended, and understood by the multitude only in distortion. Communication of intimacy is always the making of things into words, which is what the Greeks conceived as poiesis, and which is in English called: poetry. Many intimate encounters and interpenetrations of existence among men remain mute, but those which are expressed can be appropriated not through understanding but through imagination: they are such stuff as poets draw upon.

For ordinary people insight into the tragic could thus be developed on the ground of their intimate friendships and enmities, not only of their own experiences. But in most cases such insight would remain wordless, since the gift of poetic communication is not universal to any appreciable degree. To make this insight public requires then something very difficult to attain, intimacy with those who speak the language of imagination and who therein express their sense of the tragic. To become close to the most tragic poets, to feel and speak with them or after them: this is the only alternative. And great are here the dangers of failure, of distortion.

Is it then, after all, an aesthetic or critical discussion of poetic compositions concerned with the tragic, that must be undertaken? Not at all. Critical demands, aesthetic enjoyment, analysis of composition must be lost from sight completely. What must be attempted is an intimate access to men whose existence is steeped in the tragic and who have words to speak of that, to draw us imaginatively toward their tragic being. But where are such men to be found? The answer is: one such man is called Hamlet, though he was known, according to the majority opinion, by the name of Shakespeare. There are others.

Now doubt and puzzlement may erupt violently. How is Hamlet Shakespeare? They are neither contemporary nor socially equal, one lived by vengeance and died young, the other lived merrily into a ripe age; and he wrote poetry. He just imagined Hanlet out of thin air, Hamlet does not exist and never did. What conception of existence is introduced here? What is this identification by poetic composition? Is solid historical reality giving way to figments and phantasms?

What can be explained, should be. About the conception of existence the answer can be shockingly short: there is no such conception. You have direct, although not conceptual, knowledge of your own existence and no other. Unless you are speculatively minded, you accept in some way the existence of other entities and would indeed be hard put to live unless you did. This does not mean that your conceptual criteria of such accepted existence are always ready at hand: they are not. And your conviction about the existence of someone in particular is rationalized but not always very rational. You do not accept the existence of Hamlet? Then your education leaves something to be desired. Do you accept the existence of Ulysses, of Homer, of St. George? On what grounds and with what particular profit? Do you know and can you prove that a King John or King Henry existed but a King Lear did not? Are you convinced that Richard of Gloucester was really an archvillain or a hero, Joan of Arc – a saint, a charlatan or a madwoman, Socrates – a corrupting sophist, a great mind, or a fabrication of Plato's? And for that matter, what was the true name of the really existing person who imagined this greatest crowd of nonexistent people? These queries are not meant to disparage historical research and its fascination. They are meant to emphasize the simple truth that, not as historians, but as citizens of the Western world you and I cannot but live with Hamlet and Lear, with Ulysses and St. George, with King John and King Richard, with Socrates and Jesus, that they are inherent and indestructible in the network of your imagination, they are in your mind's blood; though what of them you accept as real depends on the details of your education, literary, historical, philosophical, religious. As models to imitate or avoid, as influences on the pattern you imagine your own life to take they are no less factual than people you meet in school, in business, in the street; and with some of them you may become more intimate than with anyone you have to deal with in everyday affairs. With all due respect to historians, whatever painstaking success they may have in scientifically establishing the origins of Hellenic myths, the genuine character of Socrates or Gloucester, the period atmosphere of Magna Charta or of the Crucifixion, all of their pains are likely to come too late to undermine reality in the minds of men whose imagination had been gripped earlier by Homer, Plato, the Bible – or Shakespeare. As for the latter gentleman, his existence or non-existence under this name, or that of Bacon, Marlowe, Oxford, Derby or any other, could again not in the least diminish your intimacy, if you reach it, with himself as Othello, Prospero, Romeo, or Hamlet.

But this presumed identity requires some more comment. To learn from Shakespeare about what is tragic or comic or lyric or heroic is to assume that there are such dimensions to be found in him. Could one study them by digging for details of his supposedly "real" life at the time of Elizabeth, in London or Stratford, among courtiers and players? The question defies an answer. To learn from him, you certainly have to listen as he speaks to you. Does he speak as himself? With the debatable exception of the sonnets and a few other poems, not at all. He speaks under assumed names, he appears disguised in innumerable shapes, in order to in-form what is proper to his character in this or that part. How can he "be" so many? Possibly to answer this question adequately one would have to be Shakespeare. But that each man on a much more modest scale can also be many, is safely founded in human imagination, and it is the easier, the richer that imagination can grow. When as a judge you put on a black cap to pronounce a death sentence, when as a lover you clasp and strain and whisper, when as a salesman you grin and bow and flatter, when as a sportsman you run and kick and shout, when as a soldier you swear and obey what may seem nonsense and try to destroy indiscriminately – could you be the same, see and move in the same way, use the same words, gestures, tendencies, in any two roles among all you assume? Would it be proper for you to be the same for your girl as for your employer, think exactly the same thoughts in the morning and at night, take the same ease or the same effort in business, at table, in church? If it were to be so, then – alas for your imagination. You would be at the opposite human pole from the great poet who not only can luxuriously exist as many, feel and act as many, but who also knows most minutely which is proper to which within his sensitively protean character, and puts it into words. Thus he can tell what is and what is not the property of the tragic human character, if he has lived as such, if his imagination has made him intimate there, and if yours is sufficiently close to take it in.

To be friendly with such as Hamlet, to listen to their phrases and movements, even to try and engage them in dialogue in order to clarify what may sound alien, this is the method of exploration proposed. It requires that imaginative medium alluded to above, which accommodates man ordinarily, from childhood on, into the world where he is born, which he accepts as a frame of existence but always tends to fill by painting in colors and details proper to himself, mostly without being coerced to decide the question of their reality beyond their reality for him. An objectively "real" rapprochement with Aeschylus, Shakespeare, or Goethe, is an idea as absurd as that of a "real" intimate friendship with Prometheus, Hamlet, or Faust. But what makes this absurd is not the supposed difference between the existence of the former characters and the non-existence of the latter; it is rather the inexorable bond of time and space over any human reality, which is not thus extended over what is there for man's productive imagination. The roles of your character which you try to play imaginatively populate the world in which they are to be acted. A child could not live his adventures in a world lacking dragons and magicians, even if they come from Mars and manipulate over the speed of light. A lover could not spin his romance in total absence of Juliet, Laura, or Dulcinea, even if he knows them as Mary, Rose or Jean. A man could not initiate dreams and drives of dominion without emulating Caesar, Tamerlaine, Napoleon, even if he thinks in terms of companies rather than campaigns, stocks rather than stockades, markets rather than marches. Thus to be intimate with Oedipus or Orestes you need neither time-travel nor the power of raising the dead nor a special conception of real existence; what you do need is to discover within yourself a tie of kinship and resemblance to them. To see what was tragic for them is to imagine what may have tragic meaning for you. And it is this thrust of your imagination which can shape itself substantially thanks to the words of those who speak of what is tragic: those words you might not be able to find for yourself, although they speak of what perhaps is also yours. How a tragic poet can be a tragic hero, giving him words and gestures of his own, you can indeed wonder; but not disbelieve. For this is in fact the very same problem as: how you can be anything, a student, a statesman, a criminal, how A is ever also B, how transitive "is" is in being. A problem, and not a shallow one, but definitely not a delusion.

So much for what can be explained here concerning the manner of access to the tragic. It will have to deal with what of it has been put into proper words, in such records as are vaguely known by the name of tragedies. Once more, however, let it be stressed that an aesthetic, critical, or historical definition of tragedy is here disregarded altogether. For a stringent critic, some of those records to be examined may not qualify under some such definition, to which he is certainly entitled on his own merits. That all of them formally belong to dramatic literature, is no more than a coincidence. Only extraneous factors prevented the inclusion of other creations which do not there belong but which could also be effectively used toward the exploration of the tragic, such as "Brothers Karamazov," "Moby Dick," "A Farewell to Arms," or "The Heart of the Matter." On the other hand, some answer is certainly due to such questions as: What tragic conceptions are used to make a start with? What qualifies the seven "tragedies" selected to serve as bases for this enquiry? If the more usual tools of dissection, such as completeness of plot, compositional structure, source materials, are not to be used except incidentally, at what points is the analytic scalpel to be inserted and what must be watched in its path?

For the answers which will complete this task of introduction, the most natural and also venerable source to turn to, for some perhaps surprising is, Aristotle. "The Art of Poetry," practically simultaneous with the birth of tragedy, contains its first and simplest examination, as articulate as anything subsequently conceived. It is true that Aristotle's purpose in discussing the tragic is by no means identical with the one announced on these pages. For that reason his statements will require a certain amount of adaptation. But if that should be accomplished successfully, it would be presumptuous to deny that there is the authority best qualified to function as point of departure for the present excursion, since his words are most widely available, most influential throughout the ages, most sanctioned by common sense and tradition.

What is the nature of this adaptation to which the Aristotelian description of tragedy can be subject? For one thing, the aesthetic and literary objectives of Aristotle are to be disregarded here, both because of what has already been stated about the direction of this enquiry and also because dealing exclusively with the specifically Greek attainments in art they might be considered too narrow in scope. But further in view of the neutral imaginative path between art and life proposed here, the Aristotelian statements must be read somewhat differently, concentrating not on what the tragedian describes but simply on what happens to whom and how: it is the character in existence of someone like Oedipus that is to be explored and not the outer shell of presentation of this character. And last but not least, if one is to win through to what is tragic as such, one must strip it from temporary and incidental accompaniments, phases, adornments. This means a rather risky attempt to read Aristotle up to date, to find in his words what is capable of appeal not only for the fourth century B.C. but equally so for the twentieth century A.D. Reading Aristotle this way should imply neither disrespect nor blind enslavement in his doctrine.

Here are the main Aristotelian views on tragedy, presented in a loosely adapted order so as to yield initial meaning for what is to be considered tragic. Tragedy, Aristotle says, relates a single complete human action. How are the words "complete action" to be understood? They may mean at one extreme any gesture or intended event like raising an arm and striking, and at the other extreme they may be insisted to correspond only to an entire lifetime. The meaning is probably best understood as median, a complete action being neither too short, episodic, trivial, nor literally extended to a whole life, in other words: a significant temporal part of a man's history, completing itself by its significance. Such a reading is further supported by the next point in which Aristotle tries to put simply what is tragic in the events of a tragedy. In this action, he says, the man's fortune turns from good to bad. This seemingly innocuous statement is actually the one subsequently exercising the most widespread influence on Western languages into their unthinking, labeling applications of today. For the average newspaper readers, everything turning for the worse, every slight adversity or pretended misfortune is conceivably tragic. I shall plunge into this broad stream of linguistic expression and move against it trying to reach narrower waters toward its sources.

But since this is the ordinary popular sense of "tragic" from which I have to start, let me at least note for the moment that neither the meaning of the word "fortune" is obvious to the popular understanding nor can it be taken for granted which kind of fortune must be accepted as good and which as bad.

The last comment has some relevance also with regard to the next Aristotelian point concerning the man who is the subject of tragedy. The tragic hero, he says, will be neither too good nor too evil. These words may have been striking in a milieu of fairly established values and criteria. They must be taken with a pinch of salt in an age of melting, lost, and searched values, such as the present, for people contemporaneous with Gandhi and Hitler, claiming mastery over all natural existence and trembling about the likely loss of their own, aiming at divinity and mourning the death of God. Today one can hardly have the Aristotelian assurance about which man is good and which too good, which man is evil and which too evil. All that these words can probably suggest for current life is that the tragic hero is not exceptional, that he is to be understood as a fitting representative of humanity; even this latter phrase will have to be questioned further on. But Aristotle adds to this statement. On the one hand, he says, the subject of tragedy should be a person sufficiently elevated. These words have been long cited as sanction of attention paid exclusively to individuals socially predominant such as princes and leaders. Must they be? In this democratic epoch of the common man can they be lastingly appealing if taken thus? Perhaps the Aristotelian purpose is sufficiently well served if it is said that a tragic hero or any hero should have a character of his own and not just a common anonymity, that he should be elevated by virtue of common interest of men vested in him but by no means necessarily of social privilege. Titles and functions pass and change; there are actions and roles assumed by men which elevate them no matter what tribal hierarchy they belong to. On the other hand, Aristotle says, the tragic hero possesses always a defect or flaw of character. This again, taken out of the perspective of serene Hellenic surroundings, is hardly demanding much. The men of today are not very used to perfection even in dreams, and for the most limited of mentalities to be human is to possess flaws. But Aristotle has a special aim in mentioning this point, since he goes on to say that this defect or flaw, while not too significant or offensive in itself, is yet the origin in the tragic person of his eventual misfortune This must be noted well for future consideration. The man's own defect that which in the root Latin sense means "something undone" is seen as leading possibly to his whole undoing. The defect is small and unnoticeable, the misfortune sometimes great and destructive. There is a hint here not only for insisting that what happens properly to a man is anchored inevitably within what he is, but also for a beginning wonder pertaining to tragic happenings: is in this bond between character and events perhaps something disproportionate, unmerited, out of balance, improper? Is this precisely tragic?

The remaining points to be noticed in the Aristotelian doctrine concern the whole medium in which the complete action of the hero brings about his undoing due to a defect in his character, turning his fortune into misfortune. He emphasizes that there is in the tragic story more than singular or private significance. Tragic events do not just happen to happen, uniquely, irretrievably; they proceed from the bourn of what may be, of what is possibly in store for any human being; therefore, he observes, they are of legitimate concern for men. On this is founded the perplexing but hardly dismissible doctrine of catharsis. In witnessing tragic actions, Aristotle says, man is relieved and purified by being moved to pity and fear: pity because what happens is not properly deserved by the character of the hero, and thus awakens wonder; and fear which goes to the marrow of self-concern since that character is not alien but akin. And so you tremble lest what happens to him should likewise happen to you – just as improperly as to him. Are you then maybe relieved that thus far it only happens to him? Yet what may be is proper neither to him nor to you. This may be tragic.

One other word must be added to these observations, though at first glance it appears quite superfluous. The tragic story, Aristotle says, is a serious one. Of course, one can say: a turn to bad fortune, undeserved though self-made, how could it be anything but serious? Still, the point is, need one take what is serious seriously or merely at face value? There is cruel laughter, there is an all but univerdal sadism in comic effects of misfortune. A man slips on a banana skin; this is rip-roaring. He breaks his leg; this is all in good fun. He lies in hospital, good for him; this is nothing to worry about. He dies; the humor of the situation half-heartedly dies out with him. What then is serious, so as to introduce the tragic? Death, it would seem. A saying of a modern author, which does not sound very modern, states that the only serious affairs in a man's life are those which have to do with him and his God. This offers a hold for thought. But then an atheist would be barred from seriousness. What can be conceived for those to whom God is but a neurotic phantasm? They are, after all, human, their lives can be tragic. Perhaps to avoid commitment to a restrictive faith, the statement could be modified to say that what is serious in the life of man has to do with his whence and whither, with some foundations, forces or factors, other than himself, which are for him the first and the last, thus embracing his whole existence and all its doing and undoing. Let "them" be nameless, and thought of in neither plural nor singular, and still be thought of. To what affairs could this notion of seriousness be applied? Not to business or trade, where a way of living might be intricated for a while, none too greatly involved, and laid aside without regret; but perhaps to something a man will speak of as his vocation or mission. Not to sex which one bears as a biological accident, enjoying in passing, forgettable entrancements, anonymous, inacccessible, drifting; but perhaps to love, an inevitable wish for possession. Not to sociable friendships, acquaintances, communal undertakings, indulged in for lack of weight and substance in one's everyday time, to be renewed, duplicated in all towns and places of all countries; but perhaps to what is felt as one's home, as where one belongs, as what one owes life to. Such phenomena, of an assigned mission, of self-transcending love, of a true belonging, are apt to guide this pursuit toward the unnamed dark from which and toward which the human being stands out in existence. Dark? If all man's light and reason stems from there? To the religious mind they are paths toward what is named God, but even there light is fragmentary. Named or un-named, what is enlightening man is never light enough but also dark; indeed, we cannot know darkness except where some light shines. This cannot be taken by you in any other way but seriously if it is yours: the source and goal of your enduring and genuine concern in your life and death. Your relation to the choice which makes you; your resting place in that future which preys upon your existence; your abandon-ment to yourself in self-dependent lonely creation and your inherence in that man-entity which goes under the name of your society, your species, your nature; such are the ideas which, according to the greatest of modern thinkers, cannot help being thought by you, who-ever you are. And these are the ideas which serve best to stake out the core of what in man's life is serious. No philosophers' monopoly contains them; on the contrary, as Kant suggests, it would be im-possible to imagine a man in existence to whom they could be entirely alien. It is then well to notice that on this interpretation of seriousness the dark essence of the tragic radiates such universal thoughts as to be the proper concern of each man in his own way. Need it be added that among the serious ideas dictated by the actions of a tragic hero there can be plenty of causes and contents for protest?

These are the indispensable preliminary explications of what is to be understood as tragic, reverently borrowed from Aristotle's words. From his theme some variations arose here in the effort to bridge the gulf of centuries. This is indispensable too, this contemporary embroidery upon an ancient text, if it is to be taken as live. Imagination must revive it. So words will be spoken on the following pages of Zeus and his dominion, of angels and the devil, spoken perhaps among those who cannot believe the reality of such. Yet all the lay thinkers of a secular time can, if they wish to, imagine what Zeus or the Evil One must be for a believer, no matter when his life. Equally so, modern man cannot be awed by the elevation of princes; he can shrug his shoulders on men too good or too evil; on defects of character he may not agree at all with the old sage. But if one is to learn from Aristotle, and one certainly can, imagination must be stretched to picture what tragic princes were for, why a tragic hero should not stand out too far, what tragic significance a defect of character can provoke. That has been the purpose of the preceding explications of criteria under which the tragic character of all seven following illustrations can be viewed.

And now, my reader, the challenging territory has been outlined as well as it can be in anticipation, the directions and starting bases of the exploration are assigned, the mode of proceeding suggested. I shall now, one by one, light the lamps for that way toward the dark grounds of tragic existence. No curtain goes up – this will not be a spectacle. But, if you wish to stay with me, try to open your eyes and ears, and watch and listen to and converse in imagination with men who lived in what you and I may one day live through; men who expressed the tragic protest of humanity. Aim at understanding them intimately, give them for a brief duration your feeling of nearness, of concern, of participation: your consent.

CHAPTER II

The Tragic Defiance - Titan Prometheus

AESCHYLUS: PROMETHEUS BOUND

There is light – and space. A great morning over a great and empty world. The sun above, radiating, heating, burning the whole expanse of time, seen so clearly, as if standing still. The upper reaches only of this world live and strive; here where you look down you find scorched emptiness and silence of ages. "Here at the furthest verge of earth we stand ..." On earth already, but not of the earth: at the limit of that earth man is to inherit. Where is he? Not to be found. Only his voice from afar, only the forces menacing his being and shaping it. But man is not yet ready to appear. What can be listened to here in this world is the prelude to the human being.

Humanly timeless is the titanic scope of Prometheus. You need a faithful effort of imagination to put yourself in touch with him, to grasp in heart – not in reason – what is not mortal, thus cannot be human. Prometheus, the outcast of the gods for his "love of mortal man," cannot be reached completely on his heights from down below, from the human vale. If your genuine sympathy extends to him, you can assimilate that in him which is like you, but no more. His isolation between heaven and earth is more than a primal type of a man's aloneness; yet as such only can it be interpreted. The Titan's features have to be humanized for human consideration; so one must speak as if one were in a man's world, knowing full well that this vast universe is not yet of man's time. Who knows? Perhaps this is the way to find how man was made to be?

There is probably no need to convince you of the tragic being of Prometheus; you may wish to question, though, wherein it is tragic. Vision achieved in this prehuman world can provide the first and best example for the contention that it is not events that can by themselves be, or make anyone, tragic: since of events one cannot say much here. From the first moment when the figure of Prometheus appears, to the last, when it moves away from your view, you cannot be dramatically gripped by any single thing that happens. You listen to him, reminiscently surveying the throw of his present lot, looking ahead to the threat freeing him in inconceivable distance to come. Mostly you stay with him, drinking in the painful, monotonous taste of his timeless present in which no change occurs, in which none could be as decisive, as determining as those which happen in your life, since you are mortal. To see Prometheus tragically at all, you must see what he is in his world and not what happens to him. The former may be reduced from those inhuman dimensions, the latter not, because it is all toyed with in endless future.

Another opening advantage can be enjoyed in this view. Prometheus imposes in gross, enduring lines the basic frame of tragic protest:

> ... O Earth, O Mother mine
> Most holy, O thou Sky divine,
> Whose light is shed on all, ye see
> This anguish and this wrong!

The world of Prometheus is viewed as a scene of suffering, not only of his own; of suffering in which man in his still insignificant role participates on his own scale, but which antedates humanity and is displayed as ready, awaiting man to grow into it in his full stature. The world is seen as a battlefield changing hands, where on a humanly supertemporal scale rulers succeed and absolutely refashion all, and just as absolutely fail and vanish, where ruthless might is dictating all rights except one: that of DEFIANCE. Already in this divine or demonic world defiance is what one appropriates without question, without title. This defiance Prometheus hurls at Hermes: "My prison chains against thy servitude I would not change!" And no one, not the ruler of the universe can compel him into servitude. However, the fruit of such defiance is not his own, since: "No victory is his who wars 'gainst That which Needs must be.'" An imposing and mystifying word, not much clearer to man today than in that world of dawn. Necessity, which many have called "fate"; it is here, on this horizon, and will be present on all others to be explored. In the Promethean world it is the power above, or perhaps better, around all things, the framework of all that is and therefore cannot not be, of all temporal combats, hopes and fears, for gods and men alike. It is here mythically personified in the three Erinys or Fates; but it is not the mythical expression which is crucial, but rather what the myth offers for thought. This can be advanced by the claim that this more than divine necessity is choice par excellence, choice responsible for the birth, the course, and the end, these "three" fates of all entities; as such, itself is neither one nor three nor any number, since it is not an entity but what makes entities be, the ground of their reality in time. Despite his recognition of necessity, does not Prometheus dare to raise his head against it? In that daring will have to be sought the tragic aspect of his defiance.

What does this defiance amount to? The sound of "defiance" should not mislead into any such word connections as "de-faith" or "de-fiat." Prometheus can neither disbelieve or abolish faith in the present rule of the lord of the world, nor can he successfully destroy his enemy by some negative fiat of his will. "Defiance" means withdrawal of fidelity and trust. Yet it must be observed that precisely in his defiance, with all hatred and contempt he feels, Prometheus remains involved with the defied Zeus, tied as to a brother by these very negative attitudes. A withdrawal which brings closer; has something like that not been mentioned already? Yes, in reference to protest. And this is what the defiance of Prometheus must resolve itself into, as long as he remains "bound": to stand witness, protesting, to invoke the sky above and the earth below for confirmation of his stand. Because the witness is defiant and calls out his suffering and suppression, therefore his protest is protesting against. But he is bound and impotent. Would it not seem sensible to say that his defiant protest is entirely pointless? Here Prometheus supplies a basic insight applicable to subsequent illustrations. The point of the protest may be outwardly none, his impotence and impossibility of success in the present world guarantee that. Inwardly, however, the protest is all-important; to surrender into subservient silence would be, for Prometheus, to deny his own self, to accept a break between what he has stood for in his past and what he would prostrate himself on in his future. The significance of protest is not to be measured in terms of worldly success. The invisible potency of it for one's own existence, the right to defy, which neither Zeus nor any other divinity can annihilate, this is what makes the Titan's example so pregnant for the forthcoming shapes of human characters. And that his defiance is bound, that even he, more than a man, is helpless toward all that which needs must be, this lays the pattern of a protest's being tragic, for future men, the creatures of Prometheus.

～

To look deeper into this vast world on which man has not yet put his stamp of possession. it is necessary above all to enquire how it is fashioned and held together. The answer seems to lie in one name: Zeus. But it only seems so. Standing at the limits of human earth, watching and listening to the Titan's torments, one can gain some varying perspectives on the position of Zeus, which make worth questioning the being of God above all gods.

Zeus is the lord of all things and spirits. While other deities may here appear as natural, dwelling in and weaving through all nature, the role of Zeus appears ex hypothesi super-natural, since all that is nature here and now is subject to his will. There is great distance, characterized by fear, from all other immortal spirits to the single one who rules. Hermes, one of the privileged, accepts the epithet of "Olympians' slave." Hephaistos, another important god, groans: "Woe to him whose mind shrinks from its task, beneath the eternal eyes!," as though his eyes were not eternal. He is driven and ordered about by Zeus' household attendant, Kratos, who in his turn has this to say: "All ways of life are hard, except to be King of the Gods: since none but Zeus is free." Although divine, all of them, orderly subordinates of the one they acknowledge as their master, they identify his being only with freedom. The freedom in question is conceived on the pattern of all those who are dependent: to do as one pleases and escape punishment, to be exempt from law and command by standing above them. It is in this sense only that they begrudge Zeus his freedom: because his will lays down the law. So the person of Zeus appears as the single source of order in the nature of the whole universe; he is above it.

But wherefrom obtains the supernatural might of Zeus? The answer is clear: from conquest. He is the master in virtue of having mastered the older rulers. In this world of battles change and succession is in continuous order, the younger and healthier usurp legitimately the seats of might from their ancestors, the right to rule rests with the might backing it: such is the law. Now, what is this, the word just mentioned – the law? This law cannot be subject to the will of Zeus. The law of law-making in its succession is indeed what Zeus himself trembles about. The order of nature which is his, is present; it is but a fragment of the order in time. This is what eludes his mighty spirit. When his confident servant Hermes proudly asserts that "woe" is a word "Zeus knoweth not," Prometheus answers: "By Time and Age full many things are taught." Of time Zeus has yet to learn, and of its law. No wonder then that his law may not claim undivided loyalty, that even Okeanos' daughters may dare themselves into an expression of seditious reserve:

> Strange hands are now upon the helm
> Of Olympus; with new doings manifold
> And lawless Zeus fortifies his realm.

It is the temporal aspect of novelty and youth which can give to the law of Zeus the semblance of lawlessness, hard and selfish: his "heart listeth not to prayer, but conquerors all are hard in the early days." Once a breach made, a detachment conceived from the attitude that "the king abides no questioning," it is possible to see not only the free glory but also the loneliness of his supreme position, and even its insecurity, as long as his person, however mighty, is but single:

> In every tyrant's heart there springs in the end
> This poison, that he cannot trust a friend . . .
> When first he mounted on his father's throne
> Straightway he called the gods, and gave each one
> His place and honours. So he wrought his plan
> Of empire.

A lawless tyrant now is Zeus, rather than the unique source of law. His order must be "fortified" into empire, when all the potential rivals and significant servants are bought off by imperial favors. In this plan there is, however, no place for that insignificant and harmless creature, creeping somewhere below, in a corner of the divine universe: man. Of him, perhaps understandably for the imperial interests, Zeus "had no care." Man could appear from his distant throne as some useless weed to be uprooted, created pointlessly and defectively, not by him – he is no father to that race – but by his incompetent predecessor. Again the limits of Zeus' ruling spirit must be noted. Had he but known that his disfavor toward those mortals would prompt the rebellion of Prometheus, would he not recoil before depriving himself of the indispensable alliance with this "Forethinker?" And still he has not found out that from this breed of mortals one day in Argos a rival will rise to thrust him off his throne; may his name be Herakles or may it be – Orestes of the flies? The limits of his imperial awareness are imposed by that to which the God of gods must bow: the temporal thread of being. His dominion, however absolutely present, is absolute only in the present. The future, forever not known to him, not real yet, not a part of nature, is not his to rule; nor is his the past, where has been chosen what is now given him to rule. If his contempt for man were a decisive hatred, still he could not make man nonexistent, only destroy him; nor, after the revolt could he have taken away the gifts of the rebel. If annihilated, man still forever will have existed, forever will have been the creature inspired by the divine Promethean spark. This is what needs must be, even for the lord of all nature. Such may have been the thought which held back his thunderbolt while binding his destructive intent toward mankind. Later – it may have been too late for Zeus. Time does not stand quite still, not even for immortals.

If now the necessity of the law is understood as extending through time, then a merely present law-maker, whatever his supremacy, shows himself in his will as arbitrary. The supernatural will of Zeus is the will of one and of now, therefore subjective. It is possible to ask about the choice which makes him the one he is, to set off the oneness of his will against the temporal manifold of all there is, and so to find it capricious. The will of one cannot be the law of all, however over-mastering the one. In this widened perspective it is then possible to escape subservience and to defy Zeus. His ways may be "fathomless," but they are only his and have to contend with what is not his, has not been, will not be his. Zeus is seen in strife; the result of strife, far from acquiring automatic legitimacy, can be tyrannous persecution, such as that of Io. It may be, and now is right, that he is the lord enslaving all others under his freedom; but then it also may be, not now, that he will "learn the difference between lord and slave" from the other side. No thing is necessary just in its present. The rule of Zeus, consequently, is not necessary. Its future overthrow may be, now, just a dream, and still it may be. If one of the ingredients of that rule is arbitrary hatred, is such hatred the law? On the contrary, it need not at all be mad "to hate the hater." Does Zeus expect, can he expect, devotion of the heart, or only devotion of service to the master's order? To yield innerly to such service, to come to love the hater merely because he is the master, is actually the sign of accepted enslavement such as Zeus or any other universal ruler can never enforce, if there is choice in reality. Defiance remains as a contrary alternative, also for man.[1] Also, to a certain extent, it remains possible in thought with respect to a Zeus who would have created the universe and man: as long as such a God is not identical with all there is and

---

[1] "I'm on my feet and fully dressed, to show this: it's not I who am dying. No, I'm not dying, I am being killed ... You wish I'd lie down? Like a cowed dog, offering his belly to his master's kicks, to soften him?" – the singular intransigence of the sick man of Vercors, *The Insurgents*.

remains one amongst many entities, a temporal mind is free to resist his rule and to long ahead to another or to no rule. Such is the temporal escape from present subjection in nature.

Of the other spiritual presences in this world there is no need to enquire. They are the cohorts of Zeus, all those powerful Olympians who could be, but are not, relevant to the destiny of man. One only of them will have to be studied carefully: the suffering Titan. But what of the human being? It is not yet in the scene, it is only described as in process of arising. No humans appear: the daughters of the god Okeanos cannot be strictly held as such, nor can even the long-persecuted Io, daughter of another river deity. Are men not yet important? Yet the whole revolt and conflict concerns them and their fragile mortality. They are weeds ripe for extinction, orphans whose parent vanished, flies for the sport and whim of all stronger spirits; their being in the world continues just on sufferance and seems without any import whatever. They are objects of contemptuous pity; so the Okeanides speak of them:

> Shall they comfort thee, who perish in a day?
> Didst thou see not that Man was ever thus:
> Little-doing, and his strength hazardous
> And dreamlike? In such weakness, every way,
> His blind tribes are chained, and his thought
> Shall escape not . . .

For now, for the present nature, this description clearly fits humanity of this world; but is the concluding forecast of gloom justified? Does not Prometheus know better? For the time being, men are only capable of sympathy: "Every land is loud with a travail of compassion." They bewail the enchainment of Prometheus; they know of it. And that already is significant. To think about the future of mankind, it is necessary to look closer into its origins as revealed here.

Kronos, the god of time before Zeus, made men and endowed them with enduring but mortal bodies – and no more. They were "a thing of no avail," without "a living mind": "Sight they had but saw in vain . . . as shapes in dreams they moved." Was that the being of man or merely the search of it? Surely, if you are scientifically minded, you can fill in this mythical speech with reference to Neanderthalers or even older ancestors of yours? Those were mindless "humans" of pre-Promethean shape. Then came the revolt in heaven, the stealing of fire for the benefit of mankind. What is the meaning of fire here? Clearly, it is the weapon Zeus himself uses in his conquest of the universe, it is the divine gift: for destruction and transformation. From that mankind is to "learn all arts, all greatnesses." Their long list follows: sheltering, the use of seasons, knowledge of numbers, writing, dominance of beasts, the arts of sailing, healing, mining, telling of dreams and of predictions. Is this not the creation of mankind such as you yourself belong to, the slow passage of cave-dwellers on the road toward tomorrow? It would thus seem that not the bare physical emergence but the appropriation of the gifts of Prometheus is what most properly made the human species; to him it owes filial recognition. But then, there is another characteristic feature of the human rise. Before he even mentions the divine spark of fire transmitted by him to earth, Prometheus speaks of something that he may consider as an even more basic gift of his:

> From thoughts of coming death I saved mankind:
> Blind hopes I planted in their hearts to dwell.

That these hopes are called blind attests that they do not save from death, only from thoughts of it. Why then is there such a great significance in them? Because this is what Prometheus gives of his very own to his creatures: the Fore-thinker, the spirit superior to Zeus himself in his awareness of time necessarily coming, makes men in his own likeness into temporal creatures casting themselves in hope toward the future, toward "vision of things to be." This is the threshold dividing the cave origins from what can be homo sapiens: temporality. Without it divine fire would soon be quelled, all arts and skills would be rootless and not to be progressed into. This benefice, however, carries with it what many might consider as a dark curse: the possibility already pointed out, to defy the might of the present, to turn one's care away from nature as it is ruled, to suffer overpowered and not to yield – in the name of a future hoped for, even blindly. Here is a seed of tragic protest.

Is something still missing from the scenes? They have been described now, those Promethean descendants, those temporal, hoping men who build and strive in their common earthly lots. Why does not one of them appear? Precisely because there is not yet one. They have been created in multiplicity, of a kind, in the crowd down below. A human being does not exist yet. Perhaps not even Prometheus could make him. He has to find himself, to accept his own time of life and death, to respond to his own "I" and to the others' "you," to become responsible for his existence. He will then be all-one, maybe a more tragic one, when he stands out from amongst or even against "them" as a self-avoiding species. One such fully human being will soon step up into the light; he will be a king known as Oedipus. There are none in the world contemplated here. It takes time to fashion a human existence. But the Titan who fore-knows, expects eventually a mortal deliverer of himself:

> One born of thine own blood he needs must be –
> O'er Argos reigning ... Io, 'tis he
> Who from these bonds at last shall set me free.

∾

The earth is germinating, laboring in the preparation of man's dominion. The gods, preoccupied in their heavenly empire, care not. In between, within this vast panorama, hangs on the heights suspended the intermediary: the first tragic hero, setting in above-human dimensions the frame of tragedy. Who is Prometheus? How is he to be conceived so that from him man can be said to descend?

Asking in sympathy about his tragic character, the first insight that one may readily grasp could be to say that the "fault" for which he suffers is no more than love of the human being, love of man such as he may be, "dreamlike and little-doing, with his strength hazardous." This is true and suggests, although one may not want to see it, that he who offers himself to human love, must pay for it dearly. There is, in the tragic perspective, something poisonous or rotten about the human race so that, without intent to harm, it stings in return of love, imposing pain upon the one who would save or beautify it. This will be later euphemized as sacrificial love. When Prometheus exclaims: "A piteous sight I am, to all who love," is it not implied that all who love must tremble lest their love produce a similar fruit of stakes and nails and chains? To cite the only other example available here, though but slightly similar, observe the effect of love on the life of Io. This love of which so little is told, burns her trail without the slightest shade of justice, provoking the outcry: "Do such things lie in wait for the innocent?" This love in which Io is involved has nothing in common with Prometheus' suffering, except that in each case there is love leading to disaster, and – one might think – innocence. The undeserved persecution of Io, however, develops not on the human horizon; it is connected with the attitude of the "Tyrant of the Skies." And so, it may be thought that such a painful picture of love is somehow due to the present nature of the universe, to the hateful rule of Zeus; that with his fall love, even of men, may be freed from this stigma of suffering. This thought leads back to the consideration of

Prometheus' heart. It would be naive to consider him as a sacrificial lamb floating in coy purity. In his heart, inseparable from love of man, lodges just as deeply the want of revenge upon the ruling god who shall "atone in tears" and "bow low his head." Does this suggest that evil intent must be balanced with evil before a good and loving freedom can emerge, that reparations must be paid in injustice according to the order of time, as Anaximander was said to demand? Possibly. One thing, however, transpires above all: that Prometheus is not innocent. It is neither false nor fanciful to picture him as the prototype of loving redeemers; but that is only a partial picture.

More essential even than his love, because providing that love's foundation, is his character of a dis-ordering spirit. If the stage of this world can be watched to reveal another Genesis, a more heroic and dignified Genesis, then here is the first rebellion. Prometheus can be an Adam, but an Adam noble rather than schoolboyish, knowing rather than ignorantly curious, resolute rather than henpecked. "With firm resolve and knowledge I transgressed, nor now deny it." This statement could not be made by the stunned, whipped exile from that garden replete with food and laziness. Better then, Prometheus can be seen as Lucifer, about whom the more common Genesis is so reticent whose forbidden character meets with only invective or silence – except that he is the "Lightbearer." Could he be, by coincidence, bearing the light for men? And why, why, did he rebel? Prometheus can answer that. Whomever he resembles, in this Genesis the titanic dis-orderer is the founder of what is commonly called "original sin."

The tragic undoing of Prometheus lies in this situation of choice: humanity versus order. The creed which puts him in chains is that persons are more important than principles, that the reality of living and suffering beings on earth takes precedence over the ideality of an organized, systematic, lawfully ruled nature. In Zeus' imperial plan there is no place for men, their freakish existence is outside of his care, but that is such a minor lack as offset against order for the whole serene universe; can the whole plan be condemned on that account? Prometheus is to be bound "till he learns to accept our Master's plan." Is this such an exorbitant demand from the God above all gods, is not Zeus lenient and reasonable, must he not discipline obedience in the name of his law for all? But Prometheus' answer is: "Never." The superhuman plan, idea, order, is rejected in toto, because it is inhuman. Zeus sacrifices not much, in his terms, for the sake of universal law; for the Titan even the insignificant sacrifice of that mortal race is enough to rouse him into rebellion against immortal nature.

It is easy to argue that Prometheus defies Zeus' order in expectation of a superior order to succeed Zeus; but the dangerous moment lies in the rejection of the order which is, which binds nature now. It is a transgression which can open the door to anarchy. The seed of disorder has been sown; the Promethean hybris. Such a choice, for him and for many men inheriting from him, may be excused in love – which is not exactly an orderly phenomenon – and will be accused in suffering, deserved and undeserved at the same time. Tragedy is opened in disorder, in rebellion, in a break with nature. This is the forbidden "light" borne by the first hero in the tragic genesis of the human being. Yet, to prevent too easy an identification of Prometheus with the demonic spirit of negation and destruction, who will later appear in a Christian world-view, let it be noted in this place that Promethean defiance represents assertion, not negation, assertion of himself, of mankind and of the future. It is expressed on behalf of existence and against destructibility. The protest of Prometheus is against the turning of something into nothing, against the mortality of man.

The odd, impenetrable feature of the Titan is that he can rise to this protest despite his own being in no relation to nothing: immortal. But what is or is not attainable in the character of an immortal and how far this immortality sets him apart from all things human, that is not to be demonstrated. Even an appeal to your imagination can be attempted in vain, within these dimensions. This can only be pointed to, negatively. Thus, try to sound the depth of the expression: "How should I fear, for whom there is no death?" Consider that you share with your fellow-humans their generally persistent trait of fearing annihilation, that you can rise above this fear in courage or indifference but never in total disregard of your mortality. How can such human fear belong to Prometheus?

To illustrate it further: the same alienating chasm divides the Titan from you, even more crucially, with regard to his torments. In an immortal, the capacity of bearing pain should be unlimited. He is aware of what is happening to him now; Hephaistos' compassionate description can be taken as correct: "Alway the present pain shall be the one most hated." Such suffering is like that of men. And yet, the merely present affliction by pain may be only a circumscribing feature: when you are in pain, seriously, agonizingly, your consciousness can adopt this pain as coextensive with your finite being; what makes the pain unbearable is the thought so threateningly close that the end of this pain can be also the end of you. Such an awareness of pain, filling one's whole identity, seems inconceivable for an immortal. When Prometheus speaks of himself as of a "watchtower of eternal pain," he speaks figuratively; first, because he knows he will be eventually delivered from pain, second, because even if he did not know that, still being infinite he can always expect to outlast his pain. Pain "everlasting," in the sense of "pain which is all that remains to me" is, paradoxically, possible only for a being which knows that only a little remains to him, a mortal. How then Prometheus suffers, one cannot tell. It would be certainly an exaggeration to claim that his sense of forthcoming triumph makes his pain not genuine. Although immortal, he is in the order of time, where the present which is, weighs more heavily than the future, even known, but which is not yet. He confirms this temporal subjection quite clearly, when he catches himself:

> I groan; Oh, when and in what guise
> Cometh an end of misery?
> And yet what say I? Clearly I foreknow
> Each pang that cometh: no unlooked-for blow
> Can touch me ever ...

The certitude of each coming pang – does this not sharpen it? Is not Prometheus speaking of his own knowledge when he suggests – and not only for humans: "Ah, not to know were happier than to know?" He knows. Or – does he? Again, his transtemporal, inhuman omniscience, like his immortality, raises difficulties of understanding, which permit only of guesses. Does he in fact fore-know what happens and will happen in all its infinite detail? Then how is it that he misunderstands the friendly intentions of Okeanos, is uncertain about the identity of his daughters when they come to him, and even more definitely admits about his own misfortune: "I dreamed not such revenge as this?" It seems more plausible to believe that Prometheus can only foresee the outward outline, the fundamental fabric of events, but not their complete concrescence. And it is, indeed, that gift of the general rather than concrete prediction of what may happen, that man's mind will inherit from him, for its better or worse but strictly human fortune. But here, in this world of origins, the human being plays as yet no part. Prometheus is the only one in possession of fore-knowledge, however concrete it might or might not be. This is what ties the time-powerless Zeus to him. This anxious need links the ruler with the bound rebel for the whole duration of the present rule, since that rule itself depends on fore-thought. "Only by thought, the conquerors should prevail." The dependence of this uniquely "free" Zeus is the obverse of Prometheus' defiance of him.

His exclusive position makes for his exclusive solitude, between heaven and earth, solitude such as no mortal can ever know. To the Olympians serving Zeus he is the outcast, the fallen one. To men, he is the first in a long line of half-known benefactors, to whom will be rendered as much of vague gratitude as of nameless oblivion: what of those men who first spread the use of fire, of writing, of all the arts, are they known or appreciated any more than their ancestor, Prometheus? The human race is dream-like and forgetting. Nor is Prometheus looking for companionship, of gods or men. He knows of sympathy, resting in common past, among his kinsmen and comrades. This community with gods he leaves behind; and the community with men he does not yet expect. "I will drain unto the lees, alone, my cup of fortune." He feels, and assents to, his isolation – why? Because alone he dared to feel differently, alone he waged his deed of revolt, and – what is most important – alone he reaffirms it in his defiance. In this no god is his equal. What companionship can Prometheus find in all those who, with kindly intent, feel themselves into suffering such as his – but not into him? Kratos: "Why vex thyself with pains that profit none?" Hephaistos: "Thou dreamer all too daring!" Okeanos: "Away, O sufferer, cast thine angry mood!" His daughter: "What hope for thee? Canst see not now, thou hast the law transgressed?" And Hermes: "O madman! Try, try even now to know thine own helpless misfortune, and be wise!" His alienation then is his madness, his daring to transgress the normal, his daring to be mad. Or – are all the others mad, while he knows it? What is the course of wisdom here? As the normal mind would describe it, divine or human, it is to avoid suffering, to reconcile oneself with the arm of might, to support it even. Would the Titan lose anything apparent by renouncing his defiance and resuming his seat of honor on Olympus? No, perhaps men would lose, but not himself. Is then his persistent mood not completely mad and pointless, rather than wise? Must he not through it stay alone, against advice, feeling, wisdom, of all? Yes, he must. To stay alone with just as "firm resolve and knowledge" appears to be his choice. Perhaps this choice rests merely in a "reason" of the heart, perhaps in no reason at all. Perhaps reason needs such choice to arise?

To be alone, to be oneself, at the cost of isolating pain and pride, at all costs, as if all present nature were immaterial and uninfluential; to shape one's reasons and deeds in accordance with what one is, rather than to shape what one is in accordance with other deeds and reasons: is all this not the emergence of what men will call "freedom" – and another Promethean creation? Is it the adversary of wisdom, or the foundation of it? No man has ever attained to wisdom by doing just as the others do, nor has anyone reached it without standing up for himself and for his own future. The light of reason shines from the ground of Prometheus' madness, from his casting himself fore-thinking ahead into the temporal stream of existence.

There is a strange, from without hardly accessible correlation in Prometheus' way to be. The choice which he claims as his own lies at the source of it. It is the conflict of value, between the existential significance of the human being as such and the essential order of nature as organized by the law of Zeus whose care does not extend to men. Having taken his stand for man and the future, against nature and the present, Prometheus shapes his character accordingly. He expropriates himself from his legitimate Olympian heritage into indefinite lonely exile. He appropriates the unique responsibility for his deed, the right to suffering, defying, unyielding, all-one, all by himself. From that issues his vision of the world around him, in which hatred is indispensable, in which his love for man is only a fragment. The vision is vengeful, aiming at a necessary twilight of the gods so radiant now in their morning time; even if he were not endowed with true foresight, still he would have to posit the fall of Zeus and his empire. To all the other spirits bathed in the light of their present greatness, he is mad. Is there not method in this madness? Would Prometheus be Promethean without it?

To understand the protest of Prometheus, one must first see that its point is turned inward. In the arrangements of the world, present and even future, it would be vain to search for that point. Because even if his prediction failed him, if the might of Zeus were to hold sway indefinitely without peril, his protest would be just as crucial for the Titan as ever. In it he affirms his being, his creed, his judging disposition. He stands witness for it, although no one is ready to listen. He puts himself on record, stamps his indelible trace through the temporal universe, invoking sky and earth for confirmation: this is what I am, and will be, this is what I have done and what has been done to me, this is what I stand for. Such a self-asserting will lies below the distinctions of right and wrong. Man will take it over from

Prometheus: in a similar disregard of common evaluation. Faust will lay it down as his final stamp upon existence. Perishable or imperishable as the universe may be, as long as it is there it will have contained this Promethean being. No more is needful: triumph and defeat are in this respect irrelevant. Bound for ever or victoriously unbound, Prometheus will have been all-one, will not have broken with and denied himself. This is what his protest is for.

Yet it develops also – necessarily? – as a protest against. Its core is the defiant liberation from Zeus which the Titan desires but which, as has been noted earlier, actually ties him to the God of gods, by his own intention. This defiant Prometheus must remain bound; as long as his defiance must last the power of Zeus. If Zeus falls, a new Prometheus will emerge, perhaps cruel, perhaps lenient in victory, perhaps supremely indifferent, but no longer only defiant. In this relation then, in the fact that his defiance is binding and not fighting, that it is held within the scope of only protest, lies the clue to its being TRAGIC.

What is tragic in Prometheus? That which happens to him? But on the contrary, while you can observe him, after he is bound, nothing happens, and you can become exhausted with the unending view of time stretching ahead, in which there will be no dramatic events, in which Prometheus will stay chained, tortured, alone. If you are seriously sensitive to such a monotone view, not thirsting for change to happen for the sake of happening, but hoping for change because it would be a change from what afflicts you now in your encounter with the suffering Titan, then you can feel that the tragic root lies here in the very being of Prometheus as you watch him. What is that root? It is not quite enough to say that it is his relation to Zeus; this must be interpreted. The defiance of the Olympian tyrant is tragic not on account of the personal hostility involved. If it were, you could harbor some pious reverence justifying the unfathomable ways of the ruling God and thus weaken your sympathy for the rebel; thus, penetrating into this horizon of pain and power, you have to try to understand who Zeus is, how he rules, and why Prometheus rejects him. But this does not yet suffice to elicit the tragic essence here. That consists not in what, how, or why Prometheus defies, but in that he defies now what is now in force, and therefore can be only protested against. The tragic root of Promethean being is temporal. It is not only rebellion against Zeus as Zeus, it is the daring defiance of the necessary order of time. Prometheus longs for the better future; that such a future is founded on, and can only emerge to succeed, the present nature of things, which is not evanescent but drastically real and continuing – that he would abolish if he could, even although this is against his own better knowledge:

> One thing being certain, that no victory
> Is his who wars 'gainst That which Needs must be.

Does he not war against it? Is not the enduring essence of his defiance the outwardly impotent protest against what he is clearly aware of as the enduring might of Zeus? Acceptance of the future with rejection of the present which bears it – this is the dis-ordering and "binding" aspect of Promethean protest. To describe it in these terms is certainly not to condemn it, but to say wherein it is tragic: in an affirming cast toward time which brings on that which is to come, but identical with a dissenting turn away from the "same" time – which must be lived now.

Should men embrace the alternative in flight from tragedy? Many will. The prevalent attitude and "wisdom" will be to "kneel, worship, fawn on him who now is great," to abandon a cause as soon as it is known as lost, to avoid self-dependent solitude even at the cost of losing the self. Such is and will remain the opportunist mind of the crowd, of the human kind. But some will choose to stay alone, deeming themselves free, to stand up for their own being, to exist as unique men. To those few a protest, even if always a lost cause, even if only a protest against, in bounds of time, will be worth their while, their short while in the world. To those the Titanic challenger of heaven opens the temporal entrance into tragic being. They will live as proper creatures of Prometheus.

CHAPTER III

The Tragic Fear - Oedipus King

SOPHOCLES: OEDIPUS THE KING

The hills and high ways, the bays and valleys, and in between them, clinging to slopes and hiding in curves, sparse settlements of city-states. Such are the seen aspects of the small, tight world in which Oedipus dwells. A world very tight and narrow for the pressures of FEAR which fills and overflows it, a world inhospitable in concealment for a man who tries to flee. Is Oedipus a coward? Does he not show that impetuous, arrogant bravery which may seem the cause of his downfall? Yes, and many times. But his prideful drive, facing up to enemies and obstacles in his way, is no more than a shell, a shield covering what all the while moves him and shapes his character: the choice of fearful flight with no expected refuge, the choice to sever himself off from the inseparable, to run away from that which in running is still carried along – his self to be, his own future.

> ... I went to Delphi secretly.
> Apollo gave no answer to my question
> But sent me off, anguished and terrified,
> With fearful prophecies that I was fated
> To be my mother's husband, to bring forth
> Children whom men could not endure to see,
> And to take my father's life. When I heard this
> I turned and fled, hoping to find at length
> Some place ...

The place he hoped to find he could not; a place where he would be other than himself. Not because the oracle must be infallible, but because he believed it. To disregard the prophecy would have been a possible choice. It was not his. The choice which made him what he became, whether self-made or imposed upon, was that of fear. This started the absurd flight to preserve and assert his own existence of the present in escaping from what he in faith accepted to be his own existence in the future. The tragic king whose words will sound in terror exists from that choice onward. The fear which drives him through his small, dark world, does not stretch out to things or people around him. It relates nowhere, it stays within as severance, as a cut where no such cut should be, between his now and his tomorrow; this fear is about his own being in time.

~

The world in which one can find Oedipus has many aspects not seen overtly, which can give occasion and nourishing substance to fear. It can yield a picture of awaiting traps in a great web. That web, so often called by the name of fate, is yet spun and expanded in time, willingly or not, by what is known as human actions. It is spun in the dark, by steps and gestures which are undertaken without sufficient insight, but undertaken they must be, if men are not to lose the spark of spontaneity they cherish. The predicament is hinted at in the words Oedipus speaks to fend off the charge of overhasty suspicion and condemnation of Creon.

> When a conspiracy is quick in forming,
> I must move quickly to retaliate
> If I sat still and let my enemy act,
> I would lose everything that he would gain.

Oedipus is fearful and suspicious. Granted this much, does this alter the problem he is faced with? Would his words not bind someone not known as fearful and suspicious? How should he proceed in a similar situation? With reasonable prudence, it might be said. But the essence of reasonable prudence is not only not to act with undue haste but also to act with due promptness where justified. The junction, however, at which justified action fits, is clearly displayed only in abstractions. If the conspiracy against the ruling order were real, Oedipus would, like Cicero, earn only praise for crushing it before it was obvious to every citizen. A conspiracy by its nature is not likely to be publicly obvious, unless it has already gained such strength and self-assurance that it can permit easy discovery. Then Oedipus as king would have failed in his watchful duties toward his state. To fail to act is also to act.

It is not only kings and leaders who are weighed down with the demand for action. It is the common lot of men, to judge themselves and to be judged for the value of deeds they commit and also of those they omit. What Oedipus sees, or rather the way in which he sees the living structure of his world, you can but try to glimpse and assimilate, to share with him the tragic vision of his world. It does not sink into a crushing inescapable pessimism saying that no matter how you turn, act, and decide, you must be trapped and overwhelmed. Oedipus does not believe that to be the conclusion of his tragic life. Rather, the view resulting is that no matter what, you must decide and act, and so with your own hands prepare what may be a tragic failure and misfortune. The tragic vision here is not that this world is no more than a web-trap where like caught flies you just rebound from the walls, but that traps abound into which you run of what seems to be your own free accord. If the presence of such traps were to point to a trapper, he would have to be granted a good knowledge of his game.

Oedipus is only too human, neither titanic nor immortal, unlike Prometheus in his solitude. And so from his proper story hints of universal human significance can be derived, a pattern of what may be, of what may be tragic, not only for him but for you or me. This pattern of what may be need not be particularized, it need not linger with the horrible details of his own adventures which can happen to be considered unusual and unlikely. Likely or not, they have their own empirical individuality, they are purely his. But there is more, much more in Oedipus' way to see and to be, which is not exclusively his and yet with him is tragic. What is it like to exist within this fearful world?

There is, first, what has the aesthetic function of a symbol, but deserves a deeper psychological name of a trauma:

> Oh, narrow crossroad where the three paths meet!

The crossroads of Oedipus: the place where Laius was killed and where his son committed his terrible and only conscious crime. He knew he killed a man there, but he thought it a deed of valor, provoked by the vanity of the unknown man whom he fought and vanquished in his prime, along with his followers; this deed turned out to be parricide, not known, not regretted, not attended to at the time. It is the mention of the crossroads that begins to open Oedipus' eyes and starts him on his doomed search of his self. It is the crossroads that he invokes at the end, when his search is successful, when all is revealed in the sight of everyone but himself, when he has looked at himself and refused to look any more. This is the literal crossroads, the forgotten point in his past flight, which traumatically embraces all his destiny.

The crossroads which may be are everywhere, at all stages of a man's progress, not attended to, not recognized as crossroads. The human way winds and branches off continually, through all steps, all deeds, all decisions. A man does not know it, though, which unimportant step is to be his traumatic crossroads. As Tiresias suggests, men can "have eyesight and cannot see" what they do and become and are. So many incidents happen, require to be received, appropriated, directed; men have to handle them, to respond, to move. Their crossroads are built by their own acts, committed or omitted. They cannot help acting. But how? A word spoken at random may offend and produce an enemy; another equally light-weight may arouse sudden interest and initiate great love or friendship. A single look or gesture may return a manifold of happiness or pain. The roots, occasions, promptings of grave happenings in life are minuscule crossroads, too trifling to be noticed, too unpredictable to be planned. They often are not serious: laughter greets the new guest who kisses the maid's hand and tips his host. Yet comic or disastrous, man's vacuous, random acts have this germinating power hidden from his view, to confront him with unawaited sequels of what he indisputably does, unbeknownst. Not only must he move but he must grope. The full weight of every present action cannot possibly lie in the light, since it rests in what is yet to come. Passing all action crossroads, man is ahead of his own awareness. Not ever fully knowing what he does, can he in clear fairness deserve rewards or punishments? Glorious or tragic outcome, is it ever proper?

The crossroads crime of Oedipus is his only one. It can hardly be cited against him as a misdemeanor that he had fled from his supposed home and parents at Corinth, terrified by the oracle, or that he was wise enough to answer the Sphinx, thus liberating Thebes, or that from its grateful citizens he accepted their throne and their queen, admittedly a lady older than himself, but to his knowledge no more than that. Wedding a well-preserved widow is not exactly criminal; especially having left one's mother safely behind in another city. The crossroads killing appears indeed as criminal. But even there extenuating circumstances could easily be brought forward in an intelligent court of law. How strong might have been the provocation suffered by Oedipus? Who in best evidence struck the first blow? How much could be made of a claim of self-defense, and being outnumbered? Was there intent to kill or was the death of Laius largely accidental, due to bad heart condition or blood pressure? The irony of such a phantom trial is that no matter what its verdict, even if Oedipus were to be found not guilty of any crime, the chain of consequences could still stretch untouched onto his royal seat at Thebes, his search, discovery and condemnation. Thus his "objective" guilt does not seem to be of primary import.

But still, you could probably say, there at the crossroads Oedipus was at fault: acting in pride and anger against strangers he did not know as enemies. A fault, a clear fault to be punished; you would be satisfied in feeling justice done. Are you then his better, casting stones? Cool, cool reason you boast of, reject emotional, irresponsible motives of unforeseen impetus? Is this a human character or a rationalist fancy? The saintly seer, Tiresias, is as much apt as Oedipus to move in pride and anger, under provocation, as much at fault then, as much to be punished. Where are those beings who move without being moved inwardly – are they human beings? Is not responding to challenge in a situation a part of man's way to exist not only ineradicable but admired? Men climb mountains, fight wars, run races, knowing and accepting the odds against success, the odds in favor of damage and destruction. When Creon asks, appealing: "Who would choose kingship, if with the same power he could sleep in peace?," the answer is: all men looked up to in history's annals, all men who want their name to last, all men who choose their ambitious drive. Men reason sometimes, and offtimes their reason allows them so much more ardently to strive. The truth of a possibly tragic existence is that a man has to act and in acting cannot eliminate the unknown risk, cannot destroy the power of others to move him to love, anger, jealousy, cannot avoid exposing his naked weakness, cannot enshroud himself in static, abstract virtue, but must exhibit flaws, failings, and faults. For man to be is to be finite, vulnerable, wanting; and to know himself as such. To be never at fault, never in expectation of this fault's claiming a result that may come, is to be at least dead. Life is an adventure of passions.

What of the values found along the crossing roads of action, so appraised now, so looked forward to in future? Again, the world of Oedipus and his journey through it reveals some new clearings, and obscures some old, familiar ones. It is only too true for Oedipus, when he is told by Tiresias: "It is the same good fortune that has ruined you." True, though amazing, What is the goodness that ruins? For him, it is his greatest feat, his strongest claim to celebrity: his conquest of the Sphinx. If he had not been able to unravel the riddle, he would have died, there and then, without continuance toward his final humiliation. If he had not encountered the Sphinx, not gone on the road to Thebes, he would not have become a king and a criminal known to all. Yet this would have been possible without changing the fact of his already having killed Laius. Here is then a fascinating example of causal analysis: the effect, his eventual disaster, follows not from the "evil" cause, his slaying of his father, but from the "good' cause, his saving of Thebes from the Sphinx. The direct ground of his suffering is not what he can have reason to repent but what he has a reason to prize and be proud of. Is it now easy, for him or for anyone, to discern where his fortune is good and where bad? When the old shepherd, trembling before his royal might. pleads in confusion? "What have I done my lord? What have I done? " what should he be told? There is the old and orthodox outlook in which the shepherd performed a purely good deed an act of kindness, charity and pity, preserving the life of a defenseless, abandoned child. Oedipus cannot adopt this outlook, cannot approvingly thank the shepherd; he curses that deed. And if you stand by with sympathy for Oedipus, watching his fortunes unroll, watching the brink to which the shepherd's testimony nears him decisively, can you still unhesitatingly assure the shepherd: Rest in peace, you have done what is good?

The truth of values in tragic existence is not reassuring, quiescent, reliable. They could be that in a Platonic heaven, not in the world men inhabit: men with a sensitive conscience such as that of Hamlet. In their life values radiate inescapably in two ways. There are no human deeds, experiences, events, which could be nothing but good, nothing but evil. Every value is valid in ambivalence. Is not too much said here? No. This could be only a rough generalization, admitting counterexamples of situations and happenings which taken by themselves show nothing positive or nothing negative in value – but for the fact of temporality in man's existence. There are no happenings or deeds of man which can be isolated by themselves and then conclusively evaluated. That can be done only for purposes of theoretical abstraction, but not in life which stretches historically between where it has lived and where it has to live. The consequential paths from all crossroads one has to pass are, if not infinite, at least uncountable. The indefinite if finite future harbors indefinite, un-guessed value for all of the past and present. Casting about for a single case of a human event which would be not only good in its happening, but founding, breeding only good in time, you must look in vain. Not even the Crucifixion stands up to these requirements, if as a Christian, you reflect honestly and without fanaticism. There perhaps, it might be said, a balance can be drawn at any rate, a balance in favor of goodness. For the present age, perhaps. But thinking so, you are apt to forget that any balance drawn by any man is no more than provisional, subject to change until the end of times. This ever-looming, indefinite future is the reason for the inescapable ambivalence of all values for man. And so with anguish or with irony you have to learn from Oedipus' good fortune which has ruined him that no man ever knows what he does himself in his time, if such a knowledge were to amount to saying: What I have done, seen, lived through, is good. Not for a tragic vision is the child-like faith that a good tree can bear good fruit only.

Such is the world in which Oedipus exists. Can you still wonder that fear is proper to it? When what a man undertakes can always be crucial for him without his being aware of it, when to act and pursue with feeling is to expose his vulnerable nakedness, when to reach ahead toward what he values is neither to attain nor to deserve it properly, when what he counts to rely upon, with assent of ages, gives way under his hand, yields, vanishes or turns bitter and crushing? Where in this world may fear not be at home?

～

To widen the scope of this vision of the world one can glance further at the alternative dispositions of the others amongst whom Oedipus lives. None of them share in his tragic character, to none of them are his fortunes proper, yet being close to him they cannot be blind to what is there for him and may be for them. His tragic aura reflects in their eyes. How do they bear it?

One personality which appears equally prominent, although very different from Oedipus', is that of Tiresias, the seer who not only stands up to but actually is capable of looking down upon the king. Where is his height obtained from? Is it genuine? The haughty stand of Tiresias is erected upon his possession of the unique gift of prophecy, of seeing things concealed from others, both those which have happened and those which are to happen. Whether this gift is as powerful as Thebans believe, with his encouragement, is one question. But that its possession does not create such a gap between himself and all others as Tiresias wishes to maintain, that is fairly clear. His very first words lament the uselessness of wisdom – at the same time claiming its attainment by himself. But is his second sight, a supernumerary

sense equipment, equivalent to wisdom? He attempts to remain above
the common stream of human adventures, indeed he hardly admits to
being human, to sharing in the vicissitudes of the life of man. Is this
the course of wisdom? Does one not rather understand by that word
an achievement toiled for in the rough school of experience, developed
for oneself but inmidst of the common throng of aspiring fellow-
humans – as was the case with Socrates – rather than a gift freely
given by the capricious favor of the gods? The behavior of Tiresias
in his confrontation with Oedipus also scarcely demonstrates wisdom.
To a courteous demand, to a reminder of his citizenship, to an appeal
to his sense of duty, he finds no response. He does make use of his gift
only under provocation, reacts to insulting taunts of the king, showing
himself to be a man of flesh and passion, just like the other, no higher.
And how is to be interpreted the curious impotence of Tiresias at the
time when the Sphinx threatened the city? He was either unable or
unwilling to remove the plague. In one case this gift of hidden knowledge appears not only capriciously given to him, but also capriciously
restricted in use by the giver. In the other case, if he could and would
not contribute his help, letting his compatriots wait for rescue by a
stranger, justified respect for his nobility cannot be exaggerated.
What of his claim to power? Even if it be true that Tiresias knows
about the destiny of all men, his foresight is certainly not the making
of that destiny, just as the man who accurately predicts the time of
arrival of a ship is not thereby an agent of that force which moves the
ship toward its port of call. Tiresias then is rather like the child who
overheard a secret of the mighty, and struts and boasts as if it shared
their might. In addition, his phrase, so well repeated after: "What is
to come, will come" – is a one-sided, limited truth, if truth it is at all.
What it omits or denies is that it is you yourself who by your actions
make come that which will come, that it is your very own character
which determines your future, that unless you are nothing, without
your participation what will come "is" not yet to come, though it
may come. Your part in the shaping of your destiny cannot be disregarded: for that you would pay the penalty of consciously intended
self-negation. Thus again Tiresias in his too simple fatalism shows
himself remarkably similar to the submissive crowd of Thebans
around him. A semi-god removed from human horizons? Not at all.
Why then the distance, the self-elevation he insists upon? The answer
seems to be that while Tiresias certainly does not know everything,
he does know enough of the genuinely human lot and its tragic perspectives to wish to remove and alienate himself from it. Not success-

fully, by any means, as has been indicated above. But he endeavors, and persists in trying to be more than human, because he is thoroughly frightened of what it means to be a man, and no more than a man. Fear is his motive, from which flow both his submissive exaltation of non-human fate and his assumed grandeur in face of the whole mortal race. His attitude can be summed up in one word: pretense.

As Tiresias openly rejects a tragic human role, so the people of Thebes, even their elders, are incapable of casting themselves for it:

> ... Great king,
> Glorious in all men's eyes, we now beseech you
> To find some way of helping us, your suppliants...
> Apollo, thou healer, to whom in our dread we cry,
> We are anguished, racked, and beset by fears!...
> All-ruling Zeus, if thou art king indeed,
> Put forth thy majesty, make good thy word,
> Faith in these fading oracles restore!...
> Look to the end of mortal life. In vain
> We say a man is happy, till he goes
> Beyond life's final border, free from pain.

Suppliants they are, crying, beseeching, shaking, despairing beggars. The refrain of resignation runs through all the words and speeches one can hear from them. They are pious – if piety can be set on a par with a continuous demand for help, shot through with imbecile distrust of those even, whose support they seek: "Zeus, if thou art king indeed"? They are too crushed by fear to gather themselves for a self-dependent response, to rise from their knees and move, to look out and judge where they stand. Sheep delivered absolutely into the hands of their shepherd, though he may choose to play butcher. They flatten themselves imploring Oedipus, previously a satisfactory redeemer; they will flatten themselves before his successor the moment Oedipus disappears, glad to be rid of this human who seemed a king and proved a horror. They will obey all commands loud enough; they will believe in any force superior to their own, above all that most unfathomed, unnamed, unresponding divinity of fate. The deserts of their worship? They have to serve such gods as they are worthy of. With their own distrust and feeble hostility they infest heaven itself, praying – or is it praying? – "O Zeus, hurl down thy lightning upon Ares!" In their self-confessed ignorance and impotence anything unexplained and not humanly usual, hence not of unworthy human origin, such as Tiresias' sight or the intoxicated words of the Delphic priestess, deserves unswerving, humble reverence: "I cannot go in full faith unless men see that omens never fail." Who could here sift and

separate the serious, fruitful grains of faith from the chaff of super-
stitious terror? To doubt, to test, to unmask a man posing as prophet
or oracle is for them as clearly impious, insolent, profane and presumptuous as to defy the Olympians themselves. Any daring, any
original, any protesting expression, anything strong of human origin
merits in their eyes, and must encounter in their fatalist prejudice, an
immediate, disastrous downfall. To act on one's own, to try and find
out rather than be told, to choose one's strength, be it limited, all that
is beyond their supposedly human level, and therefore wrong. Woe to
king Oedipus and his proud hybris! If such blindness, inaction, lack
of inward movement with the single exception of fear could ever be
called tragic, then stones would have to be the most tragic creatures
in the universe. Of tragic light suffusing Oedipus all that transcends
toward the Theban humanity around him is fear, of themselves, of all
that may be theirs, of death the unknown from which they cry to be
saved, and of life more full of pain than death.

Pretense rising toward the superhuman in Tiresias, and trembling
resignation self-enclosed in immobile humanity among the Theban
elders. Still another and not less fearful attitude is suggested by queen
Jocasta. Here is a reckless, almost cynical surrender of her human
character to all the winds that blow through existence:

> Why should you be afraid? Chance rules our lives,
> And no one can foresee the future, no one.
> We live best when we live without a purpose
> From one day to the next.

A seeming conquest of fear. At what cost? As the result of exchang-
ing the life of a human person for that of a butterfly. Because that is
what Jocasta proposes: to destroy forcibly the temporal structure of
man for whom his past and his future are equally proper to his present
day. An interesting if not a very promising enterprise, obviously
arrived at, for lack of another solution, in the course of a close look at
human experience. Jocasta is by no means stupid: her intelligence
has seen through the rigid emptiness of the orthodox beliefs and
superstitions of the surrounding crowd. Nor is she entirely irreligious:
she comes praying before the altar of Apollo and offers a challenging
prayer: "Deliver us from fear!" And yet her religious tie to the world
around her, apparently directed by the gods, does not remain whole,
is shattered in the installation, above the orderly deities, of a negative
one: chance. "Chance rules our lives." If chance in fact could rule –
regulate, order, organize? It would not be chance any more. Instead,

perhaps Jocasta should be saying: Our lives are not ruled, nor should we rule them ourselves. Hence the shattering of temporality, of order, integrity and roundness, whatever of that a whole life-time can achieve. If chaos is the rule – or no rule – for passage from day to day, if there is nothing proper in what has been nor in what will be, then oracles must indeed be out of business, then one must be ready for anything whatever, for any wind, any breeze, any hurricane. What may be one's own must remain completely unrestricted. To aim, to hope, and to fear would be equally without foundation. Here is Jocasta's apparent triumph over fear. But does she remain faithful to her own proposal, does she verify the possibility of sustaining this attitude of being ready to cope with anything in the strict and only present? No. Very soon it is Oedipus' turn to say to her: "Do not be frightened." Because Jocasta, reckless without a future, begs him now: "Give up this search! I have endured enough." She breaks, when the gates of future and past are opened in Oedipus' search for himself. Fear has reclaimed Jocasta's humanity. Can you blame her, this palace lady whose dominion has been anything but untroubled, this mother of royal power, powerless to save her first son, this wife whose first husband vanished and whose second husband now reappears as her son? She has indeed endured enough; and yet perhaps not more than many other women around her, around you. What wife and mother ever lived free of fear?

These are the people of Thebes whose expression is sufficiently determined to disclose what is proper to them; this is not the case with others appearing there. None of them are without fear. But none of them enter into the tragic mode of human being: neither Tiresias whose superhuman pretense rouses suspicion, nor the elders whose despair of humanity deserves contempt, not even Jocasta whose reckless abandonment of human possibilities awakens at best a tolerant sympathy. None of them try to give their sense to being human, none choose to be themselves. The cyclone of fear which blows around the person of their king is too strong for them, devastates what could be their proper existence. How is it with Oedipus? It is quite different.

After trying to imagine how Oedipus can see the world in which he exists with the people related to him, it can be asked next how his character is shaped in fear. He first appears in serene majesty:

> I have come to you myself, I, Oedipus,
> Renowned in the sight of all. Tell me what desire or fear
> Brings you before me? I will gladly give you
> Such help as is in my power.

No fugitive, no suppliant. A giver, not a seeker of help, aware of some power within himself. Aware, too, that the world pattern is graven by many universal forces; but such a force he accounts himself to possess, in virtue of the rule vested in him:

> Each of you suffers for himself alone,
> But my heart feels the heaviness of my sorrow,
> Your sorrow, and the sorrow of all the others.

Because he feels "more for their sakes than for my own life," therefore he wants to live on an open pedestal of truth, accessible, supervised by all whose interests cross within his actions. He is an agent, not only for himself but for the people entrusted to his care; more than an individual. He is the shepherd; and more even than their lives to him, he belongs to them in his care. He belongs. Then he is at rest, has found the place he had set out to win for himself long ago, where he can be and live with others, with himself, free of a future menace? So it would appear. Yet in his super-individual place, where his identity covers that of the whole state, he cannot and does not forget that he is also human. He will act in the enlightened interest, of his own as well: "For my own sake, since the murderer may strike at me as well." More likely it is, in fact, that he, the king, is in danger from an alien enemy of Thebes: uneasy lies the head which is his own. What he, an individual, has gained, may be wrested from him, it is his conquest only at the cost of constant watch against tomorrow. The place he has acquired is of enough worth for him, the homeless or home-forbidden one. He, more than anyone else who could occupy it, must cling to it desperately. His kingship has become and is, his proper, but will it stay so? The enemy or competitor, besides, does not have to be alien. Jealously power must be guarded within the state and without. Is there any wonder now in the pressing strain of suspicion already cited, which goes against Creon and his possible, definitely possible, conspiracy? Any king would have to respond to such possibilities, but king Oedipus has drastic personal reasons to watch out. His established being may crumble, leaving him not only without royalty but without any self. No factors, none at all, dare be considered, which could be disposed against him. Law and rightness, traditional customs, links of former friendship, all must be disregarded for Oedipus to remain himself: "I am the king. I rule." So quickly is this claim counterbalanced, so reasonably, by Creon: "Not if you rule unjustly." But if ever absolute dominion could be claimed absolutely, with all the demand of existence, it is so in case of Oedipus. More follows. Driven by his need, absolute against all less immediate influences, to assert himself in his proper place, Oedipus defies the external power of fate worshipped by Thebans, and sweeps away his bondage to oracles, hearing the news that the king of Corinth is dead. Here he stands now, the ruler of Thebes and not a parricide, with the threat removed forever:

> Hear that, Jocasta! Why should anyone
> Give heed to oracles from the Pythian shrine,
> Or to the birds that shriek above our heads?

Why should anyone? Well, and why did he? Here is the culmination of Oedipus' active might, of his striving to be someone: raised above the common run of men, proud against society and law, daring to challenge the voice of the gods. This, in the judgment of Thebans and of many for centuries after, is his hybris, his undoing defect: pride unpermitted in the human being. This is his source of downfall, this is what justice tragically must punish; then all is well, proper and in balance. But in such thinking is it seen that his is a very unsafe, very frightened pride which speaks because it dares not stay silent? Because it wants to soothe and convince none other but Oedipus himself? This, the vertigo of his royal summit, should be the cause of his tragic reward? What kind of causality is in question here? All the causal links have been forged well before, and now only the effects remain to strike. The cause of Oedipus' disaster impious pride? This can not be meant in earnest. The cause of his now irrecoverable future lies in his youthful flight, the choice of fear which took him from Corinth to Thebes. Had he not so chosen, then no matter what his history might have been, he would not be who he is, he would not pass through the crossroads of death. Once such crossroads behind him, were he meek as a shorn lamb, he is open to suffering, though by no means inevitably. If the genuine first source of his fortunes, good and bad, is sought, there is only one: the choice of flight. And that choice can hardly be described as impious hybris. It expressed not defiance but belief in the oracle as divine; hence his fright. Of course, it can be argued that then Oedipus tried to get the better of the gods, to outwit them by running away. What was his alternative? To believe that he is going to kill his father and mate with his mother, and to wait calmly in place until all this came to pass? When once his faith and affection of the time are posed, to expect from him anything but fear, to expect him to stay inactive in fear or without fear, is to take him for something less than human. What then is Oedipus being "punished" for? For accepting a choice, for being human, for sharing the faith of his home. That is his original hybris. And now, as king, he is just as anxious as in his youth, to prove his faith-full fear unnecessary, to be able to stay himself.

Then the next phase devolves pregnantly: the king who unkings himself, Oedipus in his search of the criminal he discovers himself to be. It starts from the unknowing, anonymous curse, thrown on the person, whoever it may be, of Laius' killer. This person and his deed, unexplored, untried, is condemned as evil. Here perhaps, rather than elsewhere, there is an overhasty step, not wholly required by Oedipus' quest for security of his crown, his life, and his state. It is that step which nears the loss of all for him. It does not, however, make it unavoidable. The curse is thrown in what appears to represent parallel interests of his, public and personal. It produces a conflict of these interests and faces him with a choice, when the identity searched for is revealed. He could then renounce his curse, deny his word, stay on the throne and sacrifice the interests of his subjects. He does not choose so, and is not very likely to, but he could. This should be noted for weighing the balance of his motives in catastrophe. He does not choose to remain king, because Thebes would suffer. Perhaps he is not even quite aware of that open choice and that motive. The fact remains that in deciding against himself, he keeps his faith with Thebans belonging to his care. To the end, he acts as their king, not as only one individual.

The search goes on, with the aid of Tiresias, provoked into speech. He then speaks clearly. Does Oedipus grasp and examine the shocking accusation hurled against him? No, he remains quite uncomprehending, showing that those who search are by no means always disposed to find. All that Tiresias' words evoke in him is distrust, and suspicion of a plot. These lie ready just below the surface of his fearful consciousness. The truth begins to dawn on him with the mention of the crossroads. That mention constitutes another crucial point on Oedipus' way. Because from there on the search is changed, and changing the character of Oedipus. Now it is no mere hunt for a remote criminal, undertaken dutifully as well as selfishly by the king, but with remote chances of real danger or of success. Now success of search and its danger are no longer remote – and the criminal draws close. Now Oedipus is in search of himself, and thoroughly determined to complete it, and to ruin the place he has reached: "I stand on the brink of horrors – but I must." What goes on here? Some kind of perverse compulsion? Hardly. This is the stage where Oedipus catches up with his fear of himself and stands up barring its spread. The name of this perversity is courage. And yet – can one maintain that he has destroyed his fear, that he has ceased trembling on the brink of horrors? This obviously is not so. One must then conclude that courage is not at all the opposite of fear, its killing antidote. No, courage is no more than another species of fear, such fear as holds a man still in its grip but which he refuses to admit as proper to himself. It is this courage, this disowned fear, which Oedipus chooses now and drives himself on with. Inevitably, he must; he will not choose otherwise. This search is now his own. This search, so fearful, so courageous, is now the home stretch of the long run, begun in Corinth, years before, the run toward the dreaded meeting with his future self. And this is the reason why none of its stages have been devoid of fear: because fear is his disposition toward the future, just as his rage is turned to the present, just as regret can be a way to his past. When the run is completed, Oedipus comes home, to himself. His fear is then gone.

To appreciate the character of Oedipus is above all to realize that he has a man's character, or more precisely that it is his character which makes his story proper to him. The early choice of flight he sees as his own, and never denies; the same can be said about his anxious clinging to the royal place he has won; and the same about his courageous drive toward self-discovery. If this close look at the path of his life is true, then the continuing thread through it is that of fear. But this fear is chosen, appropriated, and lastly faced by himself. That could scarcely be said about fear which surrounds him and dominates the other people in Thebes: neither Tiresias, nor Jocasta, nor the elders would acknowledge their fear as proper, as chosen, as belonging to them. It is theirs, but neither accepted nor rejected; it is beyond them, a feature of their world, not of their character. It happens to them, as it might to millions of others. If human character could be a qualification for royalty, Oedipus must be truly a king. Perhaps after all it is not so easy to be human and not only to happen among the membership of mankind?

~

The resolution of Oedipus' tragic action opens his protest. It is more telling as a deed, a gesture, rather than as an articulate expression. The deed is to deprive himself of sight, by his own decision and hand, with his own reason:

Why should I see? What sight could have given me pleasure?
What is there now to love? What greeting can cheer me?
... Could I endure
To look my fellow-citizens in the face?
Never! Never! If I had found some way
Of choking off the fountain of my hearing,
I would have made a prison of my body,
Sightless and soundless. It would be sweet to live
Beyond the reach of sorrow.

Beyond sorrow, grief, painful remembrance, misfortune – as these words of Oedipus can also be interpreted: beyond all care. Escape from care, this is what Oedipus wishes for, and later much more fully Faust will echo him. To be without care, sightless and soundless, to retreat from the world, not to stand out into it, not to exist, but to curl oneself imprisoned into a moodless body, nowhere, out of time: that would be – not will be – sweet. This is the inclining, unreasonable reason in his self-destruction of sight. His vision of the world is more than full. His being in the world is condemned, and not only for himself in isolation: his protest must comprise the expanse of his care, the mother-wife now dead, the children now deserted and shamed, the Theban people he was to guide now suffering from a plague he induced. Not in solitude his ruin; to curse his own existence is to curse the affliction it involved others in, unjustly, improperly, but unavoidably.

While Oedipus commits his deed of protest, the elders lament, in fitting expression of how they conceive themselves to be human:

Men are of little worth. Their brief lives last
A single day.
They cannot hold elusive pleasure fast;
It melts away.
All laurels wither; all illusions fade;
Hopes have been phantoms, shade on air-built shade,
Since time began.

Must Oedipus join in this chorus of resigned abnegation of humanity? No, he does not. And here is the Promethean difference between him and the humans around him, who feel phantom-like, withered leaves in the air blown around, of no self-motion or worth. Oedipus is the one who can and does condemn; but condemned by him is Oedipus only. What worth he finds, negative or positive, what moving agency of glory and of downfall, he finds it in his own hand. "My curse can rest on no one but myself." That the event, the outcome, is unmerited, he knows; and that the world contains overpowering forces and sources of events, against which he struggled and failed. But he does not discount or abnegate his own agency among them. Why does Oedipus not commit suicide like Jocasta? Is it self-preservation in that life which has nothing more to offer? Is it still fear, of crossing the bar? Or is it perhaps a wish to expiate in this same world his crimes which are doubtful crimes but which he nevertheless acknowledges as no one's but his, and standing responsible, demands punishment for? Be that as it may, the one clear insight which is opened in his parting words is that Oedipus, mistakenly or not, is conscious of his freedom, of himself having acted. Despite the undeniable fact, stressed by Creon, that "even you will now believe the god." Oedipus accepts the oracle's truth, but does not have to submit to it. His actions were "fated" from outside, from before; this need not mean any more than that they were correctly predicted in time, this need not mean that they were made, undertaken, chosen, by anyone but Oedipus. His history now stretches before himself in review, and he finds it strictly his: to respond to, to place blame on, to curse, there is no one but himself. Now he recalls his crossroads, now he can look back to his first choice of flight, in Corinth. However – it seems so easy to "determine" that choice, to relieve him from responsibility for it, to make it look imposed upon him, by reasons of youth, upbringing, religion, natural human reactions. Or to "determine" his crossroads fight with Laius, as provoked, as justified defense, as ignorant instinct. This has been spoken of. But the point of the present assessment is not that he, or you, or anyone, can know that Oedipus' actions were free or not free, that he chose to perform them or that he was chosen to. The point is that to the end Oedipus accepts his choice as his, that otherwise he would not be the man he is.[1] And that is the compass of his protest: to be always with others in the world, to care for oneself and others and thereby to spread unwanted affliction, to act on one's own and thereby try to verify one's freedom without possessing knowledge of it in the dark – and to fail, on one's own, too.

The protest in the sense of dissent is expressed by Oedipus in brief, undeveloped plaint at the conclusion of his story. But the protest in the original, neutral sense of bearing witness – is not his whole story an expression of it? His initial flight says: I am here now, innocent, I have taken notice of what my future is supposed to bring, but I, Oedipus, am in the present, I do not know the criminal Oedipus of the

[1] "Isn't it awful a man should be driven to do a thing like that – and be responsible?" – Conrad, *Lord Jim*.

future, and however I move, only this here and now is I. All his subsequent steps and crossroads and gains are to bear witness to this preservation of identity in the present, are to declare his lasting present innocence and merit. And then, when the flight and the search are over, Oedipus protests, but in different terms. By limiting his curse to himself, he assumes responsibility. In what sense? Not in the sense of a guilty plea or confession before any court; as indicated above, in any trial he would have plenty of excuses. What he responds for is his whole being. This is his acknowledgement of the limited incompleteness of a man in the here and now, the reunion with the future he has fled and the past he admits as belonging to himself. It is his confession that no man is ever just in the present, there to be described as innocent or criminal, as worthy of merit or of contempt. A man exists also in his future and in his past, and those phases of the same identical existence he can neither grasp, nor deserve, nor change; "they" are beyond him, yet his; not necessarily in control of an alien fate but necessarily within that temporal human being which is his own. When Oedipus thus finds himself, embracing his future and past in his present, then and only then is his fear destroyed. That certainly does not mean that he is now in possession of some self-contained serenity. On the contrary, he cries and curses. He now protests against this truth of existence which is by no means easy to bear calmly. His temporal responsibility is not equivalent to acquiescence. Yet this in the fullness of his vision is the truth. A tragic truth.

If you now ask why the life of Oedipus is TRAGIC, an interesting situation is revealed. Because I neither can nor need to answer this question. The answer to it lies already in the exposition of what it is that Oedipus protests against. This is a noteworthy confluence, casting light on the reason why the concept of protest is a fitting clue to the exploration of what is tragic. That is, if you still heed the view that it is not events which make existence tragic but vice versa. As events go, the story of Oedipus could lend itself to a humorous, parodying interpretation, granted a sufficiently cynical and macabre dose of sense of humor. To dispose of the old man without his knowing what hit him? Why should one care a hang about that? To settle the matrimonial ad of one's own old lady? Well, it is a sort of silly situation, but she was still not so bad to look at, and anyway she is now gone and buried. Other people have nothing to boast of in their mates, and that business about incest was exploded along with the stork. And so on. Are you amused? If not, this is not the story for you. The limits of humor are unpredictable. So of course is the individual approach to what is serious, which can be only suggested, and only to those who wish to approach it seriously and relate to what is most likely to be serious for themselves. Aristotle, remember, holds that when you experience what is tragic, it must strike you as serious. In such a spirit, it would seem that what has been elicited about Oedipus' protest above is less open to parody – if you are at all like Oedipus. Then his truth which was tragic for him, may be equally yours and equally tragic for you. In other words, it is a question of vision available to a man of Oedipus' character. Not that he killed a father and married a mother, but that it was his father and his mother whom he acknowledges and respects as his own, yet whom he has treated improperly. Not that a prediction about him came true, but that he has striven with all his might to prevent its fulfillment. Not that his home, family and town did not prosper, but that by his own actions, unknowingly, he has brought disaster to those he cares for. These are the tragic aspects of Oedipus' life; and that in such light he has to see the truth of his life, maybe of others' – that is what he protests against.

It is the inescapable unity of human time that changes Oedipus' protest into protest against. And the latter is more true than the former, it incorporates a fuller vision. Why? What makes for this transition? It is that disposition of Oedipus which has been so strongly emphasized on the preceding pages under the name of fear. It is, however, a specific phenomenon, not to be equated with all types and modifications of fear. It is not fear of anything or anyone in the world. It is fear of his own future being, which thus induces a cut in his existence, limiting him to the assertion of his now and trying to annihilate his tomorrow. Oedipus protests in the name of his present existence of today, fearing his future as alien; and that protest is inadequate, it has to give way, and will, together with his fear. The present Oedipus accepts and believes in is continuous; he does not fall into the unrealistic attitude of Jocasta in which she herself does not persist for long. And yet his future his fear cuts off, until his day of reckoning. That future he treats as an object, an object other than himself, the object of his fear; for that reason his fear must be distinguished from anxiety which aims at no thing other than oneself. Why is this fear tragic? A complete answer to this question would presuppose a theory of tragic being, here in the stage of exploration. What can be said at this point must bear upon what is tragic for Oedipus. Within this scope, this fear is tragic, because it is doomed to remain futile and self-denying; because it circumscribes with limits his attitude to his world, his people, his parents true and adoptive, his origins, his identity; because it severs him from being which is and will have been his, which he can only assume too late, when it is his past. Then he sees truth emerge from the ruins of his history, that truth as tragically proper to his existence as the fear whose choice made it so.

CHAPTER IV

The Tragic Conscience - Prince Hamlet

WILLIAM SHAKESPEARE: HAMLET, PRINCE OF DENMARK

> How weary, stale, flat, and unprofitable
> Seem to me all the uses of this world!
> Fie on't! O fie! 'tis an unweeded garden,
> That grows to seed; things rank and gross in nature
> Possess it merely.

This is a new voice. The Titan gloried in his deed of rebellion, and called the world to witness. King Oedipus eagerly searched for a place in the world, withdrawing from it only when overwhelmed by the truth of his own acts. What kind of man speaks here about his world, dejected about its rankness yet well aware of his want to weed it? Is he in an unusual mood, so that his voice can be disregarded as unnecessarily dissonant, if not morbidly sick? Is his gloom aggravated by the prods of disappointed ambition? Is he then impotently paralysed between the worth of a goal and the worthlessness of its fulfillment? Whatever the truth of such assessments, they do not disclose the root of Hamlet's way to be. That root in his ethos is CONSCIENCE.

Those who speak of Hamlet as if he were no more than a prematurely decadent soul biting into its own sick flesh, and hence of no "objective" significance, tend to forget several things. They might forget that a black-and-white criterion of sickness is a fiction; that disgust could be a clear sign of health; that anyone who carefully avoids everything unusual and everything morbid must be very far from an "objective" look at the world. If Hamlet is sick, his sickness transcends the need and the use of any human healer. It does provide a vision pregnant enough to be cited and referred to, for various manners and occasions of human life. It is by no means a joyful or complacent vision, it speaks through a melancholy mood; but does that decide anything as to its truth? Hamlet's detractors might assert that his insight is valuable only in or for certain moods; but then perhaps some kinds of truth are only accessible through the aura of some moods. The belief that man must be moodless and dispassionate to advance in his pilgrimage toward truth no longer deserves such credit as is given to fairy tales: this discolored version of truth may be of some interest to superhuman or subhuman "brains" – it is of none to men of flesh and blood. And what seems also to be under-estimated by the unconsenting critics of Hamlet's morbidity is its vast fascination for the human race, such that in this world of Hamlet, if anywhere, is unanimously found the voice of poetic greatness. Is this a danger signal then, that Hamlet speaks to so many? Are so many sick and unusual? Because such widely recognized greatness of that imaginary world centers wholly around the person of the prince: without the character of Hamlet with all its dissonance, the universal fascination would be unthinkable. The prince is the play – so much so that all the other characters, compared to him, are almost echoes, are merely "mutes and audience to" his act. Only as such will they be treated on these pages.

Hamlet is a prince. It is significant that he is neither more nor less than a prince. That in his ambition he aims at being more, that much of his vision is tied within this disappointment, that his claim to the throne of Denmark cannot be disregarded in the proper understanding of his activity or inactivity – all of that is true and must be discussed. But if that were all to be said, it would miss – Hamlet himself. Crucial is the enquiry in what way and to what extent that princely ambition is proper to this existing individual Hamlet, unique among so many disappointed princes and pretendents of so many states and societies. The meaning of his ambition for him – that certainly is a question.

And those who are impatient with Hamlet for lack of action for his seeming paralysis of mind so unfitting in a prince, in an avenger, in a hero, may also hold only a superficial fraction of truth. How Hamlet acts, what for, and when, and when not, will have to be seen more closely. But to rest with that would be to speak of only "trappings," without questioning "that within which passeth show." Such an approach may suffice for someone interested in outward experiences, actions, events, someone formally examining what is dramatic. It is insufficient, if the attempt at exploration concerns the tragic being of Hamlet.

The utmost care is needed in a supposedly systematic search of his world in which, he warns, "there are more things ... than are dreamt of in your philosophy." And yet, an entry into this world is certainly worth trying. It is a universe of protest and dejection, and at the same time one of ambition and nobility. In many respects Hamlet's way to be in the world is antithetical to that of Oedipus. To Oedipus' ethos of flight and haste Hamlet opposes a standing in readiness. Compared to the brief, mainly gestured protest of Oedipus, Hamlet presents a most sensitively articulated protest against what he finds in life. The basic contrast between them pertains to their attitude toward action. While Oedipus by acting wants to identify himself, vanquish his fated guilt and justify his present innocence, Hamlet discovers plenty of temporal reflection between himself and his own activity.

What then is the core of his predicaments in acting, which may or may not morbidly paralyze Hamlet, but which on his own terms are not to be denied? This core envelops a moral problem: how is man justified in his actions? First of all:

> ... What is a man,
> If his chief good and market of his time
> Be but to sleep and feed? a beast, no more.

This is what Hamlet cannot reconcile himself to. Thinking of man, of himself, as more than a beast, he cannot admit his restriction to blind movements in search of bodily necessities, he cannot wholly rely upon the animal "native hue of resolution," he cannot rest in being a "passion's slave." He must strain further thinking, using "that capability and godlike reason," using it precisely or "too precisely on the event," using it with reference to practical imposed tasks, sensitively, honestly, conscientiously. The consequence of this strain?

> Thus conscience does make cowards of us all.

In what sense, though? What is the "cowardly" effect of reasoning conscience? It is not that of preventing some immediate rushing responses of "bravery": no one calls Hamlet "villain," breaks his "pate across," tweaks him "by the nose," gives him "the lie i' the throat." There Hamlet would obviously react, as he does to the challenge of Laertes. He does not lack the physical disposition to annihilate fear: "I do not set my life at a pin's fee." Very clearly, something else, more strictly human, is involved: not an instinctive fear of death or danger, such as may appear in "a beast, no more." What his conscience affects is his will toward responsibility, toward

that owning of decision, of self-direction which may turn out to be
unjustified by reason – afterward: too late.

> ... I do not know
> Why yet I live to say, 'This thing's to do';
> Sith I have cause, and will, and strength, and means
> To do't.

There is a contrast here for him, a challenging interval between
thinking to himself: "this thing is to do" – and the doing of it, between
killing a man in thought, permitting oneself to kill, justifying and
willing the kill – and the real act of killing with one's hands. The
former remains within the private sphere of what is one's own, under
control of reason, to be evoked and revoked as conscience may
instruct; here one remains sovereign, and safe, and still innocent. But
the latter? Through one's hands it slips out and remains for ever real
in the public world, to be recalled in vain since impossible to unmake,
no longer one's own, alienated; and yet it is to be recognized as one's
own deed, risk, or guilt. That conscience must have power to bring
about a man's human acts, and that it must be powerless toward those
acts, as soon as done, through all ensuing time – this is what Hamlet
finds in his conscience to be tragic.

Hamlet is a prince. This is the first clue to the understanding of
his situation in the world. He is neither a king, tied by his care to his
subjects, nor a commoner, lost in a sea of citizenry. This suggests a
specific isolation, of one elevated but not bound, not a symbol yet
not one of many. If he were other than he is, he could perhaps cherish
this princely solitude without qualms, able to "sleep in peace" though
in "royal freedom," as Creon imagined it. But as he is, his princely
conscience imposes upon him alone a double tie. Well he knows that
"on his choice depends the safety and the health of the whole state,
and therefore must his choice be circumscribed," that whatever he
does, the future of Denmark is likely to be affected by it. On the other
hand, since now he does not reign and cannot directly interfere in the
shaping of that future, he may well be plagued by a sense of helpless-
ness: "Sir, I lack advancement." Thus, thinking of him as both prince
and Hamlet, though without any need to reflect on his title from
historical or dynastic bases, one can begin to appreciate the predicament of this particular prince. His isolation is also his impotence.

The problem which he faces – assuming that it is a problem for a man of conscience – is revenge. If he were not a prince, how do you imagine he could proceed? Rush blindly for the blood of his father's murderer? Yet Hamlet, even without his title, retains his humanity; and such a rush, for him, is not a human action. Also, the murderer – is there one, to be sure? And who? Quite concretely, the sequence of action and inaction, which could be taking place in an entirely irroyal house, is this.

The son receives intelligence of suspicious circumstances surrounding his father's demise. He receives it from a source which, with his educational and religious background, he cannot unequivocally trust: a supernatural apparition. A ghost, if not a phantasm of one's own brain or a collective hallucination of a group of midnight watchers enervated by the warlike situation, could still, being genuine, be genuinely evil, an emissary of the powers bent on temptation. Whether or not you hold with supernatural phenomena, would you proceed to murder on the ground of a nocturnal vision, or, for that matter, on the ground of an entirely natural but dubious information? To sit and sift the substance of your evidence, that seems to be the advisable next stage; it might conceivably occupy two whole months. Then the young man is ready with the next step: his doubts not allayed entirely, he devises a test, at least to strengthen his suspicious, perhaps to ascertain the guilt. Does the persistence of doubts and the coolly empirical approach to them deserve the censure of impatience? Certainly not from someone imbued with the spirit of experimental method. The play is the test; its result is confirmatory. The son is about to avenge his father now; what holds him back on the next occasion is his acute sensitivity to what is proportional, seemly, adequate. The punishment should fit the crime – do you by any chance accept that doctrine? And if by any chance a man dying in the midst of prayer should have a prospect of improving his ultimate destination, should that be the punishment chosen for one who took your father unprepared, thus might have speeded him on his way, not to bliss but to "the other place?" No, a more proper occasion for revenge will definitely occur. It does, very soon; only the victim is not proper. So another is killed, a rash, intruding fool, but yet a man. Would such a mishap not brake the impetus of any conscientious avenger? Before he can dispose of that braking inhibition, the course of events sends him away from home, into another country. By wit and luck, he manages not only to arrange for a return earlier than anticipated, but also to get hold of evidence which incriminates his suspect. It is evidence not of his former crime but more directly, of murderous intent against the life of the avenger himself. The situation now obtains the critical pressure of self-defence: either you take the life of the man who most probably took that of your father, or else your own remaining life is likely to be very brief. The choice is made inevitable, a step must be taken. The opportunity arises soon, and gives even the weapon to hand. Alas – that weapon has been used already; revenge must be immediate, since not half an hour of life is left to accomplish it, this revenge which now properly presses, for not just one but four victims of one and the same person. Action results: "Then venom to thy work!" It is the last action.

In this forcedly brief survey of Hamlet's events, do you find any particular stage which would be accounted for by the epithet of "morbidity" and which is not accounted for in terms of conscientious reasoning? If not, then the serious question reaches deeper than a pathological label. The question concerns the relation of Hamlet's conscience to his tragedy. Much remains to be said, much to be listened to, before that question is tackled.

The complexity of the situation increases, when upon this outward outline of what happens to Hamlet is superimposed the fact of his princely ambition. The enterprise of personal revenge now acquires the dimensions of a crown conspiracy, dimensions not personal at all: "Never alone did the king sigh, but with a general groan." Claudius, criminal or not, is the king of Denmark; attacking him is very different from an accusation against a common murderer. The prince knows that quite well. This knowledge does not deflect him from his accepted goal, but it makes his progress toward that goal more winding, more circumspect, more reflective. Public issues are at stake; in these, his own bodily welfare and mental mood are inevitably involved.

To the ghost's revelation of fratricide, Hamlet responds: "O my prophetic soul! mine uncle!" Clearly, his soul has already "prophetically" cast some suspicion upon king Claudius. Indeed, before he ever hears of the apparition, Hamlet suggests in his behavior that he is conscious of being a rival to royalty. For some reason, he does not succeed to his father's throne. How human then is his suspicion born of resentment! His very first words are brooding upon his royal relation: "A little more than kin, and less than kind." His first, not very firm, intention is to remove himself to Wittenberg, away from disappointment, doubt, or danger. Later, he receives the message about the ghost and immediately wants to possess himself of more knowledge, but exclusively: secrecy is enjoined upon Horatio and his watch companions. Suspicion feels the thread of a possible plot, for or against him. It hardens, when the ghost has spoken. The prince is on the point of sharing his "wonderful news" with people he can probably trust – and yet he refrains from it: "There's ne'er a villain dwelling in all Denmark ..." compared to him who now wears her crown – this is what Hamlet might have cried. He does not; he improvises wildly: "... but he's an arrant knave." From this one moment's holding back for a choice of silence – followed by more "wild and whirling words," by jests about the ghost, by exaggerated insistence on sealing silence by oath – can it not be assumed that here, almost incidentally, is born the project of concealment in dissembling, the project of isolation in feigned madness? This project is brought to fruition gradually, later, but it has to be reflectively organized throughout the intervening period. Then this secret of a very public import is quite effectively disguised in the pattern of a very private madness: love-madness. Ophelia is introduced as a ploy; yet Hamlet is not heartless enough not to warn her father against taking this love affair seriously: "Friend, look to't." And he continues to use his madness as he wants it, against Claudius, Polonius, Rosencrantz, Guildenstern, Laertes. To distinguish sharply what Hamlet does not mean, speaking "only" in madness, is impossible. Thus to discard his mad words as not expressing any truth, would be presumptuous; on the contrary, his madness provides him with an opportunity to say what is quite "pregnant," true and meaningful for him, yet shocking to hear for others. "Madly" it can all be safely said and meant, in irresponsible guise. Hamlet refrains from exploiting his "madness" only with Horatio, the man he wears in his "heart of heart," the only man he afterward chooses to entrust with the awesome secret of royal murder. Also, just before leaving for England, when he is both sure of his suspicions against the king and confident of his ability to outwit his escorts, he opens himself to the queen. There he can count upon her maternal feelings, not for support – in view of her strange infatuation with Claudius – but for protective secrecy. His mother would hardly betray him, knowing that betrayal must mean his immediate death. Hamlet even threatens her, quite confidently bidding her to stay silent. His disclosure to her has then no air of filial trust; it is perhaps prompted by his wish to sow dissension between the royal couple during his absence. On his return a new complication awaits him in the form of an unexpected rival candidate: "Laertes shall be king!" However serious this pretendent might be, Hamlet approaches him with caution and friendliness, but not without using the cloak of madness, his most reliable device of dissimulation. And then – time stops, for Claudius, Gertrude, Laertes, but for Hamlet, too. Horatio is to live but to tell his story.

Throughout his approaches to action there are these indications of suspicion, secrecy, self-concealment in madness, suggesting the attitudes of a man who knows he is dealing with a dangerous affair, an affair of state, but an affair which disturbs him very intimately.[1] Hamlet acts as a thwarted but patient insurgent against the throne. His princely ambition is a continuous thread underlying the deeds he commits and omits. One must not disregard this factor, if one is to appreciate the sense of his proceedings, He himself does not particularly disguise his ambitions. In his first encounter with Rosencrantz and Guildenstern he receives them cordially, until he hears that "the world's grown honest" – the world ruled by his uncle! As soon as they express themselves critically about ambition as an insubstantial "shadow," he wants to end the conversation: "Shall we to the court?.' He bears with them, only for the sake of penetrating into their spying minds. Again, speaking to Ophelia in a "mad" pose – which need not make his words "mad" or unworthy of consideration – he confesses: "I am very proud, revengeful, ambitious ..." And to the king: "I eat the air, promise-crammed" – but promises will not suffice for a royal heir. The same to Rosencrantz: "Sir, I lack advancement" – incomprehensibly for the latter, since the prince has "the voice of the king himself" for his succession. "Ay, but 'While the grass grows' – "is Hamlet's reply. And later, losing patience with the inseparable/pair of his escorts who but thinly mask their lack of regard for him: "To be demanded of a sponge! – what replication should be made by the son of a king?" To them, and also to Claudius, he assumes more and more of the haughty contempt of a legitimate prince; yet still he takes refuge in his "madness" to keep the edge off his well-aimed darts.

These are the main features of Hamlet's situation: a prince of royal kind but without royal power, challenged by his vindictive mission, but unwilling to grasp it as less or more than a human task, ambitiously moving toward a complex crown conspiracy, but hiding his preparations in the guise of a private obsession. There are ever so many

[1] Listen to the words of a man in a similar public-private predicament, but who is not generally blamed for inactivity – Brutus:
> Between the acting of a dreadful thing
> And the first motion, all the interim is
> Like a phantasma or a hideous dream:
> The genius and the mortal instruments
> Are then in council; and the state of man,
> Like to a little kingdom, suffers then
> The nature of an insurrection.

warring "but's" in the effort to appreciate him as he is. And this is not surprising – Hamlet himself has always a "but" in his vision of the world. "My fate cries out" – but this does not mean for Hamlet that fate relieves him from his spontaneity; fate puts a task in his hands but it need not fulfill that task for him. "The time is out of joint" – but this is not a calm description; it is a demand prescribing a future for him: that he was "born to set it right." "What a piece of work is a man" – but for all his pride and glory, his noble reason, his infinite faculties, his admirable movements, "man delights not me"; the human being remains for Hamlet the source of puzzlement and exasperation quite close and drastic inasmuch as this human being is his own. To understand and preserve the being of man and yet to respond to the timely call of his fate: that is more than a problem for Hamlet, it is the challenge of his existence, as he sees it. Trying to cope with his vision in all its tension, he becomes tragic. Might he not have avoided tragedy, if he were willing to let go of some "but?"

There is then a cleft through existence in prince Hamlet's vision: the world out of joint is a direct challenge for anyone genuine and human enough to embrace his ambition of weeding this garden possessed by gross and rank things; the world cries out for action – but: action, again for those who are genuinely human, is never free of handicap in thought. To "have a father kill'd, a mother stain'd," to live in Denmark as a king's son and see the heritage "traduc'd and tax'd of other nations," see it turn into "one o' the worst" dungeons in the world – this is indeed to feel the pressure of living time, the call to actions. And yet the human actions, for this prince, must needs bear much shamming, seeming, guile, must needs await much planning, plotting, guidance; and even then they are so apt to founder and fail. Are actions only what "a man might play?" But the playing of them is gambling for the highest stake: for one's own self. Blind violence spurred on by "native resolution" is not one's own, is not engaging one's humanity. And those true actions which engage one's self, are they, as actions toward a future world, any less opaque, any less dark to one's thoughts?

> And prais'd be rashness for it, – let us know,
> Our indiscretion sometimes serves us well,
> When our deep plots do fail: and that should teach us
> There's a divinity that shapes our ends,
> Rough-hew them how we will.

Planned plots do fail, and unplanned indiscretions serve; does that relieve man, though, from the conscience of planning? Does even the reference to divinity provide such relief? Not for Hamlet, whose trust in Providence is none too firm. Even if it were, the judgment of divinity with its aid and approval, lies hidden in the future, obscured in the goal, while the predicament of conscience presses the now, the present commitment. One's decision for now, one's heeding of the cry for action, one's weighing of the godlike reason: this is the burden not to be passed off, not even to a God. Divinity is not a substitute for the suspenseful call of the human being who needs his actions to remain his own. Hamlet is not a puppet pulled on the strings of some fate. Against all alien powers he can call: "Though you can fret me you cannot play upon me." With qualms, he has to play the game of his own blood. That is what his princely ambition means to him. It means an existence demanding, desperate and doubtful of its own deserts, yet an existence unavoidably human, unavoidably conscious, unavoidably proper.

~

What, in addition to his ambitious cast into a wearying world, is proper to Hamlet's character? What does he claim for himself from God and men, from life and death?

I cannot see Hamlet's tragedy as a Christian one. It is not only a matter of its main raison d'etre founded on vengeance, a phenomenon not usually classified as Christian. It is also the impression evoked by Hamlet, of a complete absence or disregard of the "good tidings" of hope. The fixed framework is that of Christian belief; but the living motion within it is pagan. Thus a formal consideration of heaven and hell holds back his dagger from the praying king; but is there real or desiccated Christianity in such use of its tenets to apportion vindictiveness? Never does Hamlet reflect that his whole mission is irreligious. Nor does he expect anything serious from the official faith he shares with his age and country; not the salvation of his father's soul, nor of his own. The trust in a merciful, rewarding God of love – where is that in Hamlet's inward life? The "undiscovered country" merely "puzzles the will," threatening it with ills "we know not of"; what is to come "when we have shuffled off this mortal coil" is for him a shadow of terror, not a ray of hope. How close is this attitude toward the afterlife to that of Homer's Achilles: "Rather – I'd choose a weight of woes, and breathe the vital air, a slave ... than reign the sceptred monarch of the dead!" Except that Hamlet does not even have the Hellenic joy in "breathing the vital air." On the contrary, death

"– 'tis a consummation devoutly to be wish'd ... to die, – to sleep, – no more." What "more" has been projected in the Christian tidings, leaves Hamlet unaffected, inspires in him no choice, unless it be greater reluctance, further weariness with the calamity of life. The Christian God may be for him the ruling lord of all, but if Hamlet obeys "His canon 'gainst self-slaughter," his obedience is no blessed loving zeal but rather an added "fardel" to "bear, to grunt and sweat under." And an eternity – what point would it have? The finite human time has enough "whips and scorns" of its own. A policy of tired but not trusting tolerance seems to characterize Hamlet's stand against Christendom's promise and its deity. Nor could one find a model of faith's inspiration for the prince among the personalities of Elsinore's court. If Christianity means a way of men's being with their God, this court and this prince are less Christian than the open apostate Faust.

How does Hamlet stand toward the mankind around him? His story is essentially one of isolation, approximating within human limits the solitude of the Titan. But it would be a mistake to account for this solitude only in terms of his social elevation as a prince without peers and mates. Hamlet is alone, and would remain so probably in any station of human society, because he makes himself alone by with-drawal, precisely like Prometheus. Disowning his surroundings, first and foremost he keeps his eye, his mind's eye, on the image of memory: "Methinks I see my father." This unique image which made him mourn by himself, soon strengthens into an imperative demand, claiming all of his mind, and exclusively his. Thus Hamlet forms his own mission:

> Remember thee!
> Yea, from the table of my memory
> I'll wipe away all trivial fond records,
> All saws of books, all forms, all pressures past,
> That youth and observation copied there;
> And thy commandment all alone shall live
> Within the book and volume of my brain,
> Unmix'd with baser matter: yes, by heaven.

Unkindly, one could say that this is how an obsession is formed, and also, that from this moment Hamlet moves with a fixed, rigid mind. If these derogatory words be despoiled of their barbs, the facts they mean are certainly correct. Hamlet withdraws from ordinary interrelations with men, toward the fount of his mission; what is to be his own self is all devoted to its task. To him that maxim supremely applies, which is so falsely mouthed by the spying, suspicious, servile

Polonius: "This above all, – to thine own self be true!" Only for Hamlet, thus to be true is not yet to reveal one's truth. Truth to one's self is a disposition not publicly accessible, not objectively measurable, not susceptible to judgment of others; it is the unique feeling of weight in the task of one's own existence. Is it then any different from conscience?

Because to embrace one's proper fate in truth is a task no alien can participate in, therefore Hamlet is alienated from his entourage, singled out or singling himself out in his choice. The legitimate princely heritage, the true filial devotion, the risk and blame of vengeance, these are his exclusively, as are his moods and intents about them. Hence his dissimulation, his sworn secrecy, his public cloak of madness: "These, indeed, seem ... these but the trappings and the suits of woe." It is not what he seems like to others that is of primal concern to him, since none of it can "denote truly" Hamlet as he is. All that is overt with men in their world, all that can pass as "show" and be hastily adopted as communication, all that is incidental to the man within. His cast upon the past in remembrance, his throw of future fate, his bittersweet presence in living – how could this ever be reached from the public world? Well Hamlet knows that the self's own truth is all his, all-one and beyond all show. Perhaps this pains him, too, perhaps some pangs of isolation rise to his lips, to be silenced there. A curt "no matter" even to Horatio, even when all's ill about his heart, even when dying: "O, I could tell you, – but let it be." The taste of death, as of existence, is incommunicable. True to himself, Hamlet remains alone. So are all men, feeling as he does. The prince reminds them about the "heart of mystery," about "much music, excellent voice in this little organ" which no one else can ever make speak, in play or in earnest, in love or in hate; the sovereign, self-enclosed magic of a human heart.

From that heart of mystery, all worldly tasks, challenges and despairs adopt their mass and color, from there it happens that any man's existence acquires glory or gloom, solitude or success. From that ground time can appear as out of joint, fate can cry out, from there life and death are embraced. Why? "For there is nothing either good or bad, but thinking makes it so." Thinking on the events, their pressure into one's own heart, their conscientious judging, that is for Hamlet the privileged projection and the anxious autonomy of a man's way to be in his world. It is an independence infrangible by anyone or anything alien: even though the "canon of the Everlasting" be "fix'd 'gainst self-slaughter," this does not preclude genuine longing that "this too too solid flesh would melt." No God and no man can make one's life good or bad in the living of it, against one's own verdict from the heart.

Although prince Hamlet thus clearly claims and recognizes the ground of private thinking independence in the human being, this does not lead him toward any acceptance of man's equality in the public, social, competitive world, in which they are interrelated throughout. On the contrary: there, in surface service, some men fulfill themselves only as "sponges," mouthed, squeezed, swallowed by the mighty ones. But what must be noted about such subordination of service, even servility, is that it does not take place entirely without the acquiescence of the sponge-individuals themselves. This is perhaps the strongest point for the understanding of the prince's ability to dispose in a carefree manner of the lives of Guildenstern and Rosencrantz: their naturally inclined and voluntary acceptance of their enslavement within the bonds of public power, plot and peril.

> Why, man, they did make love to this employment;
> They are not near my conscience; their defeat
> Does by their own insinuation grow:
> 'Tis dangerous when the baser nature comes
> Between the pass and fell incensed points
> Of mighty opposites.

The stress in this utterance falls toward its end: as the world goes, it is the might of men that gives the clue to action and authority. The king, though a villain despised by Hamlet, is nevertheless "high and mighty" and his shadow looms large on the horizons of Elsinore; respect him Hamlet will not, but regard him he must, as socially his equal. The two "natural slaves" merit neither his respect nor his regard. "So Guildenstern and Rosencrantz go to 't." This happens, it may be added, in the last stage of the prince's plan, when it is open to him that his choice lies now only in killing or being killed, when the spirit of vengeance sits full-blown upon his shoulders. Also, though this may seem to be a casuist distinction, it could be noted that Hamlet neither performs here nor witnesses the deed of blood: he does not kill the pair but lets them be killed. The range of what a man lets happen in his world is much wider than the size of his own hands' actions.

Such special attention has been paid to the end of Rosencrantz and Guildenstern, because it may easily be imagined that here is the one and only instance where Hamlet acts without heed of his conscience. The above considerations suggest that this is not so, that his at least

permissive attitude toward the doom of the two spies is just another
consistent example, of his social approaches, on the whole conser-
vative rather than egalitarian. Within their hearts, all men are
sovereign; but by their indispensable entries, chosen entries into the
public world of interhuman relations, they make for permanent
inequalities. Conscience may rule men's thoughts; it is might that
rules their acts. Human society is a multiply interwoven network
whose wholeness is maintained or readjusted by ambitions and
attacks as well as by submissions and services. Herein no one is on
an island or in irrecoverable exile, but each one pays the others all
his time through his pride, his pain, his patience:

> Why, let the strucken deer go weep,
> The hart ungalled play;
> For some must watch, while some must sleep:
> So runs the world away.

The world's stage is set for continuous performance, the scale of
roles available is limited. It is the players who pass through it in
variations, who undertake such or other part assignments, who com-
pete amongst themselves for the brittle glory of protagonists. If there
are to be leaders who could play and rest, there must be those led
who would acquiesce in watching and weeping. A leader is to spur
himself into greatness, "greatly to find quarrel in a straw when
honour's at stake," and those led are for him to "debate the question
of this straw," and ultimately fall showing "no cause without why
the man dies." Such is the common world of men, in which prince
Hamlet has a part to play. His part, however, even if unwillingly
assumed, he assumes to be that of a leader, entitled to look down upon
the sponging mass, entitled to be royally selective, but then also called
upon to bear the weight of his eminence. His selective preference
shines in his words to the court-players whom he recommends to
address their art as an appeal primarily to the leading taste of the
judicious whose judgment "must o'erweigh a whole theatre of others."
To be disregarded is the crowd of "barren spectators" whose limitation is "capable of nothing but inexplicable dumb shows and noise."
Another, more subtle example of his conservatism seems to lie in his
advice to Gertrude whom, again, he does not respect as mother yet
does regard as queen. "Assume a virtue, if you have it not," This
means: put on the trappings proper to your elevation, play in the
world's social game if you can not find significance in your own moral
role. Hypocrisy? Why not? Is not Hamlet's own dissembling a proper
part of his character? This only confirms what was suggested above,

that for Hamlet the truth to one's self definitely need not coincide with "objective truth" to the people around him. On the interhuman stage the mighty and elevated ones must rely on "that monster custom," even though it "all sense doth eat." For one's spontaneous thought mere custom is senseless, deadening, "of habits devil"; not so for the role-playing business of society where it provides "a frock or livery that aptly is put on." Whatever their own truth and will may be, the show demands a distance between a royal person and a sponge.

And yet – the prince is friendly, unassuming, gracious toward his subjects and succeeds in gaining genuine popularity amongst them. This is attested in the words of a witness certainly not favor-biased, Claudius himself, who speaks of "the great love the general gender bear him." While fulfilling his royal role, he deserves their love as a man amongst men. He can be lovable because the greater weight of reality attaches in Hamlet's mind not to the objective distances and inequalities of the world's show but to the subjective independence of all men; because beneath the pomp and circumstance of the passing stage he is moved by a deeper and desperate human equality of frailty. That holds true in the moral and mortal being of men, in the flight of their longings and the misery of their deserts, in their dreams of self-glory and their stopping in dust. "Use every man after his desert, and who should scape whipping? Use them after your own honour and dignity: the less they deserve the more merit is in your bounty." The high, unreachable aim of humanity, which Hamlet holds to, must reflect in his dealings with others as human as himself. There is no need for him to thirst after severity, to trample on his subjects, to take tokens of superiority. On the contrary: enough to each life is the evil thereof, enough punishment will always be gathered in men, since "foul deeds will rise, though all the earth o'erwhelm them, to men's eyes." Without a search for it, there is enough necessity impressing upon each to be "cruel only to be kind," to create suffering with benevolent intent, to impose bad "while worse remains behind." To limit evil is ambitious enough; to eradicate it exceeds what is possible for man.

Again a contrast then, a division, a "but". In the world's show men are at distances, unequal to each other, set up for preconceived and alien parts. But is this all they are? No, for they all equally share in the desperate, abiding ambiguity of man as man. "In action, how like an angel! in apprehension, how like a god! the beauty of the world! the paragon of animals! And yet, to me, what is this quintessence of dust?" In his thought he emulates the divine, in his aims he aspires to infinity, in his beauty and goodness he often impresses himself – yet he falls back into his finite humanity, into his vice and ugliness, into his dusty death. Having dreamt, sinned and revelled, each man is equal to another when he yields to forgetting: in two hours, or longer – does it matter? "O heavens! die two months ago, and not forgotten yet? Then there's hope a great man's memory may outlive his life half a year." Great or petty, base or mighty, all men's longings as well as their evils are subdued by leveling oblivion.

What in such sight is humanly proper? What does prince Hamlet claim for his own stay in this passing world? Little, so very little – but truly. "What should a man do but be merry?" His mirth, though genuine, has an air of dancing upon his grave. What else? Smiling at his own end, stay calm and self-possessed; use mercy, use restraint with other mortals; be not a passion's slave but rather "as one, in suffering all, that suffers nothing." Ready to acknowledge his own wrongs, his blows, though not purposed, yet by him caused to others such as Polonius and Laertes, the prince stands poised against any future. Neither as fearful nor as haste-pressing as Oedipus, Hamlet embraces doom, defying its auguries, careful above all else to stay himself and to himself be true; although he knows that his truth is perishable. "Had I but time –" Yet no men has: let be.

Only too soon will crack a noble heart. And then – good night, sweet prince.

Hamlet's proud reticence places him painfully so that for his world any plaint would be dishonorable and any praise dishonest. Distinct from those, his voice sounds in protest. The protest of Hamlet, considered in its negative or critical thrust, is sweeping and devastating; that is, if you are willing to take it seriously at its value and not to dismiss it as merely an immature or morbid evocation of uneven moods. If you find true the impression of Hamlet, suggested above, then listen to his protesting words as complementary to the way he sees the world and claims his part in it.

What may be mentioned first is a point of consistency, which has not occurred explicitly in the visions of Prometheus and Oedipus, the former not belonging to the framework of mortal humanity and the latter expressing his protest in a much less definite articulation than Hamlet. To put it simply, it would not be logically consistent to protest directly and equivalently against both existence and non-existence, or against life and death. If evil is found negatively in annihilation, privation, absence of being, then life as such is invested with positive value. On the other hand, if the judgment on life is one of rejection, then death as absence of life cannot be entirely devoid of appeal, since it is a deliverance. On the whole, it is the Promethean attitude which shows affirmation, particularly of the unlimited horizons of future being; hence his central compassion for men who are deprived of such horizons, being mortal. But this disjunction does not shine there as clearly as it does in the opposite sense with Hamlet. His protest is about the paradoxes and predicaments of the way the human being has to exist, and in his sensitive mind he feels that consequently the end of these, non-existence, cannot be condemned. Death – "tis a consummation devoutly to be wish'd," death greeted as that which ends "the heart-ache and the thousand natural shocks that flesh is heir to," death as freedom from living. But is death just that?

Before exploring the wide scope of what Hamlet protests against, the question may well be asked what his protest is for, in the name of what he protests and condemns and rejects so many facets and occurrences of life. The answer is that Hamlet protests in the name of conscientious thought, of honest grasping of the human truth. If this is seen, an important step will have been made toward approaching the tragic essence of his conscience. But at the moment, this reference to what he protests for, can appear as a merely paradoxical assertion. How can anyone refuse and dissociate himself from life as such, in the name of what can only emerge within life?

Here it is time to call to mind the roots of the word "existence." To exist is to stand out: it is to cast oneself from concealment into the open, to be exposed to the warring winds of the world. That human life exists in the world, may seem like a trifling truth. It is not trifling but tormenting to some existing individuals. "It would be sweet," Oedipus cried, to withdraw from the world beyond all care. And Hamlet feels himself existing under sharp tugging of dualities; this is what was earlier alluded to as his "but" outlook. There is such a duality for him between the self and the world. His self he wishes to preserve, in loneliness, in dissimulation, in seeming security; his self is what he stands for – but in contrast to this self's world which to him is temptation, degradation, calamity. What he is and protests against is living "out" in the world: existence. How such a split is possible at all, how that which otherwise may appear as necessity, as glory and privilege, as absolute precondition of being human – existence in the world – can strike this prince as jeopardy for his self, that will still have to be asked, later. For the moment, let this suffice as a basis for the negative sweep of Hamlet's protest against life. His starting, startling stand: "How weary, stale, flat, and unprofitable seem to me all the uses of this world!"

To prince Hamlet, the world is a prison "in which there are many confines, wards, and dungeons, Denmark being one o' the worst." The world, far from being an open horizon of opportunities, is confining, constraining, crippling. In such a frame, it must be noted as rather inappropriate even to think of the "outer" world; on the contrary, the world seems to be the place "within" which imprisonment can bind. Again: why is Denmark one of the worst dungeons in this prison? Why is it that to Hamlet who admits to his pair of spics: "Why, then, 'tis none to you?" Is it not obvious that the prince's judgment on Denmark is related directly to the fact of its having been polluted and plunged into debasing darkness by its present king, queen, and court? If that is the ground of the world's being an oppression to Hamlet, then this follows: how one is based or debased in the world depends on human hands. It is men's presence, men's relations and deeds, that can make the world into a confining place of imprisonment. This is confirmed further: the world's oppressiveness has nothing to do with any crushing tightness of limits in physical dimensions. Hamlet is not a claustrophobe. "O God, I could be bounded in a nutshell, and count myself a king of infinite space ..." – but – there is always a "but" for him: "... were it not that I have bad dreams." The world, then, "in" which he is "bounded" is not the physical universe of space; it is the human universe, temporal in its dreams and drives, of daring and of deadly defeat. And what are the "bad dreams" of Hamlet? Guildenstern suggests, and the prince does not deny, that these dreams are nothing but ambition. Bad dreams could be of fright and fog, of danger and despondency, of hell and hopelessness. They are made worse, if out of the dark immobility voices call out and up to deeds, to vindications, to stirrings of honor; such calls are heard by the ambitious prince, at night as well as in his waking. Then does his dream, his shadow, plague him, oppress him into feeling bound. He dreams – of what? Of thriving freedom, justice, purity? But the world of men, into which he is called, confronts him with gross weeds, rankness, drag of dungeons. Were his dreams not so demanding, were his sights not set so high, how could he criticize so condemningly: "To be honest, as this world goes, is to be one man picked out of ten thousand?" How could he, with such astringent assurance, parry Rosencrantz's "The world's grown honest" – "Then is doomsday near"? It is this doomed and self-dooming world of debased and debasing mortals, within which he has to do and dream and die: that is a prison for Hamlet. And the main defect he finds in it is: "Man delights not me."

It is not a matter of mere idiosyncratic aversion against particular humans such as the king and the court. It is a protest against the scheme and spread of this world, against these innerworldly but impersonal interrelations of parts among passing actors, over which rages fortune – a strumpet – rewarding in life's blind lust, crushing in contempt of merit. Is corruption individually earned, is it proper to you or me, is it genuinely appropriated in character? Not as prince Hamlet sees the human lot; it lies in wait at men's being together within the play of their judgments upon each stage of action. Therein is hidden dread of ambitious acting for and amongst people. Why? Because –

> So oft it chances in particular men
> That, for some vicious mole of nature in them,
> As in their birth, – wherein they are not guilty,
> Since nature cannot choose his origin, – . . .
> Their virtues else, – be they as pure as grace,
> As infinite as man may undergo, –
> Shall in the general censure take corruption
> From that particular fault.

What else is this speech but a drastic restatement of the calm Aristotelian view of the tragic defect? Improper and proper at once: improper is such corruption in the scales of individually just punishment only due to crime; proper in the disbalanced belonging of tragic necessity. But what Hamlet brings out more sharply still, is this. As in your birth, so in the birth of all your worldly projects, your nature cannot choose your origin: you arise and arrive beyond yourself. In what you are and choose and become you can strive for property, for integrity, for being true to yourself; all that is not yours, when acting you intermingle with others. Not to be out of yourself, not to overreach for a future, not to expose your faults, your lacks, your wounds – therein might be your safety. Still must you exist in the world! Your vices and your virtues can be your own, proper, particular; but your censure is general, can always tend to be improper, unmerited, alien to you. Not only their words, but all the acts of others must intermesh with yours. The unexpectable is what you must face upon the common stage, where you are called to act. Corruption takes hold of you from beyond, not of your nature, not of your chosen origins, what you just brush against and forever lose through the stream of time. That your human existence in the world is perpetual corruptibility, this, you can learn from Hamlet as earlier from Oedipus, is a germ of tragedy. And what may develop, if your conscience like his still wants to own and to respond for this elusive realm?

The world around you, the world of nature could be perhaps a solace to the man-wearied self. Nature with its soothing power, its reliability, its beauty. Thus to be solaced and to remain open and natural, not every self can gather sound response. Hamlet can not; to him beauty is a temptation, breaking over the senses, arousing frustrating passions enslaving godlike reason, and thus, again, a gateway of corruption. "For the power of beauty will sooner transform honesty from what it is to a bawd than the force of honesty can translate beauty into his likeness." Not for him is the classically serene assurance that beauty, truth, goodness, are one; to his cutting view they are at odds, splitting and tugging at each other, against all unified longing. Nor is this surprising, since the most intimate and accessible of aesthetic charms, man – "the beauty of the world" – is so corruptible, so trembling, so futile in his morals: "Man delights not me." Another mode of consolation for the trapping disappointments of the world is equally disappointing to the prince. Books, studies, elevation of the spirit – he tried that, he used to be a careful scholar, with Horatio, at Wittenberg. But in his present disposition he does not seem to miss much by having renounced the plan of returning there. What does he find in those pursuits? "Words, words, words": a vanity of learning. Such judgment will be confirmed by someone even more deeply tried in it, more deeply disappointed: Faust. Nor does the prince assuage the pangs of his torn and seething mood by any hopeful throw ahead. What does the cruel human time ever promise? Calm, content, compensation in the feeling of conquest to come? Not quite: "That old men have gray beards; that their faces are wrinkled; their eyes purging thick amber and plum-tree gum; and that they have a plentiful lack of wit, together with most weak hams: all of which, sir ... I most powerfully and potently believe." Is this a future to look forward to? Or rather a future men try to forget about, and abhor "to have it thus set down," and blame Hamlet's madness for holding it remembered? But if these are the moods, the uncompromising rays of Hamlet's vision of the human life and its thousand natural shocks, what balance can be expected from it? What could men do? It appears consonant with the tone of his protest, when he himself poses this "madly" unanswerable question: "What should such fellows as I do crawling between heaven and earth?" In the same tone is his even more "madly" drastic solution: "We will have no more marriages: those that are married already, all but one, shall live; the rest shall keep as they are." Is this shocking to you? Yes, of course it is, to all reasonable and respectable people it must be. Is it thereby mad? "Yet there is method in't." Freezing of marriages in the status quo, a bar on procreation, stopping forever the wedded deceit of love "for wise men know well enough what monsters you make of them"; and as the ultimate result, of course – suppression of the human breed as such. What else could be expected, what other remedy more methodical and humane, how else could Hamlet speak, if his thinking makes man's existence in the world an evil? To you or me such a step of protest may seem unthinkable, absurd, and so perhaps only amusing; but then what is in question is how close you are to the prince's tragic ethos, how seriously it may appeal to you. Your amusement at Hamlet's madness may dull you like an anaesthetic, absolving you from feeling with him – until you feel tragically.

If this is what prince Hamlet tragically inclines to as his own grasp of the human being in the world, in what light then can one see the central query of his protest?

> To be, or not to be, – that is the question ...

If taken as a matter of simple preference, of unforced issues, of self-isolated bent, "to be or not to be" may not appear as a question for Hamlet. To be, through time, through a long life, through the commitments of the worldly stage, is a calamity. It is imposed from without, without choice of origins and destinies, without one's proper option. And it is from without that a barrier arises, unassimilated, unfamiliar, a barrier of dread shutting man off from his willing withdrawal. It mocks his present pains with the perspective of more severe ones, it thrusts upon him oppression, injustice, arrogant rivalry of others, the monstrous schematism of authorities, and the futility of the heart's self-torment:

> For who would bear the whips and scorns of time,
> The oppressor's wrong, the proud man's contumely,
> The pangs of despis'd love, the law's delay,
> The insolence of office, and the spurns
> That patient merit of the unworthy takes,
> When he himself might his quietus make
> With a bare bodkin?

Who would? This key question must first be reversed: who dares to stop those ills, who dares "take arms against a sea of troubles, and by opposing end them?" Who dares once say: "Enough!" and stamp down the challenge of the future, and ruthlessly defy those other ills "that we know not of?" What is to block the daring of such deed? Not the weight of one's will, not any fearful object in existence, not one's proper, discovered powers, frailties, risks. An alien barrier arises here, a cold limit strictly unknowable to one who is in being, however he may thirst and suffer, and rebel:

> The dread of something after death, –
> The undiscover'd country, from whose bourn
> No traveller returns ...

However improper, despised, hostile and tragic may be all passes and perplexities of the human being, none of them are as inappropriable, unreturnable, aliently repellent, as the bourn of non-being. "To die, – to sleep, – no more": if it were just that! But how could it be that, how could it "be" anything? To man, to any existing entity, the bourn of nonbeing "is" what alienates everything alien: from its dark fount radiates whatever resists as strange, ungrasped, non-appropriated. Yet man is the one who ever exposes himself to these black rays, who stumbles against the jutting sharpness of mystery, who is aware that he is but may not be. Thus can he be frozen in un-objective dread, against which his objective disposition in his world, be it in content or disgust, avails nothing. How does Hamlet resolve the evidence of such possible and palpable dread freezing his own protesting arm? "Thus conscience does make cowards of us all." What is man's conscience then, if therein dwells his touch upon the chancy surface of non-being?

What transpires in this sounding of sources of Hamlet's protest is the way of no return on which he is moved, with and by his conscience. He protests against existence which is the cast into the world, because in that world he finds himself not at home but in prison. Acutely he suffers "the slings and arrows of outrageous fortune," and seeks refuge from them, vainly. Condemning life, he cannot condemn death. In a certain shape he welcomes it – in death "to say we end the heart-ache" – but this shape he is unable to hold and rest in, since it is the shapeless par excellence, the elusive, the freezing in dread. Existence can be held as good or bad, as better, partially, or worse; but to find existence as better or worse than non-existence is to be repelled through absurdity, since non-existence cannot be comparably found. Man's living judgments, aspiring and desperate, grow only in the charmed circle of what he can appropriate in life; they are neither affirmed nor denied by death, only frozen senseless and still. To one like Hamlet, who leaves his grounding in the world of men, of acts and values, no other ground is available. Unless blinded by prejudice, he cannot whole-heartedly withdraw from his human being in order to embrace non-being: there "is" nothing to embrace. The only attitude which can then conscientiously evolve is one of cold indifference and readiness for all or nothing. Protest against life cannot be raised on the ground or in the name of death. Whatever death is, it "is" ground-refusing, nameless, and alien; no one can properly protest "for" it. Hamlet's protest against existence perforce must rise from his own rest in it.

Restless is Hamlet; his sensitive sight shows him that the barrier beyond his existence is infrangible, and that his wishes, hopes, and disgusts can only be concerned with the way he is and has to be. This is what so wearies him:

> O, that this too too solid flesh would melt,
> Thaw, and resolve itself into a dew!
> Or that the Everlasting had not fix'd
> His canon 'gainst self-slaughter!'

The last sentiment could be interpreted as an expression of faith, of a basic reliance upon Christian doctrine. It was observed earlier that merely formal vestiges of Christianity are found in Hamlet. To these he is not antagonistic: he would not ally himself with God's enemy, as Faust will. But whatever fragmentary religious ideas appear in his conscience, they are not what makes him move or stop his hand. Violating the canon of the Everlasting supposedly leads to damnation. And does he not violate it, in his vengeance? Quite possibly, despite the canon, he might have resolved to cross the barrier with a bare bodkin, but that his time offers him a more urgent death than his own: the villain king's. He lives on in order to accomplish his sinful mission, rather than to abstain from the sin of self-slaughter.

No wonder then that in his very opening appearance the prince coldly admits: "Ay, madam, it is common" – to die. As he views it, death is not tragic to him who dies; it may be – to his survivors. In Hamlet's conscience, the witnessed death of others is an opening of opportunity for corruption. In this intermeshed world of men, it is the death of others as possibility, that provides such plentiful chances for showing one's own worthlessness: by forgetfulness in two hours or two months, by temptation to ease such death in murderous plots, by malice designed to wound the good name of those who are beyond defense. Mortality of men amongst other men is their corruptibility on the grandest scale. But for oneself? "The readiness is all." This commonly cherished quantity of time, while it is finite. leaves Hamlet indifferent: if "a man's life's no more than to say one," then "what is't to leave betimes?" A constant touch of the cold surface of death is necessary within life, and it need not be a necessary evil. "If it be now, 'tis not to come; if it be not to come, it will be now; if it be not now, yet it will come." This only insuperable "to come" imposed upon human existence, Hamlet treats with a strictly stoic contempt, if not invitingly; there is no preeminent season for this "to come." Only in his last moments the prince strives to fulfill his chosen mission, to risk damnation for his vengeance taken on this ultimate occasion. What does this show? Not the readying of a repentant faithful soul, but the readying of what remains under his own control of conscience: his destiny, the completion of what he "was born to set right." Not death, Hamlet believes, is the destiny of man, though death only makes it possible: once more, in ending this existence to implement that "readiness is all."

And after? On one occasion Hamlet says a few words of his immortal soul. Sometimes, then, for him too glimmers that intimation; but it only glimmers and never burns him up. Those words are spoken publicly, in haste and heat, in his anxiety to pursue the ghost. Against this one utterance must be weighed his prevailing indifference to the vanity of all mortal, temporal ends, under the sway of what is "to come," under the great commoner and leveler of all improprieties of men's world. The final equality awaits all – in dust. Lawyers and clowns, ladies and courtiers, beggars and politicians, friendly Yoricks and imperious Alexanders – "to what base uses we may return, Horatio!" All of us, indiscriminately. "We fat ourselves for maggots: your fat king and your lean beggar is but variable service, – two dishes, but to one table: that's the end."

That indeed may be the end, in Hamlet's eyes, the last end. No reference is made here to anything abiding, everlasting, no hope for blessed dreams for some in their sleep in dust, no expectation for himself. And when that which is "to come" confronts the prince, what parting words does he leave behind? A brief, unsentimental farewell, with no regrets, no sympathy: "Wretched queen, adieu!" – this to his mother. A curt and manly handshake to his only friend: "Horatio, I am dead; thou liv'st." The passing bonds of the heart are being loosened here, swiftly. This world, this state, this weeded field of action

Denmark, he leaves with his dying vote to the man whose stirrings of honor and action inspired him with admiration; the voice of Hamlet's ambition speaks to ambitious Fortinbras. His own destiny accomplished, the prince is ready. And what remains? An immortality? Perhaps, of a vicarious kind. Not the divine, the otherworldly bliss, but a human abiding. What remains of Hamlet now is only his name. And so his last legacy is to preserve that name unwounded amongst men, to clear it against their judgment, to tell his story through his friend so that this name might live in honor and remembrance. And even that – how long, two hours or two months? Can this affect deeply his indifference, his readiness to step out from "within" the world? O, let it be. Dust is all men's end, the end of Hamlet, his uncle, his sponges; their passions', and their plays' end.

If so the end is set and if its time is indifferent, what weight remains to the question:

> Whether 'tis nobler in the mind to suffer
> The slings and arrows of outrageous fortune,
> Or to take arms against a sea of troubles,
> And by opposing end them?

~·

If now, having listened to Hamlet and watched him with consent, having tried to assimilate his moods and moves in his world, one wishes to approach closer toward the roots of his tragic existence, the task seems very hard. One has to ask what is responsible for such dualities in his character, such restless sway of his protest, such torn out distances throughout his whole way to be. And if the initial guiding lines of this exploration are proper, to ask in this radical manner is to search for a founding choice.

That choice for Hamlet is never clear-cut, unique and complete, has been suggested repeatedly, by reference to the lingering "but" in everything he approaches, attempts or appropriates. A thirst for vengeance – but properly human; singleminded remembrance of his father's death – but testing the ghost's truth; ambition – but carefully controlled by reason; mysterious sovereignty of men's hearts – but not of their places in the world; the canon of the Everlasting – but formally, not actively embraced; truth to himself – but dissembling to others; longing for death – but not of his name. Examples could be multiplied at will. What this predominance of the "but" indicates is Hamlet's unwillingness to cast himself unreservedly into one alternative of choice, to swim resolutely toward the stream's right bank and to forget the left one, behind. He remains in mid-stream, to drown. Choice, whether of beliefs, of moods, or of actions, is for him never single and thus never simple. Is there a possibility of accounting for this fractionalized, oversensitive imagination in regard to choice?

Perhaps there is. The primary choice of all, not only for Hamlet but for any existent, for any reflection, is the one which envelops the roots of Hamlet's awareness: "To be or not to be." And what has to be genuinely understood here is that this choice, while not illusory, can never be unequivocal, at least not in human terms. To choose "not to be," as Hamlet seems inclined to, is to remain without what is chosen, it is to be unable to grasp what one chooses, since it "is not" there to be grasped. From such a choice one is thrown back on to what one supposedly choosing rejected: to continue in being, even while reaching for the bodkin – and possibly thereafter, too. This must indeed "puzzle the will." But to choose "to be," as Hamlet does, although not in his mood but in fact, is, for one negatively disposed to it, also never a clear option. It is to throw a shade of gratuity, of indifference, of brittleness, upon that continuation in being, which one keeps in remembrance as yielding throughout to non-being. Non-being, accessible not on its own ground – since it has none – but only from the promontory of being; and being, suspended over its dark negation, devastated by the floods of doubt, denial and doom – a sterile promontory, no more. A present death in life and a future life of death, both tightly linked by time which can submerge something into nothing and emerge nothing into something: these are the alternatives in the most primordial of all choices a man may become confronted with. If he faces that choice, can someone like Hamlet be blamed and criticized as indecisive? What is it to be decisive? It is to throw oneself in one direction at any cost, to dismiss all subliminal destruction of the path built, to hold and cherish all that is made, planned, awaited, as already available and indubitably availing, fortifying, fertile. Is it still possible to remain decisive after encountering the choice "to be or not to be?" Perhaps; if one is capable of discounting the negative as unthinkable and unequal to the positive, if the choice is not maintained with concern but rather abandoned, unqueried, forgotten, if once it is enough to abdicate this choice as beyond man. Why is such a way closed to Hamlet? The answer to that question touches the root of what makes Hamlet TRAGIC: his conscience.

What is conscience? The word signifies as much as "knowing-with." This suggests that no straight self-completed knowing is in question, but some knowing which is complementary, reflecting, dependent. "With" what? Ordinarily what is complemented by such knowing could be thought of as variously acquired possessions, positions, or propositions: it would be then a matter of "also" knowing what one has, where one stands, what one believes. Yet here the English language adds a significant suggestion which is not differentiated in the original Latin: that in such static contexts the word to be used is "consciousness" rather than "conscience." While the line dividing these two is not to be drawn sharply, the use of the word "conscience" is more reserved for what can be generally referred to as ethical. It has then to do with men's ethos or way to be, to conduct themselves, to strive, act and appropriate. Conscience is clearly less a matter of intelligence than of character. It is reflective knowing, involved in and temporally gathering what one does, where one aims, what one is. Recalling to mind what was introductorily said about the sources of man's character in the process of his existence, I shall understand by "conscience" a knowing encounter with choice. To be conscientious means then: by keeping it aware, to make oneself respond for a choice.

Thus conscience does make cowards of us all.

Not all conscience, and not of all men.[1] But a conscience such as that of prince Hamlet: touched clearly, innerly, by the freezing awareness of the intertwined alternatives of being and non-being, and unwilling if not unable to break loose from this freeze on its resulting horizon. An all too conscientious conscience, persistently aware, responsively self-questioning, a conscience with a defect – self-undoing while attached to the choice beyond man: a tragic conscience.

What Hamlet is thoroughly unwilling to let go is his human being, a being aware of choice, When he realizes what follows from gripping the alternatives "to be or not to be," his grip upon them is no less firm. As a result, he must conscientiously see what stretches out before him as of no avail: a being in time hollowed out by its response to non-being. That is how he sees all men; no wonder that such a quintessence of dust can no longer delight him. "If it be not now, yet it will come." There is no "it" to come; it is man himself crawling away from yet toward that which puzzles his will: the ambiguity of his being. What weight, what validity can attach to any movements in such self-

---

[1] At least an ironical counterpart is expressed by the Second Murderer in *Richard III*, who says of conscience: "It makes a man a coward – it fills one full of obstacles – it beggars any man that keeps it: it is turned out of all towns and cities for a dangerous thing; and every man that means to live well endeavours to trust to himself and live without it."

entailing crawl? Yet they are, awhile; and what makes them be, in a human way, is the self-awareness through dust, "knowing-with" the crawl, conscience.

To himself, primarily, does Hamlet apply his awareness of the question of his being. Had he not identified himself with his conscience, he could claim to "be" more fully, more decisively, he might like Oedipus try to escape, to live longer, more happily, with less bad dreams. But if he did dismiss his primary choice, he could not choose himself, he would not "be" himself, if to be in his conscience is to respond for the choice he encounters. His fate of nature "not choosing his origins" is to be Hamlet; it is Hamlet's conscience then which must be responsible. The response is against the overwhelming role of time which mediates between the human being and non-being. "The readiness is all." This creed of readiness at any moment, what is it but an expression of dis-regard for the span of moments? If every moment is equal to every other moment in claiming his readiness, then to think in terms of more than momentary striving and decisive task completion becomes quite vain. The creed of readiness is a longing to stand still, not to expose himself to whips and scorns of time, to dis-regard such continuance of his being as must through time turn self-destructive. If consummation "is" in nothingness, to move towards it in the "real" world is of no moment; rather stay at rest, in silence, ready.

> And thus the native hue of resolution
> Is sicklied o'er with the pale cast of thought;
> And enterprises of great pith and moment,
> With this regard, their currents turn awry,
> And lose the name of action.

Such is the meaning of Hamlet's cowardice: not that he is frightened of critical occasions for action – as a "coward" in the more common sense would be – but that, insistent on responding in conscience to all his choices, he dis-regards action and inaction as equally of no avail or worth. In his conscience he is unable to choose-through the conflicting identity of being and non-being, and thus he is frozen to find not only non-being – as everyone must – but also his "own" being alienated. Stopped in the inconceivable primary choice, he cannot cope with the choice of other choices, although he is quite conscientiously aware of them. The darkness once encountered persists in overshadowing all his life. He continues to exist, "but" ... A single "but" upon existence, and all the other "but's" multiply from it.

Hamlet meets dualities, divisions, alternations, but cannot cut his way through them. No choice is single.

If "readiness" is the aim of his cold disregard for time, this aim raises a contrast immediately. Readiness can only be aimed at in the safe and sovereign sphere of one's mind, never in the in-dependent and intermingled public world at large. To maintain his being in readiness inclines Hamlet to isolate himself in silence, to favor dreams over deeds, pure feelings over impure facts. If he could, he would commit himself to no person, no placement, no part on the world's stage. But – can he? Existence in the human being is public projection as well as inward immanence. To try and abnegate that is only possible for someone for whom the choice "to be or not to be" is dubious. And so the world becomes a prison for Hamlet, although he dreams of happiness in a nutshell. His self and his world enter into conflict, and the task of readiness signifies: withdrawal.

But – the contents of his withdrawn mind are such that a static quiescence even there is impossible. No hermitage for the prince: his heritage calls him. And so he has bad dreams and cannot help judging, adjusting, accusing. To be true to himself he cannot stand still. He does not long to be, but as long as he "is," he is ambitious. Not with the ruthless, self-certain ambition of Fortinbras, but with enough inner disturbance to prevent serene renunciation of his claim to what is properly his from his father. His ambition makes him stand forth as a claimant. But – to stand forth is to act. Even though action is of no avail, even though no goal is above questioning, even though every imperiously striving Caesar must turn to vulgar clay; still there is no rest for this reluctant rebel. "O cursed spite, that ever I was born to set it right!" To reach his readiness, the prince has a task to re-move. The readiness and the task are at odds. But – none of them can be chosen at the expense of the other. The only temporal mediation between them is by way of action.

And so Hamlet has to accomodate his conscience to action. Not that he chooses action for the sake of acting; he has too little trust in his being for that. His actions are not so much chosen as permitted to happen between one rest disturbed and another rest longed for. His disturbance is genuine; his hope of being able to remedy it is not. Therefore he has to increase pressure against himself to bring about a boiling over. He needs to hear about "the rugged Pyrrhus" who in the rush of fury yet stood still and "like a neutral to his will and matter, did nothing," then, after a pause of "roused vengeance," struck against the strumpet fortune. He wants to grasp the genuine grief of Hecuba to light "the motive and the cue for passion" of his own. He revives the image of his father to whet his "almost blunted purpose." He enquires into the triviality of occasions sufficient to provoke in others a bloody, total commitment but for "a straw – an eggshell – a fantasy." Thus he excites himself to a critical self-contempt, challenges himself through words and images, tries to elicit action as an impelled response to passion, as a rush of release.

But – being himself, he cannot. He recalls: "How all occasions do inform against me, and spur my dull revenge!" – and immediately recalls in conscience: "What is a man – ?..." Action, easy and obvious and taken for granted by many, to conscientious Hamlet presents a predicament of choice. "To do it?" Yes, even a beast can. But – what about saying: "This thing is to do?" Can motions, animal gestures, instinctive responses, deserve "the name of action?" Does a man just let them rush out and happen, unaffected by what his judgment says? No, for Hamlet an action of someone who does not merely "imitate humanity" must be reflected in a "knowing with it," it must issue from an awareness of choice, it must be responsible in conscience. Is this enough, though, to stop and hesitate? With regard to his task, after all, he does live to say: "This thing is to do." Why not then – simply – do it? Why run the alternative risk that through the pale cast of thought whatever comes to happen might also "lose the name of action?" [1]

Hamlet is caught in the irresoluble ambiguity: "to be or not to be." He is perhaps not the only man to be so stopped in thought by this question of choice. It is to be observed, however, that the specific way in which the character of this man revolves within such choice is this: "Whether 'tis nobler in the mind to suffer – or ...?" For him, it would not do – supposing it were humanly feasible – simply to choose to be or not to be. For him, not the simple choice raises the question but the nobler choice. The chosen is not only to be but to deserve to be, it is not only to be accomplished but also to be responded for. Choice, in the fundamental and more than human meaning of it, can confront, and make or break, other entities. Here it confronts a man concerned at all costs to preserve his human being in his conscience. In the outcome, Hamlet is frozen not only in the orbit of this primary choice

---

[1] That this predicament was present to the man who speaks as "Hamlet," can be seen also in the words spoken by his wisest female character, Portia: "If to do were as easy as to know what were good to do, chapels had been churches, and poor men's cottages princes' palaces. It is a good divine that follows his own instructions: I can easier teach twenty what were good to be done, than be one of the twenty to follow mine own teaching ... O me, the word choose!"

but also in his approach to other choices. And so to the choice to act or not to act.

Not to lose its name, a man's action must neither rush out from a blind impetus of native animal resolution nor have its currents turn awry by force of outward circumstances which silence thought. A man's action must be a proper issue of his whole being. When this human being is put into question, as it is by Hamlet, is it surprising that the issue of action becomes questionable too? Further, if the choice of being must be reflected and appropriated in conscience, if it must be responded for as "nobler in the mind," can anything else suffice with regard to action? Certainly not. A man's chosen action must be the nobler action. It must maintain itself "in the mind" against all slings and arrows of outrageous fortune, it must be claimed and re-claimed as properly his action, not as merely one "that a man might play." A momentary whim, a simple preference, a dissembling gesture, cannot suffice as justifications of what is nobler in the mind. Such added weight demands time of reflection. And there, indeed, is the rub. Time, which puts into question even being and non-being, cannot be counted on to leave untouched, undoubted, the affirmation for the mind of what is nobler in it. Conscience, exposed to the assault of time, cannot avoid the risk of remorse, of re-negation, of rejecting response. "This thing is to do" – now; it is even nobler "to do it." But – what assurance is there that when it is done, it will still be nobler to have done it? In the speech he gives to the Player King, Hamlet observes: "Our thoughts are ours, their ends none of our own." The thing to do is yours, it dwells within your mind, it is proper to your conscience; the thing done, even done by you, is no longer yours. Before – you seem to have all control over an action, to make it be or not be; after – you know you have no choice in this regard, whether it is or not, deserves to be or not, you cannot hold it wholly in your conscience. And yet, before it is done, "is" it anything other than a suspension in choice? Your appropriation of your deeds is thus paradoxically evanescent; when they are yours, they "are not" deeds – when they are deeds, they "are not" yours. Their nobility is then as much in question for you as for anyone not properly involved in them at all. Despite that, you are to choose yourself, retrogressively, as responsible for them: this is the being of your conscience.

For many people this paradox of conscience is not visible in the least. They are capable in order to live a "wholesome" life of erecting multiple screens within the mind, of not letting their left hand know what their right hand is doing, of taking for granted their past as gone and their future as somehow coming. To them, Hamlet can appear as "morbid." To them, there is no such choice as "to be or not to be", there is no question about the power and property of conscience. To preserve the hue of health, their conscience must be equipped with qualm-proof compartments and function staying ready to relinquish its object of choice, whenever so prompted. If your character is thus functionalized, the tragedy of Hamlet must be closed to you.

Because exactly the reverse of this situation characterizes him. His critics can limit and compartmentalize themselves to maintain whole their standing in their world. Hamlet endeavors to maintain his humanity whole and in the consequence of this his relations to his world break apart. The name of his "sickness" is quest for integrity; his conscience is afflicted with it. What is remarkable is that in such "sickness" he still manages to act as firmly as he does. His critics can in a superior way point out that if he were less devoted to responding wholly to his time out of joint, then his acting in the world could be fuller, faster, easier. But the answer of Hamlet can fall on deaf ears; since therein lies his tragic distinction that his way to be can only be expressed in questioning protest – or in silence.

For his existence does Hamlet raise his protest which has to turn against it. Wondering, he speaks of man's existence in which the question of being and non-being is sounded as a choice; but never solved. He speaks of the demands of the world, the unweeded garden, thrust in bad dreams upon a princely ambition; but never fulfilled in honesty. He speaks of the heart of his mystery which can make all things good or bad; but cannot be plucked out at will. He speaks of distinctions amongst men, the mighty and the sponge-like ones, upon the stage where they are cast to play themselves out; but all end without applause in the dust. He speaks of godlike reason which, precisely thinking, is to award the name of action; but which puzzles the will instead. He speaks in such a way that each one of his answers must raise a question, that to affirm and to negate appears equally proper or improper. Yet when he speaks and wonders, he is well present and much concerned within his wonder: his whole being is there in question and his reflected conscience of it is wholly involved. And thus his protest issues as a negative affirmation of the enigma of man's existence between heaven and earth. Himself wedged between his wholeness and his nothingness, he cannot resolve this protesting query: is it well chosen to be, when one can smile and smile and be a villain – and thrive, and when another can aim at holding himself whole and honest and true – and perish of this aim? In other words – does the human being fully deserve to be? To find in conscience a noble ground for both man's life and death – that is the tragic quest of Hamlet.

But is there any placating response to this protest? Not in this human time. No more. "The rest is silence."

CHAPTER V

The Tragic Striving - Faust

JOHANN WOLFGANG VON GOETHE: FAUST

Night is on earth. While in high heavens the suns and stars chant the clear glory of divine creation, the human earth has to cope with darkness. Rising toward the straight, unbearable light, man must avert his face, look at the misty rainbow of illusions, burrow in hidden holes, wait through the short turn of his hours. Then night again envelops his view. Perhaps it lulls him into dreamy rest, perhaps it haunts him in unknowable dread, perhaps it stirs him to search for some light. Not the surpassing fullness of a sun: a human dimness for a waking home.

> Ah, when in our narrow cell
> The lamp once more imparts good cheer,
> Then in our bosom – in the heart
> That knows itself – then things grow clear.
> Reason once more begins to speak
> And the blooms of hope once more to spread;
> One hankers for the brooks of life,
> Ah, and for life's fountain head.

Between the blinding sun and the drowning dark lies the world of man. He hankers out of night, yet it is for the night he seeks his dwelling. His reason speaks in the finite circle of the lamp, of the familiar and reachable. Hope spreads as long as nourished by some light, it spreads but short of achievement; the fountain head is beyond the spread.

> So it is too when hope by yearning hounded
> Trusts and thrusts for its highest goal and chances
> To find the gates wing-open, the field unbounded;
> But now there bursts from that eternal porch
> A superabundance of flame, we stand confounded;

Our aim was life, we wished to light the torch,
And a sea of fire laps round us – beyond measure! . . .
Think on it and you grasp what lot is ours:
Reflected colour forms our life for ever.

A bridge, a rainbow, posed against the fountain head of light which makes it shine yet in which it must drown: such is man's form of life. Breaking under the strain of infinite sunlight, man must recoil and find his way in shade. Yet he must vanquish darkness, to enliven his reason, heart and hope: in fabricated light, in reflected color, in tentative, limited spread. This spread, this bridge of colors out of the night is human striving. Born in dark chaos, it evolves glimmers of guidelines, self-guarding supports, "now clearly drawn, now into vapour melting." Does it ever achieve a lasting sustenance of lightness? This is the tragic issue of Faust.

Night is on earth when Faust begins to speak. Night covers in mysterious mercy his decisions, deeds and despairs. At night he reaches for his loving-cup of death, then for his blood to sign the fatefull pact. Through further nights Gretchen becomes his, her mother dies and her brother falls, and then he finds her last night in prison. Another night revives Faust to some other dawns of striving: in empty darkness he visits the Mothers, shadows preside on his union with Helen, and midnight presses blindly his challenge of Care. Amongst ghostly torches, when Faust pronounces his last word, sinks back and ends his wandering course, night is on earth again.

Where, in such close continuance of darkness, is there an open outlook toward light? Not a perfect horizon of everlasting day – that would be too much to demand; nor does Faust expect it. All his claim amounts to stopping the rainbow brightness of a passing moment: "Linger a while! Thou art so fair!" Is even that claim fulfilled in reality, or merely in illusion? If it is, then its stopping stops into eternity, then light is also on earth to stay, then night-born blind striving can issue in a vision justifying itself. The protest of Faust against the overpowering nightliness of existence may then perhaps be taken as testament of a man's days, too. The tragic aspect of Faust's humanity depends on his STRIVING, remaining for ever in question.

～

Overwhelming is the immensity of Faust's world. The ground for his imperious striving can be no less than cosmic; and thus a panorama is laid out, to overpower all kinds of interest, more complex and unsounded than anything else in the tragic history of man. Again, as with Prometheus, a more than human universe has to be faced, richer by far, more labyrinthine, more questionable than the stark outline of that first tragic vision. Entities and elements uncounted, powers and presences ungrasped, spirits and specters unknown, all "throng the air" above and around man. And so do problems, unsuspected, unresolved yet unmistakably pressing through man's existence: of living and dying, of knowing and doing, of unity and community, of youth and its age, of care and its challenge, of "painful joy, enamoured hate, enlivening disgust" – all in excess, as Faust would have them. Again the protest of Promethean force rings darkly on, again the earth is called to witness for man. Yet here, for the first time, the tragic darkness of protesting against does not close in, unequivocally. While tragedy abounds, this tragedy may perhaps offer an issue, a thread of a question for light. That issue rises from Faust's death – and life.

The world of Faust is overwhelming, both in the sense of those who lose their way in its "superabundance of flame" and relinquish their torches of enquiry, discouraged, and also for those who persist in casting spellbound glances at what they feel to be the greatest vision ever developed by man. This world offers so much that to avoid both critical renunciation and hypnotized admiration of it – neither of which attitudes offers a possible way throughout the maze of its horizons – a consenting enquirer has to choose his steps with circumspection. There is no single path through here, no single exhaustive "meaning" which could permit dismissal of questions still untackled. Whoever enters the world of Faust will find in it various not pre-emptive vistas. Their shape and content will depend on his intelligence – what he is capable of finding, on his faith – what he may permit himself to find, on his temperament – what he will look forward to find. There is perhaps a focus which cannot justifiably be omitted in anyone's conscientious exploration, although anyone's view toward it is again by no means exclusive: it surrounds the destiny of Faust's striving through existence. It is toward that focus that the present exploration will move, and its steps will be directed in analogy with previous attempts to aim at some intimacy with the tragic hero. In consequence, attention will be paid primarily to one man's vision – Faust's own – of this immense world. But it will have to be complemented, made translucent by some words and views of others turned on to that vision; and not the least positive light will have to be drawn from the poignantly negative testimony of the witness of darkness – Mephisto. If the following exploration holds your consent, as a genuine, though by no means complete, approach to Faust, then it will have accomplished its purpose.

To outline the background and the weight of the issue concerning the man Faust, it is first indispensable to ask about the general scope of the universe in which he exists. This immediately raises many difficulties about its spiritual population, which can be only briefly pointed to. The founding and motive structure of this world, unlike those examined before, is basically though not purely Christian. The purity of a Christian cosmology is here complicated by the presence of factors and forces belonging to older or newer phases of world-faith.

What determines the preponderance of Christian elements in the framing of this world is the central convergence of emphasis upon the figure of the Lord. Although it can be questioned whether the Lord is the only origin of all entities entering action here, nevertheless the belief seems justified that it is the Lord who constitutes the pinnacle of power and even the basis of being of all. The latter appears particularly clear from a Platonic viewpoint, where all being is seen as due to good while evil is only privatively linked with inert resistance to order, empty chaos, nothingness. Because all the ordering, producing, surveying of everything that is good is here clearly attributed to the power of the Lord. Responsible for all formation and sustenance, for making visible and enduring, the Lord is the universal source of light. In the light which illuminates itself as well as any darkness, the Lord is completely all-knowing. His omniscience needs to be taken very literally. It is not sufficient to visualize it on the model of some superlative expansion of a limited mind, such as human, because such a mind loses in specific detail whenever it stretches out toward more comprehensive generality: the higher it rises above its average horizon, the more objective knowledge it embraces of fields and spheres, the less it can delve into points of depth, the less involved it must be in subjective relations. The omniscient illumination of the Lord must be appreciated in sharp contrast to such limited lighting; this is made very definite when to the accusing generalizations of Mephistopheles about the state of the universe, the Lord replies in perfect specificity, showing his continuous concerned awareness not only of all entities in the universe but also of what and how they are at any time: "Do you know Faust?" If it be thought that Mephisto's ready reply on Faust shows matching acquaintance on his part, then it should be recalled that Mephistopheles, by his own admission, is only a part of the negating force, only one amongst many evil ones. Thus his familiarity with Faust's life and with many affairs of many members of the human race may be due to a division of scope amongst the devils, this being the particular sphere of responsibility of Mephisto, of which he is well aware; by contrast, various presences and places appear later on, to which Mephisto's knowledge does not familiarly reach. But the Lord is only one, and his light does penetrate everywhere equally. This contrast of the oneness of the Lord's light against the plurality of dark negations has to be noted now for future reference in the human context.

While the omniscience of the Lord can be unequivocally stressed, some reservations can arise with regard to his omnipotence. His is the central but not the unique power in the universe. If it were unique, not only could there be no cosmic struggle between good and evil, and no contest concerning man, but also man himself could never find that his existential issue is in any real sense up to him. His serious striving would be no more than a puppet's dance, if the Lord were identified for him with omnideterminant fate. Faust's story is significant only if it is made to happen by Faust and not for Faust. Further, the Lord as well as old Zeus has no dominance over time. It is true that, unlike for the Olympian ruler, no question of arbitrary tyranny or of fearful scheming and battling of empire arises for the Lord: if he is the good, it is good that he is there for the universe. But again, if there is a real resistance of evil, its conquest must be temporal; if there is a real question and a possibility of protest within the destiny of man, he must reach for it through time. Time then, as the proper horizon for both, is beyond good and evil. Good is to vanquish evil, to mature and fulfill itself – through future time. In relation to the temporal striving of Faust, the Lord himself thus acknowledges his own role: "The gardener knows when the sapling first turns green that flowers and fruit will make the future bright." In addition, there is a genuine query with regard to the Lord's own attitude toward his power. It sounds in a dissonance after the harmonies of the angels singing the praise of divine glory, in the words of the strange visitor to heaven, according to which the Lord has "left off laughing long ago." There is no reason to take these words of Mephisto, uttered to the Lord himself, as untrue. But if they are true, what reason can there be for the Lord's not being able or willing to laugh? Could it be pity for those under his rule? Or an infinite weight of responsibility for the whole universe? Or even a doubting worry whether the universe is worth being? The answer is obviously not available. But if the question stands, it questions and thus limits the power of good accepted as good by itself, so as to be welcome with laughter.

Beneath its culmination in the Lord, this world is populated by a mass of forces which are difficult to appreciate. The angels, the ministers of good, present no problem. Their contemplative and appraising role is displayed at the outset of Faust's story; their active and militant role at its conclusion. Their status is not too unlike that of the Olympians serving Zeus. Perhaps the angels have a worthier master, perhaps they themselves are more loving and less servile; nevertheless they are dependent, and by themselves would have no decisive significance for the tragic issue of Faust. They do, because there is their Lord.

Outside of heaven, yet not to be identified or even strictly allied with its enemies, are such spirits as populate the pagan underworld. Although once Mephisto describes one of them, Neptune, as a "water-demon," yet in the wealth of the classical air, earth and water through the second Walpurgisnight, more than once he finds himself in perplexity, unable to sound or cope with these elements and their inhabitants, alien to him; while on the contrary the man Faust finds himself refreshingly at home there. Thus to assign to all these spirits an exact role in the hierarchy of cosmic combat between good and evil seems almost impossible; they represent the surpassed pre-Christian forces, kept alive mainly by the longings and memories of their human successors. Even more puzzling is the significance of those original entities which fit into the frame of neither Christian nor pagan belief, and which are in no definite relation to the mind of man. The Earth Spirit, while responsive to Faust's call, mocks this "superman" and denies equality or kinship with him: "You are like that spirit which you can grasp, not me!" Yet strangely, in an apparent misunderstanding, Faust derives the impression that his subsequent meeting and association with Mephisto is due to the intervening power of the Earth Spirit whom he later invokes: "You gave me that companion ..." If correct, this interpretation would make the Earth Spirit overlord of the devils, while yet he himself tells Faust: "At the whirring loom of Time, I weave the living clothes of the Deity." Not less enigmatic is the place of the Mothers: "Goddesses throned in solitude, sublime, set in no place, still less in any time ... to earth unknown, whom Hell is loath to name ... wreathed with all floating forms of what may be." They seem to provide some relation between hell and the pagan underworld, since at their instance Faust acquires access to Helen; but to regard them therefore as opposed to creative heaven would be hazardous. Nor can anything conclusive be said about the four dark sisters: Want, Debt, Need and Care, who creep toward Faust in his last night, who also announce the advent of a still darker brother: Death. The human race seems irrevocably though "blindly" in their power. Faust appears materially immune against the first three sisters; he is, of course, as a mortal, vanquished by their brother; it is, however, his encounter with the fourth sister, Care, that is of crucial significance for his human destiny, and will have to be properly explored. But even there, the question of the direction and allegiance of the powers of these "phantoms," by hell or heaven sent, may not be unambiguously resolved. It is precisely the possible emergence of such richly different and dubious spiritual forms on the horizon of human existence that makes this existence so question-worthy in the case of Faust.

At the furthest remove from the source of heavenly light are the multiple powers of night, thus describing their claim through their emissary:

> I am a part of the Part which in the beginning was all,
> A part of the darkness which gave birth to light.

Here arises the above mentioned query about the origin of the universe in time: if Mephisto is right, the Lord is no creator out of nothing, only a light-throwing fashioner of form out of the chaos of night. The Christian tale, of the light-bearing rebel Lucifer cast out into chaos to become the prince of darkness, is here reversed; as there the nature of the light borne and the way it becomes darkness, so here the wonder of darkness "giving birth to light" is inconceived. According to Mephistopheles, the emergence of light and all the order it forms is a misbegotten accident in the bosom of mother night laboring ever since to remove its effects, to reassume the cosmos into chaos. Thus the sons of darkness, such as himself, are particularly prey bent on all finite existence which, they maintain, has to return into nothingness, thus never ought to have existed at all: "Whatever has a beginning deserves to have an undoing." Thus is necessitated the devils' contemptuous cynicism concerning all sustained efforts, their adversaries' as well as their own: "What use these cycles of creation! Or snatching off the creatures to negation!" But while they can enjoy this quasi-superior attitude toward all that is there only for a time, the devils are also trapped in their own constituent paradox: "that Power which always wills evil, always procures good." Why? Because if evil is the negative will to retain or return all within nothing, then no "something" can be willed by evil, then to procure, produce, procreate anything is to serve the cause of good, then all formation and endurance in time can fall into the light of the Lord, even though issued and guided by intent of darkness. The cosmic conflict thus defines its application to all temporal being. Evil holds in: "If it had not been, it would make no difference." Good persists in asserting this difference which, far from being nil, may be taken as eternal. Time, again, mediates between good and evil as between something and nothing.

The destructive aim at negation develops, as already mentioned, in a plurality of expressions. The Lord speaks of the various "spirits of denial," mentioning his "favor" for Mephistopheles the ironist. There are of course different channels toward destruction, material and mental, natural and moral. Interestingly, one of such channels runs through a possible pity for the suffering humanity, in which Mephisto "specializes." Needless to say, such devil's pity is not without its ironical aspect: in claiming that men torment themselves enough even without being plagued by him, he protests against the pointlessness and evanescence of his own employment. Still, it is worth observing that the appearance of pity in a man's protest may be just what renders him vulnerable to the force of negation, and that therefore it may have to be overcome for the sake of assertion of good.

Some other features of Mephistopheles may be noticed briefly at this stage. For instance, his identification as the "god of flies"; this, while nominally rather irrelevant, can provide a curious ambiguity when recalled later, in the liberating struggle of Orestes. Or further, the characterization of his darkness as due to "the Fog Age of the North," attached to "romantic phantoms only." This not only ties well with his disorientation in the classical pagan realms. but also seems to detach the human South, basking in serene sunhine, as more life-loving, less fog-foundering, les open to diffidence, doubt and denial. Hamlet is obviously a northern character; while Prometheus bears his light toward southern Hellas. One other point must be brought out for a more proper appreciation of Mephisto's relation to Faust. It is the question of what truth can be found in the devil's mouth. While it is clear that much of his speech should be discounted or taken as its opposite precisely because it is a tempter's speech, nevertheless there are occasions when his words cannot but be accepted as informative and true. One such instance has been mentioned already in reference to the absence of laughter in the Lord. Mephisto is neither tempting anyone there nor is he in a position to say this, were it untrue, in the Lord's own presence. Another example can be found in the words he speaks after concluding the pact and in

Faust's absence, words extolling the real weight for man of knowledge and reason as against the lies of magic and illusion. Here he speaks to himself and not to any man, and his hope is actually to mislead Faust toward an opposite judgment, in order to destroy him. Here is then no ground for refusing the truth of his better knowledge and experience of men in this regard, even although it is the deceiver speaking. This need to penetrate carefully through the deceit of the deceiver to arrive at possible truth will be quite pressing with regard to the truth of Faust's destiny in his death.

Finally, in this spiritual panorama of bewildering complexity, there is a place for mankind. And how different, on this stage of the same cosmic dimensions as witnessed by Prometheus, is now the role of men! There, in the dawn picture men were not even yet ready to appear; their earth was not in the least their own; they were but helpless orphans, useless weeds waiting for extinction, solely preserved by the rebellious effort of the Titan. Here, although the whole universe has grown and filled out, not less has grown the stature of men. On this immense arena, where the Lord is supreme arbiter, where his ministers can only help to stage and applaud the spectacle and his opponents to disrupt and criticize it, it is men who are the actual gladiators in the center. It is men that the grandiose spectacle is all about. It is through men's hands that the worth of the universe is being decided. It is upon the shoulders of mankind's representative, Faust, that the whole issue of creation and destruction rests, overwhelmingly.

Some relations of man to the other presences in this world have already been alluded to. Apart from his way toward the Lord, which will constitute the main problem of Faust's story, the most interesting is his relation to the Lord's evil opponents. While it is fairly clear that in many respects the immortal powers of evil greatly exceed the power of mortal humanity, what must not be overlooked are the indications that to some extent man is superior to the devil. Thus the Lord's opening permission for Mephistopheles to do his worst by the soul of Faust is qualified by the phrase: "if you can seize it"; which implies the possibility or even likelihood that the evil ones are not capable of properly grasping the human being. Thus Faust himself loudly claims such human inaccessibility to the devil: "Your bitter malice, dour and dire, how should it know what men require?" Thus with regard to the problematic issue of Faust's last moment, what is not at all problematic is that Mephisto interprets or misinterprets the significance of that last moment in a way diametrically opposed to Faust's, and that it is Faust's appreciation of it which may be approved in heaven. And there are indications that man, on the other hand, can grasp the devil and penetrate through the surface of his blandishments; in this vein Faust says in reply to Mephisto's promises: "Poor devil, can you give anything ever? Was a human spirit in its high endeavour even once understood by one of your breed?"

The endeavor of human existence is then suspended between heaven and hell, between the light and the night. If negative evil cannot seize him in his being, he nonetheless cannot seize the perfection of good. The sun blinds him; and so does the dark. In his own proper twilight of "reflected colour," the human being is the movement from night into light, the effort to illuminate his search of himself. Man gropes to strive ahead and strives to grope further. He finds that he misses only in reaching for what he misses. His "everlasting song in every ear and every hour" aims to express what he "must do without." To be human, he must long and err; because, to be human, he must himself build the path ahead on which he himself is to go. The Lord's word of this is unquestioned: "Men make mistakes as long as they strive." What forms the question about human striving is this other judgment:

> A good man with his groping intuitions
> Still knows the path that is true and fit.

The question concerns the dimness of man's light, the path of his groping, the goodness of his existence. Because the opposing judgment, that of the spirit of denial, would maintain, and not without grounds, that man's reflected color is as dim as to fade into darkness, that his groping ahead of himself implies absence of a path, that the suspension of his existence makes it belong to vain emptiness of negation. Within the temporal universe, the question is about the power of goodness to assert itself even in mortal frame and to disprove the claim that finite being deserves not to be since its non-being "would make no difference." This is the question at the roots of the wager for the soul of Faust. Rightly or wrongly, Faust stands for mankind, and mankind for the worth of all creation.

Taken at its letter, the formulation of this wager between the Lord and the devil may suggest various criticisms. The Lord, for one thing, may not appear at his divine advantage when he descends to the level of a gamble, even aside from the attitude which sees in gambling a clear symptom of evil. As genuine rivals competing for the same stake, the Lord and the devil may seem to stand as equals: an inherent superiority of one contestant would make the contest a fraud. Also, from this point of view, the wager could be objected to as undignified, because it makes man's life into no more than a toy, a pawn in some game of struggling superhuman forces. These objections can be answered and the reality of the wager established more definitely, if the human role in it is seen differently. It can be argued that far from being played as a pawn, the man in question is one of the combatants, that in his erring and straying way he can and does cope on his own with the power of darkness. From this it would follow that the contest is a matter of any light, even human, proving and asserting itself against the night by illuminating it anew, as well as itself; or in other words, that it is the task of finite striving to show itself genuinely striving in contrast with the impotent inertia of denial. Then the Lord as transcendent source of all light and self-assertion would remain hors de combat, above the scene of man's striving against empty nothingness, retaining for himself the seal of judgment and eternal approval beyond the human horizon of time. If the creator creates man to send him into combat alone, his own struggles not only remain real for man but acquire a much more involving significance: not counting on safe heavenly support, man may be discouraged, anxious, desperate, but he is concerned throughout with his own stake, his own existence.[1]

This interpretation of the wager concerning the man Faust may appear to be inadequate if you believe, as many have done, that in all reasonable justice Mephistopheles is the winner of the wager, that Faust at death should become his property which he loses only as a result of the angels' "hoax". Drawing the balance on Faust in this manner, you could then go on to claim that mankind, in this representation of it, is clearly exposed to an unfair handicap, abandoned to struggle on its own against powers far beyond its limitation. You could say that Faust's story precisely proves that the belief in an overwhelming superiority of good over evil is entirely unfounded; that even if not a man but the Lord himself is seen as the combatant against the league of evil, defeat in such combat remains a possibility; that good can always fail, and the question of worth of being is very dubious. Such far reaching conclusions remain your privilege, but only if you have looked closely enough at Faust's life and death, and then reached unshakable conviction as to his ultimate destiny. In the present exploration I shall move gradually toward some questioning

---

[1] Precisely such a god-man relation issues from another divine desire – that of Wagner's Wotan: "A hero whom I would never approach with my aid; estranged from his god, free from his favor, acting unconscious, unordered, through his own need and his own way ... Whom I love, I let strive for himself: may he stand or fall, he is on his own."

of Faust's destiny, which cannot be omitted in a proper appreciation of his tragic striving.

~

According to the cosmic framework outlined above, the existence of Faust is to serve as a test regarding the worth of all mortal or at least all human existence. Faust is, then, not just one of many heroes but the hero representative of mankind as such. This immediately raises a problem of how to see and hear him, a problem pointing to the paradox of all representation. In an interhuman setting, the paradox is this: an individual is the more adequately representative of a class or group, the more he has in common with the others, the less uncommon, excentric or unique he is himself; but taken quite literally, such an individual Everyman who is just like all others and has nothing particularly proper to himself, would have no qualifications of his own to be selected as a representative, in preference to any other individual of the same class. This paradox may recall to mind the introductory reflections from Aristotle concerning the proper hero who is to be neither too good nor too evil and yet somehow sufficiently outstanding in his own right; otherwise, if he is either "superhuman" or "subhuman" or too commonly human, he may be unable to provoke sufficient interest in other humans. This unresolved paradox must greatly affect any attempt at intimate appreciation of Faust. If he is the hero representative of mankind, then all he thinks and feels and does must remain open to questioning: is he like me or you in thinking and feeling and doing thus, is he, here or there, standing for himself alone or for the human breed as such, is his strength and weakness valid for all or just for one – himself? A clear, all-applicable answer is not possible. To treat Faust's humanity as quite unlike your own would prevent your possible intimacy with him; to identify yourself with him thoroughly would be difficult and presumptuous. The only feasible attitude is to pick a way through your approaches to Faust, finding sometimes that he moves beyond or away from your grasp, and sometimes that his speech could properly be yours, that he is as human as yourself. Then you can let his story be his, yet seriously adapt it to your own heart. To be himself, Faust must retain his otherness for you; but to be represented by him in the question of your human destiny, you must find yourself sharing in his humanity. In other words, the question of Faust, the adequate human hero, is the question of whether anything can be adequately said about human existence as such, and what in it is tragic.

It must be noted that his role in the wager is not imposed at random on Faust. It corresponds to his own willing acceptance of a life representative universally of all men's lot:

> What is allotted to the whole of mankind
> That will I sample in my inmost heart,
> Grasping the highest and lowest with my spirit,
> Piling men's weal and woe upon my neck,
> To extend myself to embrace all human selves
> And to founder in the end, like them, a wreck.

It is Mephisto who reminds him that, all his dreams of a "crown of humanity" notwithstanding, he is but one of a great plurality, no more than just himself: "You are in the end ... what you are." Is there some significance to this disagreement at the outset of the story, between Mephisto's restraint on identity and Faust's willingness to live for all men and for all time? Is it perhaps necessary for Faust to resist the devil's negation, that he should fight in his combat with this claim? His acceptance speech may well be recalled, when his tragic destiny is assessed later.

If Faust is to fight a common battle, not merely his own but yours as well, then you must maintain a self-questioning caution in your approaches to his character, to the way he appropriates his being in the world. All the while the above mentioned question has to be ready in mind: is he like you? And this question may be immediately difficult to answer, when the central expression of Faust's character is introduced: "Two souls, alas, cohabit in my breast." Are there two, in your breast? The two souls of Faust can be variously interpreted: as signifying a realist against an idealist outlook, as expressing an exclusively worldly man and a dreamer, as a self-assenting sensuality in contrast with a self-contemptuous ascesis, as an obstinate grasp of a given present versus a cast ahead toward some future. Whatever their particular classification, it is the antagonistic activity of the two "souls" that must be clearly seen: there is will-ful striving both in the one which "like a rough lover clings to the world with the tentacles of its senses," and in the other which "lifts itself to Elysian Fields out of the mist on powerful wings." The two could, after all, in their opposition weaken and cancel out each other, into a delicate indecisiveness. Something on this pattern happens to Hamlet; but not to Faust. In whichever direction he tends, he tends in strength. The rent of violent conflict does not, as with Hamlet, divide his self against his world but rather his "one" self's whole way to be in the world against his "other" self's. This is not Hamlet's alternative of being overshadowed by nothing, of affirmation undermined by negation; this is a positive duality of choice within existence. Those who find it difficult to accept the literal possibility of such an existential rent, and argue against it with some prefabricated notion of a natural organic wholeness of each existing self, had better reflect well on Mephistopheles' ironical remark, meant precisely for them: "Mankind, that little world of fools, commonly takes itself for a whole." Of this common illusion of wholeness Faust is free: the unity of himself he takes not for granted but perhaps for a task.

If you wish to weigh carefully the way Faust is to represent man, and yourself, you must definitely refer to your own existence this question of striving against striving: is such possibility unique in Faust's breast or not? Because if not only Faust's being but the human being is thus approached, as not entirely just this but probably also that, as never integrally caught, fixed, determined, as only striving toward a harmony but striving disharmoniously, then some important limitations result with regard to the human horizon. Then the self's overcoming by the self can be seen as the natural condition of man; then dissatisfaction of some tendencies and longings very proper and very dear to you can be seen as the inevitable cost of satisfaction for others not more and not less your own; then tragedy can open up as a perpetual possibility of human existence. It is on this basis alone that the first, paradoxical description of Faust's character can become understandable: when Mephisto speaks to the Lord of Faust, as of a man whose consciousness is by half aware of its own madness, of one capable of resting neither in the near and familiar nor in the far and impressive, of one suspended in motion between his own earth and a heaven he demands to conquer. Recalling that the human being as such is there characterized as a grasshoper "always in flight," up and down, leaping toward his reason's "gleam of Heaven's light" and irrevocably falling back into his native grass – is it a wonder that Faust is chosen as a representative type of this human grasshopper?

The conflict in Faust's breast grows into the events of his two lives. It moves passionately in the continuing love for the "green meadows" of life of a man self-enclosed in the grey dust of his study, his research, his theoretical abstraction. It moves in the eagerness of a spirit "whose mad striving overleaps all joys of the earth," strangely combined with the plodding patience required in the labors over minute details of learning. It moves in the thirst for eventfulness at all costs, interspersed with brooding qualms of conscience, self-criticism and despair. It moves in the superhuman challenge of the temporal dominion of care, flung by one who is constantly awakened to himself in temporal concerns and projects. This potent mixture of inclination and fight, of embracing and despising, of innocence and guilt, makes any attempt at describing his character and prescribing his destiny appear as obvious oversimplification. But then, is oversimplification ever avoidable in the approaches to man's way to be?

When first encountered, Faust the man of knowledge is on the point of condemning knowledge. He has traversed the full Socratic circle, driving himself through many years toward ever more awareness, ability, acquaintance, to reach only the realization of "talking of what I know nothing about." He has loaded himself with the accumulation of all the most exquisite human attainments – theology, philosophy, law, medicine – only to discover in them "the junk of centuries," an inert mass of "traffic in words," which instead of immersing his mind in the healthy stream of life makes him acknowledge: "Your mind is closed, your heart is dead." Dried out in the dust of a thousand theories, abstracted from the efforts of a human past which now remains closed under seven seals, this quasi-knowledge Faust finds completely useless for the painful pressures of the present. What is it for a man now, just to know? What can it give him or make him give to others?

> Shall I find here what I require?
> Read maybe in a thousand books how men
> Have in the general run tortured themselves,
> With but a lucky one now and then?

Such apathetic awareness is not the knowledge Faust has longed for. For this classically contemplative detachment the living movements of nature appear as "only a show." Not so for Faust who cries: "Infinite Nature, where can I tap thy veins? ... They well up, they give drink, but I feel drought and dearth." What makes him suffer is precisely the feeling of his impotence in his endeavor to penetrate through the veils of nature, not to witness it dispassionately, but to work with it creatively: "To flow through Nature's veins and in the act of creation to revel it like the gods!" Yet, as far as the so-called human knowledge reaches, this is impossible. The instruments are lacking, the will insufficient, the appreciation of men is averse to such daring: on the contrary, "the few who have known anything about it – have ended on the cross or at the stake." For men, it seems safer to stay "like the worm that burrows through the dust." to pretend to spiritual security among "heaps of books, pyramids of instruments," to sift stolidly the "legacy" of learning left by their fathers. Such passive plucking at predetermined provisions of the past is unbearable for Faust's active striving: "The moment can only use what the moment itself has bred." If this is all that is available to man under the title of knowledge – only to look at the universal spectacle of nature through a far veil, and never to act in its midst – then such empty sterility is destructive of the heart's own fresh blood, then the self-imprisoning quest for knowledge must be rejected. "Away! There is a world outside!"

And yet, this attitude of rejection cannot be strictly fulfilled. Because knowledge is unlike other acquisitions of the human life, such as power or wealth, in that it cannot be wilfully eradicated. The learned Faust cannot make himself abruptly unlearned, he cannot empty the store of his mind as he could throw away his earthly possessions. Thus the initial resolution of Faust does not amount to a destructive abnegation of all ways of knowing. No, what stirs in his mind there is an intimation and aspiration toward a new kind of knowledge: imbued with passionate involvement, concretizing and not abstracting the ordinary experiences of man, a knowledge green with practice of life, not grey with theories. This, if at all possible, would be knowledge creative of events, not merely mirroring nature but effectual in it, knowledge which could do something! It would affect and transform the knower and with this force would make him participate in, and productively appropriate his own hold on reality.

In the mediaeval climate of belief surrounding Faust, such an unorthodox quest can only be expressed in turning to more than human potentialities of magic. This is what the end stage of Faust's first life literally presents: the scholar's conversion into a magician. But viewed from the perspective of several subsequent centuries, this turn to magic can be appreciated differently. Its heretical significance is the departure from the exhaustion of passively faithful humanity of the Middle Ages toward the rebellious self-dependence of man in the Modern Age. Indifferently shrugging away the sterility of inherited doctrines of the order of knowledge and faith, Faust shares with Hamlet; and while the prince remains standing in wonder on that shaking ground, the scholar takes a novel step. The quest of Faust, which turns to the letters of forbidden magic, opens the gate to the spirit of modern science. This is a dream of knowledge which can do something, which can find practice in life, tie itself to experience, transform and conquer known reality. It is Faust the scientist who thus can be taken as the representative hero of the next Promethean-endowed era of mankind. To serve as the gate opener, or crasher, of the new times, Faust the apostate must, like his Titanic ancestor, pay a heavy price. The Faustian modern men will continue to pay it after him.

Why is it that Faust goes beyond Hamlet in transforming to modern lines the vision of human existence? He shares with Hamlet the conviction that men's entry into the world of interpersonal reality is due neither to thought, which only anticipates it, nor to feeling, which can lean toward or away from it, but to action: owned or disowned, base or noble in the mind, but always temporally irrevocable action. But where the prince's conscience binds him to legitimize and shade over the worth of his choice to be and to act, Faust's great thirst for life removes the shades, gives him the trust and the thrust of himself to be a doer. What makes him modern is this ruthless claim toward appropriation of the earth through deeds, done sometimes for himself, sometimes for others, sometimes proud and sometimes painful, sometimes feverish and sometimes planned, but at any rate done, stamped in reality, regardless of what lies beyond them in the future. To be, for Faust, is to act.

> Let us cast ourselves into the torrent of time,
> Into the whirl of eventfulness,
> Where disappointment and success,
> Pleasure and pain may chop and change
> As chop and change they will and can;
> It is restless action makes the man.

This conviction which plunges him into a score of devil-led adventures, predominates in him before he ever gets a chance of meeting and contracting the help of Mephistopheles. On the fateful Easter evening, Faust is impelled to reach into interpreting on his own the light of Christian revelation. "In the beginning was the Word." The problems of translating the weight of the Logos are formidable, breeding grounds for heresy. Faust's thought, in which "faith lags behind" is perhaps still Christian-inspired, but courting an open break with orthodox attachment to a gospel. What Faust reflects on here is the ground sufficient for all creation, divine as well as human: natural. The Word he finds unworthy to be such an all-embracing root: words are only events, outcomes, produced by rather than producing what is. A word must always be rooted in the possibility of a word-wielding mind. Is it then the Mind that was the beginning? Indeed the Mind is the collecting sense of all things, their home and guard, their tie of belonging and meaning. Still, is there not a question of the mind's making words be only on some ground, of not effecting

all things since the mind itself is a thing which must be first affected?
What did then in the beginning affect all to be all-effective? The
Power. The Power to be, to produce, bring about, come out and belong.
And yet – was this the beginning or only the coming forth, the root
or the growth, the entry or the sustaining content of all? Power may
give the harmonizing balance and potential lasting when already
there, in being; but it may not provide the original thrust from a
ground which is not outstanding, available, there. The beginning,
that is: creation out of nothing. "The spirit prompts me, I see in a
flash what I need, and write: In the beginning was the Deed!" The
Deed is then for Faust the beginning of all, the ground of reality, the
surge of nature; it is for him, no matter whether still in the Christian
spirit, the right understanding of the Logos. And in his insistence on
man's unity with living nature, in his contempt for merely logical
abstraction which does not rest on the universal ground of Logos, it
must follow that for man, to be true to his nature, the beginning and
the end of his existence must be the Deed.

The end, as well as the beginning, for Faust. The sequence of striving
after deeds, making events come out in a whirl, which constitutes his
"second" life with Mephisto, concludes when Faust undertakes his
final project of fighting the sea. There he applies his magic controls
precisely in the spirit of modern science's conquest over nature.
Mephisto remains ironical, misconceiving the project as a vain search
for glory amongst men. This is not Faust's intent: "Glory? The action
counts alone." The difference between a brief glory and the intrinsic
worth of the "action alone" is not something that Mephistopheles can
appreciate. For him, the effects of this action revert to nothing, anyway: "You've only toiled for us with all your damming, all your
dyking – the elements with us have banded – annihilation is the law."
It is not the law for Faust. When his last deed is accomplished and he
comes to say his last word, the main question for him is not whether
his gift of land to men will be lastingly appreciated by them, nor even
whether the physical change in the form of land and sea will or will
not persist: on the scale of duration Mephisto's scepticism cannot be
refuted, not even in terms of modern science. Yet it is this deed which
prompts Faust to seal his existence with the closing pronouncement:

> Then could I bid the passing moment:
> 'Linger a while, thou art so fair!'
> The traces of my earthly days can never
> Sink in the aeons unaware.

Whether Faust's satisfaction with this moment is genuine or illusory will have to be considered later. What is undeniable, however, is that the moment depends on the deed. Not on the outward ripples of effects spreading from its point, through social recognition or physical causality, but on the metaphysical weight of the action itself. By it, Faust like Prometheus enters himself on record in the history of the universe. It is irrelevant whether the action's traces will be annihilated or not: the action will have been done forever. This weight of the action for the negative view of the devil is nil; for Faust's view, it should be eternal. The fundamental contrast here between Mephistopheles and Faust concerns the significance of finite human time: whether it is a swamp of destruction, sucking and emptying all into its surface to make it not be, or a path built erringly, uncertainly, in frailty and frustration, and yet pointing on to eternity. The issue of the wager resounds here: whether to be temporal is to be. If Faust is right, then to act temporally, to enter through deeds into reality, to place oneself on indelible record with nature, is for a man to be.

Again, even for men of the active modern time, the question is properly incumbent, with regard to such feeling of vanity in all mere knowledge and of the need to prove one's existence through having acted: is Faust, in holding and owning this, unique, or does he share this with the humanity he is to speak for? Do you find yourself in a common, responsive mood with him here? The answer of consent or dissent must issue subjectively from your own character; on that will depend your sanctioning of Faust's representation of you, and your possible entry into his tragic world. And Faust himself is well aware of that, when he claims that all serious speech sounds pathetically empty for others "like the foggy wind which whispers in the autumn through barren leaves," unless the bond of intimacy is joined:

> But heart can never awaken a spark in heart
> Unless your own heart keep in touch.

These approaches to the outstanding outlines of Faust's character suggest already a positive hold on what he protests for – in contrast to the sheer negation of Mephistopheles. This suggestion, so closely linked with the question of Faust's destiny, will have to be explored. But the persistent pressure of Faust's vision of existence must be vented primarily in negative terms of protesting against. His critical disposition arises from the bitter disappointment in his long search for knowledge, and floods out into a devastating wave of condemnation. The outburst is at least as far reaching and violent as anything in Hamlet's destructive reflections. What is notable about it is that Faust sees through Hamlet's dream of a self-contained, high security of mind and demasks it as an illusion. Faust's curse is mainly directed against the various lures of man's confidence in his self, which sooner or later betray him and augment the depth of his descent to despair.

> Cursed in advance be the high opinion
> That serves our spirit for a cloak!
> Cursed be the dazzle of appearance
> Which bows our senses to its yoke!
> Cursed be the lying dreams of glory,
> The illusion that our name survives!
> Cursed be the flattering things we own,
> Servants and ploughs, children and wives!
> Cursed be Mammon when with his treasures
> He makes us play the adventurous man
> Or when for our luxurious pleasures
> He duly spreads the soft divan!
> A curse on the balsam of the grape!
> A curse on the love that rides for a fall!
> A curse on hope! A curse on faith!
> And a curse on patience most of all!

Why is the last and sharpest point of the curse thrown against patience? Is it not because patience epitomizes just what Faust is cursing most of all? Cursing in disgust with the empty decades of his "first" life; cursing in the realization that whatever men may admire about the continuing struggles of the mind, for him such struggles end in a fatal futility; cursing on that particular Easter night, in re-collection how a few hours ago his proud hand was held back from the deed of self-termination by memories awakened in Easter songs, memories of his childhood's naive expectations of life and hope and joy. The empty end, the futility of continuance, the pointlessness of enduring expectations – is not this the antithesis of what patience amounts to? The temporal meaning of patience is an appointment with oneself across a future, made by a mind which is self-reliant, which trusts time to offer it safety and satisfaction which it deems proper to itself. And for Faust such an appointment is a dis-appoint-ment, temporal safety and satisfaction are despair-doomed dreams. To appropriate time, a man must reach for it, neither safely nor satis-fyingly, but risking oneself through deeds. Since patience is attending rather than tending, reception rather than caption, since it is patient and not agent – therefore "a curse on patience most of all!"

It is the self-imposed frustration of man that Faust is particularly eager to curse and condemn. But this curse, while it is the most violent expression of his protest, is not the only one. He speaks of finding the burden of existence which "weighs" upon his breast, in which the course of days "will not fulfill" a single wish; in which the nights provide no rest or release when "wild dreams" plague the mind with dread; in which the divine spark within, which sways man's "every power – is powerless with external fact" in its brute, alien strength; in which death as sign of finitude is no evil by itself but only as a blockage of the human striving, unready to reconcile itself to an emptiness of the end: "I am no nearer the Infinite." He speaks of "the pain of earth's constricted life" which starting high and wide yields gradually to ever narrowing breath and scope: in youth one cannot be "without desire," without the thriving play of trials and fancies; but later, existence slips off into stages of slow, slackening decay. The "daring wing" of imagination which once reached out, soared up, fearless, into all, is broken bit by bit in living, after "the eddies of time have shipwrecked chance on chance." The pain of it, for Faust, is not so much the incidence of misfortunes but the effect they gain by pressing in the self which becomes "contented" within the narrow limits of a self-defensive fence. Therein "you tremble at every blow that you do not feel, and what you never lose you must weep for every minute": your bare, worthless, fearful, constricted life. Cowering before mere phantom desires, man, oppressed by the age and passage of his time, falls easy prey to the temporal menace of Care. "Care makes her nest forthwith in the heart's deep places – destroying rest and joy." As Faust sees it, the course of existence deserves a curse not just because it moves toward a final stage, but rather because it finalizes itself. The decay of its own aging is its gradual surrender to Care, its passive content with limitations, its servile unwillingness to dare. In their dark, impenetrable weight for a Care-full conscience, "our very actions like our sufferings put a brake upon our lives." Thus self-doubt and outward-turned anticipation and receptive patience, all come to service in the dominion of Care.

In protesting against the self-constricting course of aging, Faust holds to the spirit of youth, well before Mephisto extends to him a full chance of rejuvenation by magic. Thus his ingrained tendency is not toward the surface signs of youth, not toward eliminating age's bodily faults and frailties or wiping clean the slate of years. No, what Faust longs to preserve is the meaning of youth for existence, and that is – freedom from Care. Youth means: to be able to dare, to guard whole the wings of imagination, to make any future well-come in eagerness, to strive as a non-contented agent. No wonder Faust can agree to be ready to die, whenever he might reach a single moment's content; because such content would be a fulfillment sufficing to "batter this present world to rubble" and to part from it with no backward glance. Without attaining it, Faust continues striving, youthfully. And it is also youthfully that he believes he could meet death in dignity, without cringing, without constriction. This could happen in a sudden break of life at its fullest, unawaited, unworried, Care-less: "with the bloody laurel in the battling swirl – or after the mad dance in the arms of a girl!" Or else it could happen with dignity, in the youthful spirit of daring, when acted toward, self-prepared and bravely embraced; this is how Faust elevates his own, freely chosen cup of death:

> It was I who made this, I who had it drawn;
> So let my whole soul now make my last drink
> A high and gala greeting, a toast to the dawn!

What dawn can Faust turn to, when he is about to end his life? The dawn of choice, of suspended possibility, the dawn of the question "to be or not to be" in death. But what a difference in his stand, compared with Hamlet's! Dominant there was the overshadowing dread of the undiscovered country, puzzling the will; bursting through here is the daring "to tear asunder the gates which everyone longs to shuffle past if he can." Faust does not choose in blind recklessness, unaware of his utmost peril; he moves to "take this step, though you should fall beyond it into nothing – nothing at all." If it is to be the end, "nothing at all," he can confront it, but not with the weary release of Hamlet: "to die – to sleep – no more." His choice is not to yield to non-being but to take it up into the question of a possible transcendence. The same inkling of a reassertion of being, of "something after death" emerges for him as for Hamlet; yet for the prince it only opens up anxiety "what dreams may come when we have shuffled off this mortal coil." For Faust, on the contrary, this is the decisive draw in his choosing, to be "escorted forth on the high seas, allured towards new shores by a new day." Hamlet's primary inclination is not to be; he moves through existence end-drawn, and when repulsed by his dread, he re-turns to being merely to find it exhausted in its temporal over-turn into nothing; patiently waiting, "the readiness is all." But the impatient Faust only readies himself for the leap, for further "struggle on and upwards to that passage at the narrow mouth of which all hell is flaming"; his inclination is, beyond that passage to re-discover being in "new spheres of energy," of "high life," of "rapture" – inexhaustible in youth-full time!

It is perhaps difficult in attending to this buoyant "toast to the dawn," to keep in mind that it is raised with what appears as the ultimate gesture of despair, the suicidal gesture. The split in the Faustian character is indeed nowhere as evident as here. It is his "idealist" soul in its everpersisting cast ahead that so dreams itself toward a future to be purchased at the cost of turning "your back on the sun which enchants the earth." The same idealist cast ahead will ready Faust for death at the end of his second life. But the "realist" in him, the lover of this earth, the researcher of present nature. is in silent and desperate consent: he has gone through all that is available in this world to a knowing mind and found it empty. Even his turn to magic, his courageous claim to kinship with the Earth Spirit, resulted only in fruitless humiliation. The realist soul then accepts the suicidal gamble, without buoyancy, but also without renunciation, for this limited chance: that being, which taken just for what it appears factually ends in impotence, may perhaps re-turn, if manfully challenged at the risk of nothingness, if not trembled for in fancy condemned "to torments of its own framing," if defiantly put into question, against superstition, against fixed canons of faith, against fear and even wish – if dared in deed.

> Now is the time to act and acting prove
> That God's height need not lower the merit of Man.

Faust's protest against the reality he has been led to traverse presses him to stand up against the God he has been led to obey. It is here that his apostasy openly emerges. As a Christian, thus far and no further is he expected to move, in questioning, in thinking and moving; but now he decides to move further. This life, this nature, this world is he expected to cherish for the glory of its creator; but now he is ready to transgress such limits of creation. Positively to assert the value of existence is the humble human service of God; but in his suicidal rejection Faust chooses to defy the height of God across the gate of death. This proud Promethean rebellion, still claiming an ungodly merit of man – could it be ever redeemed?

Faust does not commit suicide. The Easter bells stop his upraised hand. But his mind is not thereby converted: "I hear your message, my faith it is that lags behind." The Easter message does not ring in for him a miracle of heaven. It is his earthly soul that is summoned, not to believe in resurrection of Christ, but to admire resurrection of nature in spring; not to look up to "those spheres whence peals the gospel of forgiving," but to be moved back in memory to " childlike feelings," to "lively games of youth, the lovely freedom of Spring's own festival." The realist unbeliever in Faust is reawakened not for a future heaven but for the life he holds: "My tears well up, I belong once more to earth."

The reminiscence of happiness in youth does not extinguish his burning despair. It moves him soothingly for a decisive moment, but only for a moment. It is soon swept away by the annihilating storm of protest in his curse against all dream and trust, against "all things that encompass the soul with lures and jugglery." On Easter night Faust is no less without hope than on its eve; nor is he more of a Christian. And so it comes about, with ease, that when offered the devil's services, Faust simply changes his suicidal project for the sale of his soul. Either through death or through the devil, what he longs for is radical novelty, what he rejects is life as he has known it. He had a chance only, not a real hope, to satisfy his striving in or after death; and he does not expect any more from his pact with Mephistopheles. In Care-less daring, he has defied God and a hope of heaven, and in the same rebellious spirit he lightly disregards the issue of "the other world," of "a Below or an Above," only more closely tied to "this earth – where my springs of joy have started." Thus he dismisses the appointment where Mephisto is to receive his reward, assured that it will be no more than another dis-appointment; thus he defies the devil's power, claiming from it so little, so very little:

> If ever I say to the passing moment
> 'Linger a while! Thou art so fair!'
> Then you may cast me into fetters,
> I will gladly perish then and there!
> Then you may set the death-bell tolling,
> Then from my service you are free,
> The clock may stop, its hand may fall,
> And that be the end of time for me!

Even apart from this explicit agreement – that moment of content would signify the last day of youth for Faust, the termination of striving, the surrender to Care. His fulfillment would initiate the constriction of his existence. His willingness to stop the passing of time would expose him as deserving that this should be "the end of time" for him. Thus in this formulation of his contract with Mephistopheles, Faust does not express any new outlook or demand, and does not in the least exploit the opportunity afforded in such superhuman chance. This word which puts him "in bond for ever" remains in true accord with his judgment of existence.

And then? Cast into "the torrent of time, the whirl of eventfulness," Faust passes through a series of adventures offered him by the power of Mephistopheles. The very continuation of this series – all the details of which no one can claim to know, nor do they crucially matter – means the continuation of Mephisto's failures; since, were he to satisfy Faust, his services would and there and then. This in turn means that this continuation, this second life of Faust does not suffice to lift him out of the negativity of his life-condemning and soul-condemning moods. His protest against the basic features of human existence holds valid. It remains to notice, at least briefly, its various critical expressions, transpiring at different points in Faust's wandering search:

Desire is discovered by Faust, as by Descartes, to be the sign of lasting human insufficiency. "That nothing perfect falls to men, oh now I feel that true." A perfectible if not perfect consciousness could foresee the end of its desiring, reach for and enjoy such consummation; it could contain an even light against the abyss of absence. Such is not the case of man, in Faust's vision. Not only does he repeatedly find his life submerged in darkness, but he is apt to lose his grasp of any light gained, through familiarity or restlessness: "What we don't know is exactly what we need and what we know fulfills no need at all." So man cries out his lack of light, but getting it cries out for more. "So do I stagger from desire to enjoyment and in enjoyment languish for desire." [1]

Affection – the effort of the heart to draw some simple roots from being alive with others – turns into ruin equalling Oedipus', for others as well as for oneself. Faust's love of Gretchen proves a dream too good. It is spun in her innocence, her trust of people, her natural inclinations, her openness for a simple bond between one human being and another. Unsuspectedly, it reaches into her despair, the death of those she loves, her mother, brother, and child, and the realization of Faust that he is an alien singled out among other humans. Is this a discovery singular to Faust or does it lie in wait for everyone? Is it Faust only or is it man as man that longs for ingenuous intimacy and finds in it delusion or disaster? Faust speaks hardly for himself alone

---

[1] This restlessness, but soothed in anticipation of rest, and thus perhaps not tragic, is "confessed" by Augustine: "Our heart can not be quieted till it may find repose in Thee."

when the last words of his affection for Gretchen are those of bitter remorse: "I wish I had never been born!"

Beauty is shown as not only insufficient but also detrimental to the human being. In a simple and humble form this is the intimation of Gretchen's complaint: "What is the use of looks and youth? – People leave it all alone, they praise you and pity you in one; gold is their sole concern and goal. Alas for us who have none!" In a more proud and self-conscious version, this is again the lament of Helen: "An ancient word proves true, true even alas to me: that happiness and beauty last not long together." As in Hamlet's vision, here too are suggestions of a demonic aspect of beauty. Its prime symbol, Helen herself, becomes accessible to Faust only through Mephisto's power; and the various aesthetic delights for the senses are gathered in a sinister Walpurgisnight. Already when Faust throws his universal curse, the evil spirits, Mephisto's "juniors," call out to deplore such destruction of "the beautiful world" which they claim as theirs. The pure incorporation of humanly poetized beauty, Euphorion, is condemned to short-lived flight, vanishing with no trace; another aesthetic symbol from the classical dreamworld, the beautiful Galatea, is overwhelmingly destructive for the dazzled eyes of the humanly conceived-generated Homunculus.

Power is clearly analyzed as incapable of self-sustaining, intrinsic worth, but always dependent and relying on some field outside the powerful one. Such is the quasi-royal power gathered by Faust in his castle defended by armies, in Greece; it is accumulated only incidentally as means towards his purpose of gaining the love of Helen. As such should also be understood the emperor's power: relating him inevitably to his subjects. If his rule is to be, unlike the Greek episode for Faust, a lasting content and objective of his life, he must beware of imagining that it is "practicable to combine kingship and pleasure in collusion." The emperor fails to direct outside his shepherd's concern, forgetting those he is to rule, playing "while anarchy dissolved his realm." In clear consequence, the populace no longer finds itself ruled, no longer secure, no longer joined together in imperial hands; by revolt the political entity falls apart, with each citizen claiming for himself the duty of self-defence from the right to live. The ruler, defaulting in payment of the proper price for his power in his person, is doomed, save for the unexpectable intervention of the devil's forces. Also, as shown in the earlier interference of Mephisto the economist at the still peaceful court, even the easier tasks of executing power in human society depend strictly on possession or at least appearance of material wealth.

Possession, property in material terms, so often delusively construed as an equivalent of safety and satisfaction, is realized by Faust as drastically wanting. He sees its evanescence already in the object-lesson at the emperor's court, where new financial means, secured by Mephisto, unfailingly produce new acquisitive ends for men – with the ironical exception of the "fool." But more immediately, Faust experiences this endless insufficiency of wealth in his own aims, in his last adventure. There, a land-owner on a great scale, whose "arms embrace the earthly sphere," whose property transcends the ordinary human horizons and challenges nature itself, Faust finds it unendurable that his estates should hold a hole in their midst, where an old couple of humans refuse to abandon their small lot of land. The contrast could not be put more decisively: the tiny possession of Philemon and Baucis, so completely insignificant in relation to the magnate's territory, faces his spirit nevertheless with a challenge. Thus Faust is reminded that he himself is still as human as all the emperor's courtiers, that his human striving has reached no fulfillment, and that it is not going to reach it in a series of given material acquisitions, since that series like any quantitative sequence is unterminable. This he comes to know: "Hence is our soul upon the rack who feel, midst plenty, what we lack." But the fault, if it lies in this disappointment, is not due to the material reality in itself, rather to man's relation to it. And, it may be added, not only to material property. Is it not the running thread of this sequence of protesting determinations, that the human being represented in Faust is not to find himself in any possession? Glimmering through the insufficiency of his desires, the dangerous reach of his affections, the temptations of destroying beauty, the non-containment of all power, the quantitative endlessness of his material quests – is this fundamental truth, a possibly tragic truth: the finite human being is unready to reconcile himself to his finiteness, to his concrete being there, to his possessing himself in just this being. And is not this the opening of the rift between the two souls of Faust, the one "clinging" to what is there, the other "lifting itself" beyond?

Finally, there is the issue of a wanted or needed human community in existence. It is not exempt from the cutting edge of Faust's protest. Already in his suicidal mood the curse of knowledge lies in its finding through "a thousand books how men have in the general run tortured themselves." This indeed seems to be the original ground for Faust's loss of Christian faith. Going back in memory to the early youth of his first life, Faust recalls his father's efforts and his own prayers toward an end of the plague raging through the district. Then he was still "rich in hope and firm in faith." But not when both, efforts of a humanitarian mind and prayers of a charitable faith, proved vain and helpless against the mortal condition of men. Faust grows older, grows more used to the fate of sharing the world with others, and sharing their pain; still he rebels against it! Still he finds himself unable to grasp the truth of human misery: his orthodox faith has snapped early under this weight, but still he remains at "the point where your human intelligence snaps." That is at least how the cynic Mephisto diagnoses this violent outcry of Faust on hearing what happened to Gretchen: "Not the first, you say! O the pity of it! What human soul can grasp that more than one creature has sunk to the depth of this misery, that the first did not pay off the guilt of all the rest, writhing and racked in death before the eyes of the Ever-Pardoning! It pierces me to my marrow and core, the torment of this one girl – and you grin calmly at the fate of thousands!" His protest, equal to that of Ivan Karamazov in his rejection of the world with such misery writhing, ironically, "before the eyes of the Ever-Pardoning," sees in Gretchen a paradigm of "the woe of all mankind," and torments him in his inability to avoid sharing in this human community. Still later, Faust confesses being worn down by this shared impotence of men in the vacant world, being "forced – no less – to fly to solitude, to the wilderness." But does he succeed in his effort "to live alone?" To have to live painfully in the midst of others – this is what voids him of his faith and his hope, this is what almost seals his destiny in a ruthless negation. But does it?

It is precisely here that Faust's rebellious dissatisfaction, his headlong rush into the night harboring the spirit of denial, seems to be stopped by a vision of light. It is with regard to the human community that his protest against seems to acquire a balance with a possible protest for. It is in the last moment of his existence that Faust begins to speak in a different vein, calling for himself but on behalf of mankind:

> My deeds –
> Would culminate as well as terminate:
> To open to the millions living space,
> Not danger-proof but free to run their race ...

And he continues to cast ahead toward a satisfaction he never expected:

> Oh to see such activity,
> Treading free ground with people that are free!
> Then could I bid the passing moment:
> 'Linger a while, thou art so fair!'

Surfeited with power, wealth, enjoyment, having found them all wanting, Faust now stops in his final deed, open to future and subjecting nature. And now he seems to reach his unique fulfillment in time: having done something for, if not with, other men, in his vision he stands sharing with them, upon the ground of this achievement:

> And I, who feel ahead such heights of bliss,
> At last enjoy my highest moment – this.

Faust dies, as he must, having spoken these words, promised long ago. What, then, becomes his destiny? If his ultimate satisfaction is genuine although due to the contractual services of Mephistopheles, then the devil has won his wager, then Faust's destiny is that of eternal night, then the Lord loses not only his "servant" but also what Faust was chosen to determine, the issue of temporal worth of being? What alternative is there? If Faust's satisfaction secured by Mephisto is not genuine but only illusory, then Faust's existence contains no fulfillment, no reconciliation, no balance against his manifold condemning expressions? Then again man and devil properly belong to each other, if Faust's protest remains valid in negation? The human time serves only nothingness in going by. So concludes Mephisto in his requiem on Faust:

> 'It is gone by!' – and we can draw the inference:
> If it had not been, it would make no difference;
> The wheel revolves the same, no more, no less.
> I should prefer eternal emptiness.

∻

The question of Faust's destiny must be properly approached, if not decided, in thorough assimilation by thought of the temporal weight of those moments surrounding his death. Such assimilation can not pretend to resolve the question unequivocally; those who very fervently present the "obvious" case for Faust's damnation or salvation may not be silenced. But perhaps even they might realize that this question is indeed questionable, and deeply knotted with the whole issue of which Faust's existence is representative.

The crucial moments of Faust's death open very significantly in his encounter with Care. The mood of Faust is still very dark: "Not yet have I fought my way out to the air." He feels entangled in throngs of "spectredom," bound to meet "some evil thing," pursued by magic phantoms which in his memory echo the day he cursed his "world and self." And in fact he is about to face what through his vision can be rightly judged as the supreme test of his existence. In his challenge of Care he finally surpasses this continuation of his dark, negative disposition; thus here will conclude the characterization of Faust's protest against.

The impending change in Faust's attitude is already intimated in his determination to "speak no magic spell," to "unlearn" his supernatural, devil-given powers, to revert to the straight cast of his own existence, "to face you, Nature, as one man of men." Hence he cannot commandingly disperse the suggestive spell in the words of Care and has to withstand her dangerous onslaught on his own. In what way is Care dangerous, though? Her opening self-identification suggests an answer: "I am just here – this is where I belong." In the whole domain of existence Care is at home; any place, any phase, any guise, are equally good for her influence on man's mind, "never looked for, always found"; she wants it understood that there is, for the human being, no possible escape from her dominion – such an escape would have to be an escape from himself; and what should make even Faust vulnerable to her embrace is his own way of viewing existence, in terms synonymous with "Care" – of anxious striving. Now it is necessary to probe further into the origin of Care's dominion:

> Whomsoever I possess,
> Finds the world but nothingness;
> Gloom descends on him forever,
> Seeing sunrise, sunset never;
> Though his senses are not wrong,
> Darknesses within him throng,
> Who – of all that he may own –
> Never owns himself alone.
> Luck, ill luck, become but fancy;
> Starving in the midst of plenty,
> Be it rapture, be it sorrow,
> He postpones it till to-morrow,
> Fixed upon futurity,
> Can never really come to be.

These words manifest clearly enough that the all-pervasive might of Care is grounded in nothing but human temporality. The subject of Care is the striving man, whose eyes are hypnotically fixed ahead upon his future, whose roots thrown from his past seem annihilated or unworthy, and whose hold in his present world becomes ephemeral, elusive to himself. Thus for him "even indifferent days" are transformed "to nets of torment, nightmares of confusion," in expectation of dis-appointment in his appointments with destinies to come:

> It forms and shows itself and comes to warn.
> And we, so scared, stand without friend or kin,
> And the door creaks – and nobody comes in.

Just when nobody comes in, Care does; Care is nobody, and the man fearfully in her power has nobody to fear but himself. But to himself he must stand in this anxious relation, if he is never complete, never one, never wholly there, if temporally he "never owns himself alone."

That Faust confronts Care with proud defiance, is beyond question. But what makes his defiance problematic is the undeniable fact that in the above described dominion of Care there are features clearly identical with Faust's own character and vision. If Faust is subject to Care, how can he then throw his challenge? "But you, O Care, your power that creeps and grows – I shall not recognize it ever." Did he not recognize it already in the old nights of brooding in his study? Did he not, afterward, pursue the "endless round" of striving, without a hope of fulfillment, "ever deeper lost and thwarted?" And yet, despite this, Faust now gathers strength to step forth as an exception to the rule of Care, and to propound a remedy against that which in Care is infecting, constricting, deadening. It seems then inescapable to judge that in this encounter Faust undergoes a transformation, that after his long climb he now arrives at a level height, that here he comes to terms with his life – and death.

What is the remedy against Care, proffered by Faust? It is not cut off abruptly from his former outlook. His challenging speech first wanders back to the ground of his past struggles, and dwells there caressingly, approvingly, though from a distance:

> I have only galloped through the world
> And clutched each lust and longing by the hair;
> What did not please me, I let go,
> What flowed away, I let it flow.
> I have only felt, only fulfilled desire,
> And once again desired and thus with power
> Have stormed my way through life.

This is striving, but no constriction. This is embracing future time, but without fixation. This is a dark search, but in youthful daring. This finds in the world incompleteness, but not nothingness. And then, Faust passes from his final review to his final and radical conclusions:

> Towards the Beyond the view has been cut off;
> Fool – who directs that way his dazzled eye,
> Contrives himself a double in the sky –
> To roam into eternity is vain!

The remedy is not at all painless; indeed to some it may appear harder to accept than the infection. A striving life has to see itself as unique and finite; it has to incorporate the silent dread of the unknowable Beyond and pass it by in daring. Because it is the Beyond which is the original source of Care, that questionable Beyond which may be nothingness and which therefore constitutes the danger of Care: casting a shadow over this world, constricting what is there now into negativity, reducing life to not-yet-death. It is this issue that Faust tramples underfoot as he moves into the Care-less enunciation of his gospel for man:

> Thus let him walk along his earthlong day;
> Though phantoms haunt him, let him go his way,
> And, moving on, to weal and woe assent –
> He, at each moment ever discontent!

Now it can be seen what ties together this challenging speech of Faust. It is the ultimate expression of his one personality: the self-assenting, worldly realist of the present. His remedy against Care is the storming through life after reachable goals only: "what he perceives, he can attain." The cost of it is renunciation of dreams of Beyond, delusions of duration, doubtful devices of immeasurable planning. The cost is heavy; but what it yields may be worth it: an assurance in present existence, an assent to "this world" with all its "weal and woe," an adventurous courage to pass through every moment, not only armed with discontent but enriched with joy. But, it may be wondered, how can this result from a mere self-limitation to the present? And how can a striving Faust ever agree to such limitation? Certainly no static present, self-enclosed, will suffice. What must be here observed is the accent on "moving on." The impatient Faust can only assent to a present which is dynamic, to a moment which is pregnant with its succession, to discontent which does not frustrate because it is about to yield to some irrepressible novelty. Moving on, no one will stay put in a solid prison of his present; moving on, a man will straddle across this present, treading firmly upon the past ground and stretching decisively toward the future attainable. Such living in constant touch with one's own life is the realist Faust's remedy against Care; a remedy which does not destroy the danger but lets man dare to live on facing it, lets him "go his way – though phantoms haunt him," the phantoms of Care.

But is the speaker of this speech the whole Faust? No, the dreaming, future-devoted visionary is silent here; he might be more vulnerable. And therefore Care, while recognizing Faust's exceptional stand, can still breathe upon him her final curse: "The human race are blind their whole life through; now, Faust, let you be blind at last." The blinding of Faust, which is both literal and symbolic, must remain a problem. If it does reduce him, symbolically, to the truly universal level of blindness, then that would mean that the whole human race are incapable of seeing light but only its illusion; then the fundamental issue would have to be resolved in favor of night and negation. But this cannot be meant literally, nor does it seem to be entirely justified with regard to the last pronouncement of the "blind" Faust. Because the affirmative transformation Faust achieves in his challenge of Care is sustained by him unto his death. Immediately after the cursing gesture of Care, Faust observes:

> The night seems pressing in more thickly, thickly,
> Yet in my inmost heart a light shines clear.

The intuition of light, the reaching for fulfillment in his last words, the affirmative "Yes" to his existence at its end – can such be the accompaniments of a triumph of negation and night?

Mephistopheles certainly thinks so, contemptuous of the inconsequential vagaries of the human being. He hears the fulfilling acceptance of existence, which begins to sound in Faust's words to Care, and immediately deciding that his hour has struck, commands the digging of Faust's grave. Standing on its brink, Faust pronounces his last words, turned to his fair moment of satisfaction. And therefore he dies, seemingly in Mephisto's power. His destiny now enters decisively into question.

The case for the damnation of Faust is very strong. It begins in easily assuming as a fact that Mephistopheles has fulfilled his side of the pact and is therefore entitled to his reward. If he should be deprived of his hold on the soul of Faust, it could only happen in disregard of the justice of his claim. But this is by no means the whole case, and further arguments are available against those who consider that evil can never raise a claim to justice. Even if the devil's position is left out of account, what undeniably remains is the judgment on Faust himself. In this regard, the first and to some orthodox eyes the sufficient ground for condemnation is the bare fact of alliance with evil. Faust, supposedly a Christian acquainted with his obligations, struck his contract in full awareness that it was unholy and forbidden. Thereby he had convicted himself, regardless of whether the devil subsequently did or did not carry out the terms of that contract; after all, in dealing with the devil, one could not be exactly inspired with expectations of the partner's honesty. If this single and crucial act of self-removal from amongst those who may hope for anything at the hands of the devil's adversary is not deemed sufficient for damnation, then one has to ask the further question: on what basis can rest any outlook for salvation of Faust? He lived and died as an unbeliever. In the very hour of his death he rejected any aspirations toward a human home Beyond, in eternity. Apart from the hazardous but still irreligious mood of his suicidal night, he was throughout addicted to "this earth – this sun," devoting "little trouble" in his conscience to "the other side." In one of his rare moments of attention to the demands of faith, provoked by his innocent beloved Gretchen, he expressed something like an apostatic credo. And how do these agnostically vague effusions measure up against the firm doctrine of Christianity? "Who dare say: I believe in God? – Call it what you will – Happiness! Heart! Love! God! I have no name for it! Feeling is all." Definitely, Faust departed from orthodox Christian religion into some kind of pantheism, at best. Hence the conclusion is clear: he cannot deserve salvation by faith. What of the possibility of salvation by works? What were the works of Faust, in his unequalled opportunities? Advancement of virtue, protection of the suffering, reverence for life? Hardly. Faust's works included: the ruin of virtuous Gretchen the death of those around her – of Valentine by Faust's own hand, the undermining of financial honesty in the emperor's realm, the suppression of a possibly justified revolt in that empire, the selfish exploitation of all kinds of magic controls over spirits. Even his last effort, supposedly humanitarian in motive, was marred by the crime committed against the old couple at his behest; although their death was not intended by Faust, it was his order that Mephisto perverted, and Faust could not quite evade his responsibility for it. Deserving works, indeed!

It would appear, then, that in terms of any ordinary, reasonable human reckoning there is, in all justice, an unbroken case against

Faust. And to the reasons for his conviction might even be added a point of equity: it does not seem fair that he who had such unsurpassable advantages throughout this life, should also have a chance on "the other side" and thus, unlike most men, get the best of two possible worlds. If this sounds like a voice of malice, still it is a very natural voice, which could certainly be heard in the adjudications of human tribunals.

Against this well-fortified entrenchment of the accusation, what breach, what opening can be made on behalf of Faust's defence? An opening – no more – might be looked for in the unresolved problems of the death hour. Is it a fact that Faust is wholly satisfied there with what was achieved by Mephisto's service? Already in his encounter with Care he renounces the use of spells and wishes to "unlearn" his non-natural powers acquired on the night of his curse, the night of the pact. Of course, it may be retorted, that wish does not dissolve the pact, and the satisfaction in the promised words of Faust is earned by Mephistopheles. But is it? Does Faust ever express satisfaction in any attained completeness? No. The words, apparently terminating the contract, say: "Then could I" – not: I do – "bid the passing moment: 'Linger a while, thou art so fair!'" The "highest moment" is enjoyed only in "feeling ahead such heights of bliss." It is a possible inter-human future and not the devil-given past that Faust embraces. To consider further: can this last pronouncement be assessed in oblivion of Faust's having been blinded by Care? Is it, in other words, a genuine satisfaction of the whole Faust? The parting gesture of Care, it was observed, is probably addressed to the idealist Faust; the realist has stood his ground against her. Thus it is the idealist, visionary soul of Faust, feeling ahead, "lifting" itself – blindly? – beyond the here and now, that is responsible for the death words; the same soul which, long before, carried him buoyantly to the gate of death in the suicidal "toast to the dawn." In this satisfaction fixed upon the future, Care reasserts herself in Faust; and its genuine or illusory nature, depending upon the effect of blinding, remains problematic. Can Mephisto claim credit for this satisfaction, if he so completely disagrees about its character, seeing in it only the "last ill moment of sheer emptiness?" He even clearly acknowledges that its weight for Faust is not due to his influence:

> He who withstood me with such strength,
> Time masters him and here he lies his length.

If these reflections of Faust's last hour are proper, two consequences arise. First, the dominion of Care is not sufficiently understood if regarded as only dangerous, constricting and infecting for man. On the contrary, Care, whose power is strictly temporal, provides man with the capacity of building his path ahead; it is only thanks to Care's cast ahead that Faust's fulfillment of existence can come into question. Second, if this returns Faust to humanity and removes him from his tie with Mephistopheles, then the devil is indeed alien to the human soul, all his temptations and gifts fail to enable him to appropriate that human being which he is unable to "seize" in sheer emptiness. But such alienation cannot apply in man's relation to Care: she is no demon outside the human grasp, she is nobody beyond, she is "just here" for – or even within – the temporality of the human being.

Still, as noted, the preceding interpretation provides no more than an opening of the case against the damnation of Faust. It certainly does not suffice to cancel the accusing weight on his destiny, in terms of reason and justice. But it may be asked whether such terms are ultimate in the view of a proper approach to the destiny of Faust – or to the tragic destiny of any man. The last words to sound through the Faustian universe are sung by a "Chorus Mysticus":

> All that is past of us
> Was but reflected;
> All that was lost in us
> Here is corrected;
> All indescribables
> Here we descry;
> Eternal Womanhead
> Leads us on high.

Can rational justice have any affinity with the mystic aura of this end? If the transient "past," which is the whole of life on the threshold of death, must be only "reflected" like a rainbow against the clear light of a sun, if the story of Faust is about the "indescribable" in man's existence – can a determinate light on its future be expected? Does this not raise an unconditioned demand that with everything human also reason and justice be put into question? But then, what would remain? Glimmers only of light, outlines only of a man's story, hints only of Faust's destiny. Such is the nature of what follows on his death.

First of all, there is no ground here for any claim to determinate certainty of Faust's salvation. This "story" with its conclusion is more humanly honest and serious than a "divine commedy" with playfully irresponsible scorn or glorification. Faust's destiny is inaccessible in the human light, because it hinges on the judgment of the Lord alone, the judgment which no man may anticipate with impunity. Hints abound, concerning the rich possibilities of human intercession in prayer and faith, of Gretchen, of other released mortals, of Mater Gloriosa in the end. But the distance between such human intercession and the divine verdict is that between the finite and the infinite.

Further, the divinity of this verdict must not be minimized in any anthropomorphic comparison with the human notions of justice. How men judge themselves need have no bearing whatever on how the Lord may judge them. The Lord's words to Mephisto: "Men make mistakes as long as they strive" – must be taken at their full weight. All men err, the judged and the judges do wrong, there is no absolute light in the human eyes. Hence whatever suppositions, convictions, pseudo-certainties may prevail in man's life, his transcendent destiny remains in question: no one is entitled to expect salvation. If all err, if all are inadequate and to be "corrected," a balancing of merits and demerits may not be proper at all: perhaps all should be rejected, perhaps none. Thus when the approvals and disapprovals of human reason must fail, a glorious destiny of existence may only be due to divine grace.

Such grace would elude all reason's necessity. But again, hints are available about the outflow of divine grace, about its aim and occasion. The angels sing: "Lovers can only be rescued by love." That theologically exasperating hoax, the battle of devils and angels over the grave of Faust, is resolved when Mephistopheles himself yields to some inspiration of love. The succeeding ecstatic hymns all sound in praise of "almighty love." The feminine voices, last to be heard, lead up to the final symbolic expression of love in the mystical chorus: "Eternal Womanhead leads us on high." Thus the effect of these concluding impressions seems to be that however weak, frail and inadequate it may or must be in men, love is what matters for the chances of grace. And if such is the resolving factor, then an unloving insistence on justice and equity is as improper and impotent here as in the parable of the vineyard workers.

Faust may not be a lovable character; he is certainly less lovable than the gentle prince of Denmark. But he can hardly be described as loveless. Throughout his stormy existence stronger tides of love stirred in his breast than could be ever found not only in Hamlet but also in Oedipus and even in the ancestral Titan. His simple love of Gretchen; his love of beauty, of nature, of classic serenity, epitomized in Helen;

his love of truth, holding in his desperate quest for science; his love of suffering humanity, which destroyed his faith, which moved his influential hand in the emperor's realm, which made him demand a conquest of the sea for the future freedom of men; above all, his unsuppressed and unrestrained love of this whole world, this earth, this sun – a love both real in its dominance over his thirsty striving, and realist in its acceptance of all the weal and woe, of pleasure and pain alike, of triumph and of despair. It was this great love of Faust which claimed the last moment's "Yes!" to all existence, which wanted to create, to maintain, to be – and which perforce eluded the spirit of denial. Faust loved greatly, and greatly suffered with it, and greatly suffering embraced to his soul all that he loved. None of his loves was perfect, for such is not given to man; but none was a mere dream, pretense, unrooted in his striving. Faust loved his life and lived his love.

In the great issue of being and nothing, is not love that which might break the bond of Faust's association with the forces of destruction? In all his works, however, unworthy and self-driven they may have been, the motive was never a hating, destructive intent, His faith, while apostatic and unorthodox, nevertheless identified God with love, unflinchingly asserted the worth of the created world, and though appalled with its immensity, managed to counter the devil's negation: "And in your Nothing may I find the All!" The superhumanly proud striving toward the All was the task of Faust's existence; was it legitimate? This means: can Faust belong to heaven? Let the last hint to answer this query be quoted by the angels:

'Should a man strive with all his heart,
Heaven can foil the devil.'

But one could still ask, more pointedly: is Faust's glorious immortality assured? This must remain unanswered. Because it reverts to the larger perspective, unfolded earlier on: Faust is not only a particular existent, he is the universal hero, his is the human character in the cosmic test of good and evil, his destiny is the destiny of man. And precisely this is the universal turn of Faust's story – that the destiny of any finite striving suspends it forever in question. This opens the human being to tragedy.

For the proper sense and course of the present exploration, a certain tie of these winding approaches to Faust must now be expected. The final problem is: on what ground is Faust to be considered as TRAGIC? The answer is to comprise the main features of Faust's protest, and it must seek its ground in that from which a character such as Faust's may issue: a choice. What choice can adequately account for Faust's entire vision and movement? A choice of good or evil? Not if one honestly assesses the amoral indifference of his acts. A choice of temporal aims, ot future or present or past? Not if one clearly re-members the goals of conflict between his two souls. One of the two may not be made to respond for the whole of Faust; and consequently the primary choice can not be looked for, either, as: idea or reality, immanence or transcendence, immediacy or escape, zeal or despond-ency. Does not the complexity of this questioning increase, when one recalls that Faust is to be considered not merely as himself but as representative of man? Yet perhaps just this consideration adds a resolving factor, by elimination: no specific selection needs to be explored, such as might be the ground of this character but not that. If Faust is seen in his representative character, that which originates him must be the choice of the human being as such. But what may that mean?

The choice of being: this is the starting ground – which will have to be narrowed to include the qualification: human. Can it be anything else but the choice of all choices, is it not the same as Hamlet's: "to be or not to be?" It must be the same, yet quite unlike. It might seem that Hamlet's formulation, as a straightforward set of alternatives, is the simplest and most adequate approach to this choice; yet the discussion in the preceding chapter showed that such choice is neither simple nor straightforward in its alternatives, and also that in Ham-let's approach it is self-disintegrating, subdued by negation. Yet how else can it be understood? If this "is" the primary choice, if it extends universally to all being, then it must make choosing "be," it must not amount to a self-cancellation of which the issue, at least by half, "is not" – since then no being could "be." This in turn means that the alternatives must not be regarded as equi-valent. The choice of being must "prejudice" to be. On the other hand, to remain a choice, it must not absolutely refuse the alternative: not to be. How such a choice may originate superhuman or subhuman beings, it would be neither possible nor desirable to enquire here. With regard to the human being, two unavoidable factors circumscribe the choice: its awareness, in contradistinction to entities "below" man – and its finiteness, in contradistinction to entities "above" him. Man can choose – or be chosen – to be, consciously but not infinitely. The "prejudiced" choice is what first makes him be, aware of being there, through a time. But the alternative of negation dwells in him consciously, reverting his being into question addressed most of all toward the destiny of his time. Thus the ever-questionable yet irrefusable choice of the human being can be understood as the quest to be: striving.

How does Faust's character fulfill its representation of the human being for this choice? The answer can be drawn directly from his own words, spoken not merely on his own behalf:

> What makes our rarest destiny do not ask!
> To be, though but for a moment, is our task.

These words show definite awareness that the choice is prejudiced though temporal, that destiny is in question though unasked, that asking though genuine never eliminates the quest itself as a task. What Faust appropriates in his character quite decisively, unlike Hamlet, is a possible fulness of human existence. What moves him through all his adventures and mis-adventures is "a strong resolve ever to strive for life in highest measure." Never, not even in his suicidal mood, when raising his toast to the doubtful dawn of death, does he allow an equal weight to the alternative "not to be." His thirst to be, which holds the strength of his striving, is never stilled. He is and chooses himself in the human being as such, despite its limitations. Of the latter he is hardly unaware – or else his protest would not be so resonant. But as already observed, his protest is never exhausted in a negative claim against: his voice speaks for, on the ground of, man's being there on his earth. Having once expressed his willingness "to embrace all human selves," even if it meant "to founder in the end" with them all, Faust keeps his faith with men's way to be.

And thus the question of Faust's being tragic, inseparable from his representative expression of man's existence in this world, must be pursued further on the ground of the primary choice of the human being. What is there about this choice, even in its most positive expression such as Faust's, that can revert it toward the negative and open potentialities of tragedy?

First of all, in the choice, there is the inevitable dispersal of plurality or duality, so strongly evident in Faust's two souls. The ground for this is in the pendular swing of choice awareness between self-locating and self-eluding, between a "grasshopper's" rest and flight, between "this" and "beyond." Both, or all, of these striving options are in being, are positive, pulling, productive; but mutually for them-

selves they are negative, repulsing, destructive. Choosing to be human
– does this signify an irrevocable commitment to some "this": this
life, this self, this time? Does not the choosing awareness also inclusi-
vely entertain perhaps some contrasting life, a different self, another
time? Does a realist have no dreams, can an ascetic forget the senses,
is living in the present ever divorceable from aiming at the future?
In such dispersal, no unity is ever to be taken for granted.[1] Faust
strives to be, to be one; yet with what divergent voices does he speak
throughout, even into his last night of life! Can one assume that in
his last speech his warring souls are united? A positive and a negative
verdict would be equally legitimate, particularly in view of the
ambiguity surrounding his final satisfaction with some moment –
attained or anticipated. And if one recalls the early noted contrast between creative unity of the Lord and its undermining plurality in the
devils, the question whether the man Faust finds his way to belong
at-one with the Lord must remain beyond human judgment. "No
angel could shatter the bonds of that twoness" – the Lord alone may
distinguish what belongs. But for the human vision, this self-questioning, un-unified swing of all human choice of being is voiced in Faust's
tragic protest.

Further, if the choice is a quest, if the "whole" of man's existence
in the world must struggle against an irreducible "not yet" of its goal,
then the human being "is" no more than the human striving. This is
the source of Care's dominion over man who "can never really come
to be." Care enables man to build a path ahead; but precisely because
Care is always "just here," because man's Care-full outlook is always
from here toward the Beyond, the fulfillment of his striving is tied
beyond him, his path in his light achieves no terminus, and therefore
might but might not be "the path that is true and fit." To strive is to
grope in self-made light alternating with darkness. There is more truth
than temptation in Mephistopheles' words:

> This universe – believe a devil –
> Was made for no one but a god!
> He exists in eternal light
> But us he has brought into the darkness
> While your sole portion is day and night.

[1] The shallow disregard for such inner-human plurality is ironically exposed by
Dostoevsky in reference to Pyotr Stepanovitch Verhovensky: "Life's a very easy
business for him, for he fancies a man to be this and that, and goes on as though he
really was ... When he's said of a man he's a scoundrel, he knows nothing more
about him except that he's a scoundrel. Or if he's said he's a fool, then that man has
no calling with him except that of fool. But I may be a fool Tuesday and Wednesday,
and on Thursday wiser than he."

That the universe is not for man, one need not believe; but that its light-full enjoyment is only for a god while man's choice can only accept being in day and night, in weal and woe, that is what a consenting witness cannot but acknowledge with Faust. The terminus of light and the indeterminacy of darkness are both suspended in the Beyond of destiny. In his earthly existence, not glorious sun radiance but the moon, expressing "reflected" light only, is Faust's "sad friend." His striving is under the demand of youthfully maintaining itself against decay and drag of aging which tends to constrict it into renunciation, which threatens it with extinction. This Faust withstands successfully, capable even at the end of challenging Care. But does his remedy against Care show a shining signal of success Beyond, does it resolve the wonder whether this manfully built path terminates in fullness or emptiness? The finite chosen being, even on eternal record, is at its temporal end "no nearer the Infinite." Such issue of the quest does not invalidate the striving, but neither does it invalidate the protest. Such wonder-fully unresolved destiny of the human striving can be seen as tragic.

And thirdly, the choice of the human being is involved in a reversal precisely on account of its universality. The positive choice means here: an assent to all things human, an effort to transcend individual limits, a willingness to enter combat now for all times and for all men. Quite consciously, Faust affirms this responsibility to sample "what is allotted to the whole of mankind," and before death reaffirms his desire to have lived for "millions." This willingness qualifies him to serve in the contest between the Lord and the devil; this affirmation distinguishes him drastically from the critical complaints in Mephisto's negation. As suggested before, it appears that in order to have a chance of coping with the spirit of denial, Faust must not of his own accord yield into final condemnation any aspect of his human being. To claim: "Homo sum," he must be able to add: "Nihil humanum mihi alienum esse puto." To bear the tension of this all-human assent destroys his orthodox faith and almost breaks him, at the level where "human intelligence snaps" – through pity: pity for mankind "writhing and racked in death before the eyes of the Ever-Pardoning." Still, he emerges from this tension hard and unbroken, to formulate his final joyful affirmation of the universe, bidding man "to weal and woe assent." This assent to human existence in this world is Nietzschean-hard and costly: its cost is the elimination of one humane thing – pity. Pity, as criticism of life, must be surrendered to Mephisto's denial of life's worth. To accept universally all human being, Faust must accept also all its woe. The negation of pity's negation is forced. Is the positive choice of the human being, which results in such in-humane en-joyment of the universe, not tragic?

But this choice to live as one for all men leads to another conse-quence. It adds a factor of irrevocable commitment, an awareness that the whole issue of human existence is being decided now for ever. This means that there is no recourse outside; if one stands for all, one stands on his own. The finite time for combat occurs now, and Faust the combatant preparing for "the end of time" dares not hope that it will ever recur, for himself or for any other human being. Thus the assumed community with all refuses itself into a pressure of isolated responsibility in "mastering" one's time or being "mastered" by it. Is not this, however, precisely required of a combatant on behalf of the Lord who is one? The task of striving, then, can be seen as a gathering from a plurality of evil, from a dispersal of "souls," from a community of men, toward some goodness of just one self. Is the task as demanding as not to permit of achievement? The answer may be-long to the Lord; man may only quest for it. Yet this appears as the tragic truth: to strive to be all-one is to exist alone.

As in the previous illustrations of tragic character, those aspects of Faust, which have been here brought out as tragic, need not appear as such to you, "unless your own heart keep in touch" with him, in serious consent. But perhaps the particular status of Faust, as not only a hero but the hero representative of mankind, justifies another reminder. These conclusions about Faust's tragic striving have been developed so as to approach him closely not in his individuality as a man but rather in his way to represent man as such. But then would your acceptance of them not overextend their import, if you were to understand them to take as tragic every man's existence as such? Such a dictum, even were it plausible, would clearly deprive of its point this attempt to discriminate what is tragic. Yet a strict, objective denial of tragedy in any particular man's existence cannot be expected after what has been said on the preceding pages. The men selected to illuminate the path of this exploration – and the man Faust more than any other – can only lead you in poetic intimacy toward what may be tragic for you as it is for them. Faust's character can be most significant in this regard, if it expresses properly for you most uni-versal human issues, ideas, involvements in tragic being, Such issues, ideas, involvements are also expressed in their way by other tragic individuals, those who appear here and those who do not; they, too, can claim to represent mankind. But the paradox of representation is restrictive; although Faust strives for man's existence as such, he is not Everyman – nor is any other existing individual. Therefore what Faust finds tragic in the human being, may not be found by every man; though it may be found or felt or perhaps fancied – by you.

To refuse tragic character to Faust may only be possible for those who take clearly for granted that the destiny of his striving is one of glorious consummation in the approval of the Lord; because then all that he lacks is "corrected," all his human woe is reconciled, all darkness is suffused in full light. To see him – and potentially all human being – as tragic, I have tried at length, and at the cost of a risky excursion beyond this life, to show that the question of Faust's human destiny must remain open, that possibilities of nothingness or hell must not be discarded in favor of heavenly fulfillment. To preserve a proper view of the "human portion" of Faust, the tension of both day and night must remain on the earthly horizon. The limits of dark are not eliminable. Despite this stress on Faust's tragic nightliness, passing thoughts have been mentioned, suggesting that Faust reaches an open outlook toward light, that his tragic protest is yet somehow balanced for and against, that through his stormy climb he does arrive at a height where he can come to terms with his striving. It is now only too proper, before parting from him, to reflect on this outlook, this balance, this height. To do that, it is necessary to turn once more to his last speech.

Before his death, Faust not only concludes his assent to the moment of existence, future or present, which has been questioned before. He also discovers the content of his life-taking action searching for life-knowledge. These are his culminating words:

> Aye! Wedded to this concept like a wife,
> I find this wisdom's final form:
> He only earns his freedom and his life
> Who takes them every day by storm.

Satisfaction? Perhaps. Safety? Never. Faust's pinnacle of wisdom dwells in being "beset by dangers," in taking all one's time "by storm," in the challenge of choice to earn, to gain, to make properly be. But to earn and appropriate what? Not bare life characterizing "not man but worm" not just the possibility "to stay as – a slave." That which enables the human being to earn itself, to strive and overcome and climb, the precondition of a self-built path, is freedom. Freedom, self-choosing itself into striving is thus discovered – if Faust's final wisdom is of merit – as the treasure-like enveloped core of man's existence. Eternal happiness belongs only to a god; worldly security is a deadening and constricting goal of Care; high-minded self-complacency is a cursed delusion. But freedom indispensable for all choice of love, might be the earning of grace and if it does not deny or betray itself, it might provide the only in-temporal self-contain-ment attainable for mortal man. Such freedom must confront danger, move on through woe and wreck, adventurously dare all advents of time. That is why Faust does not determine freedom as some uni-versally available endowment of the human species, but as worth to be earned, a core to be de-veloped the final form of wise discovery. Not every man searches for wisdom, not every man chooses to earn him-self, not every man views time as ground for de-velopment; thus freedom may be in being for all, un-discovered. Nor is there, in Faust's view, any set stage of freedom taken for granted as a goal achieved, then repulsed toward past laurels. Perhaps freedom goes better under the name of "liberation" – this question will return with Orestes. Be-cause it has to be earned "every day," not merely conquered "by storm" but re-conquered through time and only preserved in being re-gained from self-assurance, from custom and habit, from a dead past assumption of skill, method, procedure. Seeking the live "trace of spirit," it can not set in just "a matter of training." Free striving is only that of man re-born "every day" to earn, to re-fresh his thirst for the "green meadows" of life to be his own, to "move on" from revival of the past through assent in the present toward the advent of future. Freedom is not to have but to do. In Faust's vision, it corres-ponds to his continuing conviction that the creative beginning of all is the Deed.

How does this culminating discovery of freedom relate to Faust's protest with its condemnations, and to the destiny of his part in the cosmic contest of good and evil? In other words, can the possibility to de-velop freedom in the human being compensate for its lacks, in-sufficiencies, limitations? Is protest silenced thereby and tragedy eliminated? This could hardly be asserted. Nevertheless, in these last hours of his life's discovery, Faust appears able to give it his assent, even to reach for its positive fulfillment. Does this mean that for Faust to have been there is good? Such a finding might be easily mis-understood. In one sense discussed, Faust's choice of being is through-out "prejudiced," it inclines to be and strenuously refuses not to be; on this basis it might be said that he finds life "good," not only when dying. But this does not in the least stop him from violently condem-ning so much: for him, good and evil are still struggling in suspense within his choice of being. In another sense, it must be kept in mind that perfect "good" is the Lord's only, that even though Faust could have found his life good, it might not have been good: this is unresolved before the Lord's judgment. But that again does not completely disqualify all human judgment, protest and choice. "That nothing perfect falls to man," Faust feels very acutely. And this is why his final discovery of freedom becomes important. Both creation of perfect good and inert denial of evil are outside man's scope; only through the choice of free striving can he find his own human being. Freedom is thus a "reflection" of both good and evil; it is not their resolution but a resolved movement between them. Not a goal of rest but a task of doing, not available "just here" nor banned "beyond" but a suspension-linking bridge in time. With his life Faust comes not to set but to such flowing terms, and his last moment's satisfaction may be not a complete fulfillment but an active fulfilling. There is no perfection in it, no absence of limits or conflicts, neither in the visualized dangerous future nor in the concrete fermenting present: on this last night of his life the same Faust who comes to admire free striving of millions shows selfish disregard for the freedom of Philemon and Baucis. To strive is forever to err, to remain susceptible to evil, to feel one's lacks, and to be free to protest for and against them, perhaps in vain.

That human striving may be tragic is in no way denied in "wisdom's final form." But its content, life as striving for freedom, infuses the human quest with an inner sense. What is forever non-free, non-choosing, may only stay put, self-enclosed, without a chance of issue; on the temporal horizon, the words may be true of it: "If it had not been, it would make no difference" – it could be an empty and sterile part of night. Such, however, is not the human being, if it gains the task of earning freedom. It is then open to temporal adventure in its self-motion storming through the world; choosing its record, it may claim that the traces of its own "earthly days can never sink in the aeons unaware." Freedom gives to the quest a creative sense, indubitable though not infallible. Man's choice to be "is" striving for light. Full radiance of the Lord's oneness "is" beyond what his vision could bear; the dispersed indeterminacy of the devil's darkness "is" only what thrusts him forward and away. To be human is to search in freedom for a horizon of light – reflected, brief, but one' own worth. "By no joy sated, filled by no success," Faust has never ceased striving and never lost this sense of his path: "With night behind me and before me day – I hasten on to drink eternal light." So could his last words culminate in this tragic and free human quest: More light!

CHAPTER VI

The Tragic Idea - Stockmann, The People's Enemy

HENRIK IBSEN: AN ENEMY OF THE PEOPLE

The town; the native town of his birth, in which he wants to live and serve, to which he would belong completely, if anywhere he can belong: this is the world in which Doctor Thomas Stockmann lives. Only a town? Yes, a town, a polis which is respected as the natural habitat of civilized man, beginning in Hellas. A town which contains on a small scale an assembly of all human horizons, of powers, aspirations, fields of action, loves, discoveries, rights and wrongs. A miniature world, or better, a miniature of a whole world.

In such a world billions of humans have found themselves completely at home and at rest. How is it that Stockmann does not? Does he need a wider horizon for activity, a country, an empire? Is it the small size of his world that stifles him? Not as one hears him speak; he wants to belong just within those circumscribed boundaries of his native town – if he can. On the other hand, larger boundaries of national or supernational scope also could not contain him, would have to be burst, impatiently exploded if needs be, for the sake of – what? How can this paradox be accounted for that a small scope might satisfy a man like Stockmann, yet much larger scopes might not suffice at all? The answer is that the grave difficulty in finding himself at home has for Stockmann nothing to do with that home's size. What prevents him from fitting snugly into a factual area of life, no matter of what dimensions, is his being possessed in a way entirely non-dimensional and non-quantitative: by ideas.

The cutting diagnosis of his predicament is put forward early by that prosaic realist, Peter Stockmann, the mayor:

"Oh, ideas – yes! My brother has had plenty of them in his time –

unfortunately. But when it is a question of putting an idea into practical shape, you have to apply to a man of different mettle."

How are ideas put into practical shape? This is the basic question confronting Dr. Stockmann as well as the people around him. No doubt they can be. But to know how, is to resolve the dilemma of a man of ideas who wants to belong to the world he lives in. Otherwise he can be torn apart by his two loyalties, in agony such as mediaeval men suffered whose bodies used to be massacred by horses pulling in opposite directions. Is this not an exaggeration? How can an idea draw such agonizing power, when it otherwise serves as a fount of glory, of boons and advancements for humanity? Where is its danger? Why should an idea-proud man not feel at home in the world of his people? Some answers to such questions should become available from a close study of the history of Dr. Stockmann.

It is not each and every idea that signals danger to human existence. To assert that would be to fall prey to a frustrating misology. It is not even the quality of the idea that decides the danger, but the mode of grasping it, or being grasped by it, in a man's character. One man's poison is another man's discovery. There is a way, proper to some, maybe to many men, of holding to an idea so that in its blinding radiance the temporal world is suspended, neither illuminated nor hidden from view, showing not enough yet too much. The men are then neither willing to live a life of thought, nor capable of giving precedence to the real demands of everyday merely because they are real, no matter how ill suited to their idea. The light of the idea is here too diffuse to point up its practical fitness in the world, yet much too brilliant to be forgotten. Existence in the shine of such an idea becomes a Hegelian contradiction within itself. A thesis and an antithesis are posed, only no synthesis will come forth. It is in such existence that IDEA becomes tragic.

After the cosmic grandeur of Faust, the view of any man is apt to prove an anticlimax. Thus Thomas Stockmann is likely to appear as a little man, of no great depth or reach. This is the more likely, since greatness often dwells but in a haze of perspective. And here perspective is shortened with the entry into this familiar modern age which has not yet quite passed. Dr. Stockmann's time is in this secular history almost contemporary. It is a time of rationally flattened surfaces and streamlined whirls; a labyrinth, but scientific. It is the time of modern man who after Faust turns to "this earth" uniquely, supremely confident of his indifference for a Below or an Above. As for this present twentieth century, so for the preceding one, the strongest power felt immediately by any human individual is not an obsolete God whose damnation is just a cliché, but the living and breeding society whose sanction is public opinion, as effective as hell. Immortality becomes a question of newspaper publicity, and the place of final repose is one of social register. If there is a problem about saving, it is expressed not in terms of devils and souls but of dollars and cents. Greatness in this world has surely a more precise synonym in "prestige." Here begins a twilight of those great and serious ideas which seemed so essential for the conception of the tragic. One of them is certainly alive, the idea of freedom, of man's lonely self-dependence, although that, too, is threatened with being talked out of mind by a congregation of physicists, sociologists and psychiatrists. For a modern spirit, this idea is not worth bothering about, except for a rhetorical invocation. The others are all dead, never to return; and with them has been buried tragedy. Or has it, indeed?

The figure of Dr. Stockmann on this horizon still fits the Aristotelian criteria of a tragic hero: one who completes an action, therein sustaining bad fortune, also one socially elevated, and certainly neither too good nor too evil. How his character and story correspond to further aspects of tragic being, will have to be shown, depending on how serious his existence will be for you. Transposed out of historical perspective, Stockmann appears much like Oedipus, though an Oedipus unmindful of God and immortality, as befits modern style. Like Oedipus, he is involved in the disquiets and conflicts of a community's leadership; like Oedipus, he is ruined by his service to that community; like Oedipus, the seeds of his fall he sows by own hand in his actions. Some of that ancient ethos thus persists here. But beyond these points, the similarity ceases; and anyway, for a more intimate insight into Stockmann's existence, such an atemporal transposition cannot be more than a passing note aside. Because Stockmann acts in the modern time. If he is tragic, he is so in such ways only as modern man may be. His actions concern municipal meetings rather than crown conspiracies; his bad fortune can be expressed in terms of ostracism by society, not of oracular secret. Thus you must view him, and try to assimilate the serious aspects of what is proper to him in his temporal limits. Then perhaps you can see whether this tragic existence may also be yours.

The protest which Stockmann expresses does not obviously exhibit any roots in what endures through history of man; rather, it seems addressed to transitory, even disposable. features of group living arranged by the political animal. Such features, introduced in his own times or shortly before, can clearly be amended or abolished, again in his times or shortly after. If they are, nothing is left of proper concern for those who come decades or centuries later. No straight reference points to some eternal deficiency in man's existence, but only to specific, datable blows of inhumanity between man and man. Hell or heaven is no future destiny, it is only a picturesque description of faulty interpersonal relations which can, with some good intentions, so easily turn the corner into a terrestrial and social paradise. Such is the outward import of what Stockmann has to protest against. In such a frame of protesting mind he certainly stays within the ranks of modern scientific humanity for which there are not things which could not be manipulable, adaptable, reformable, within some time, and a relatively brief time. Thus the apparent higher speed of modern living makes problems and predicaments obsolete; what could be serious one hundred years ago can hardly be a serious concern now. Is not this another way of saying that what might have been persistently, universally tragic for man as man has been abolished in the wake of progress?

Because of this difficulty, to pursue the search of the tragic also on these modern grounds, it is necessary to dig to some depth under their surface, not merely to attend to the literal content and goal of Stockmann's protest. That deals with the septic condition of the town baths, if you please: surely no one contemporary with all the deodorized, detergent, disinfected know-how of today can seriously treat that backward problem. It is not a question of fleeting appearance and particular form of Stockmann's dramatic experiences, but of how these are tied in his proper character and vision of the world. For this reason his words and external gestures must be interrelated with what he strives for and does and is. In such an examination I expect to display some contradictions of his own being, of such a character as need not be confined to the nineteenth, the twentieth, or any other century of human history. This can be serious.

When first encountered, in some youthful, enthusiastic experience, the character of Dr. Stockmann is easily impressed in admiration as that of a martyr, and the label of "an enemy of the people" appears as a gross perversion of justice. When time admits a more thorough consideration, this epithet may perhaps be seen as not entirely inappropriate to his character. To make a beginning, let it be observed that on the whole Stockmann's protest is raised against idols enslaving the life of man. Each of such idols is transient, no doubt, and of danger only to such or such group, for a longer or shorter epoch. But whether idolatry criticized by him is as such equally transient, that is another question. A negative possibility is suggested by the irony contained within his protest: the fact that Stockmann does not declare war on idols in the name of human existence but under the banner of what may very well be another idol. His own actions and insights are not exempt from what he finds himself in dissent with. And that can provide a deeper but darker impression of him, as dark as to be conceivably tragic. But this observation must be clarified and developed. Here are some illustrations of it.

Stockmann protests against a narrow-minded, short-sighted, self-enclosed attitude toward life. It should imply that what he offers instead proceeds from an entirely open mind, a broad and far-reaching vision. Is this exactly the disposition indicated in such words as: "I will show that I am right and that you are wrong," "I have right on my side," "I take my stand on right and truth"? His dedication to what is right need not be questioned. But what about his assurance that he is in possession of, or in intuitive touch with, what is right? Is it not the case that such a unidirectional self-insistence tends to see only straight forward, not at all to the sides, that it can be hampered by congenital blinkers? If there is that danger, then there is reason to suspect that Stockmann's mind is also perhaps too narrow, that there lies in it the seed of all narrow-mindedness: fanaticism. This crucial aspect of his character will have to be examined further, to disclose better this apparent kinship between what he is and what he is against.

Stockmann protests against party organization: "Party programmes strangle every young and vigorous truth," "Party leaders must be exterminated." "A party leader like a wolf requires victims to prey upon." But what are his steps in regard to the affair of the baths? Claiming the backing of the "compact majority," assuring himself of a public outlet through the press, planning a series of manifestoes, "one article every single day like bombshells." This kind of activity looks to an outside eye remarkably like the organization of a political party, even if to the eye of Dr. Stockmann himself it may deserve some other denomination.

Stockmann demands that leaders who prey upon and oppress others, shackling their freedom, should be removed altogether. Yet what else can he be considered as but a leader manqué? He certainly exhibits signs of leadership aspirations, accepts this and that to be put "at his disposal," plays around with his brother's insignia of office and taunts him – not in earnest? "I am the mayor, the master of the whole town" – are there no notions of leadership there? Anyone who would claim that those are jokes without subconscious currents should also affirm that Stockmann, if successful in his crusade and carried on by his spirit of mission to his town, would definitely refuse any political responsibility for himself; such a speculation is not too well supported by evidence.

Stockmann desires independence, fresh, free air and initiative in living, deploring official shackles of organization and dependence. All this, very clearly and explicitly, on his own behalf. At the same time he is unwilling to extend his cry for independence to others without limitation. He cannot believe that human "common curs" are also capable of independent living, that even if less clever in making use of free movements, they might in their own dim way appreciate freedom no less than his own "poodle's brain." "I don't intend to waste a word on the puny, narrow-chested, short-winded – life no longer concerns itself with them." Values, advancements, privileges, these are to be justified for the poodle race; because it is stronger, more developed? No interest is shown in the narrow-chested curs, no hope for them. Only at the very end of his activities, when isolated from his town, Stockmann is reduced to this brilliant idea: "I am going to experiment with curs, just for once; there may be some exceptional heads amongst them." Restricted to curs, he is still interested in and looking for poodles amongst them.

Stockmann in his "poodle" creed finds objectionable the rule of the majority because of its implications of equality of human voices and of its foundation in overwhelming numbers. This equality and those numbers have turned against him and held him powerless. But before that happened, Stockmann felt no qualms in exclaiming: what a good thing it is "to have behind me the compact majority, to feel this bond of brotherhood between oneself and one's fellow citizens!" He finds definite attraction in the idea of citizenship, yet that idea precisely implies being one surrounded by many who are akin, alike, equal. It is hard to think of citizenship under Nero or Ivan the Terrible, yet perhaps they were poodles whom majority rule of curs would have overwhelmingly frustrated?

Stockmann protests against trickery and mishandling of truth, as though he believed in its lasting dignity and power. It comes then as a great shock to discover him in the act of introducing a view of truth in which it appears as relative to use, to possession and to time: "A normally constituted truth lives at most twenty years ... Don't talk nonsense about well-ascertained truths! The truths of which the masses now approve are the very truths that the fighters at the outposts held to in the days of our grandfathers. We fighters at the outposts nowadays no longer approve of them; and I do not believe there is any other well-ascertained truth except this, that no community can live a healthy life if it is nourished only on such old marrowless truths." This is amazing. If truth belongs among such perishable commodities for quick consumption, if it is something too many people can not and should not share, then what is Stockmann talking about, when he declares, before his catastrophe: "Truth and the people will win! "Do you imagine that you can silence me and stifle the truth?"; or after the disastrous meeting, when he claims he has been fighting "for freedom and truth?" Can it be the same truth, worth fighting for, which cannot be stifled? Is the winning power of truth contingent upon individuals' approval? Is it possible that some linguistic coincidence is interfering here and that a distinction must be made between "truths" and "Truth?" But a worse suspicion lingers: could it be that the qualification for capitalizing "truth" is that it should be yours, that it is truth which you hold to, fight for and consider as invincible? It is conceivable and natural among mortals among whom Stockmann belongs, to hypostatize truth which they consider as their own, appropriated in their existence, But such a tendency may overlook that whatever makes truth your own need not be the same as what makes it true; and further, that when it leads, as in Stockmann's case, to a double standard, to aggrandizement of "Truth with me" and destructive contempt for "truths of others" – despite their being true though not approved by him – then such a relation to truth is divided against itself and dangerous.

Stockmann in his devotion to ideas protests against overestimation of what is material. He would wish to disregard the gross and degrading necessities of earthly living, those merely incidental and secondary realities of food and domicile and income. Early in his story he boasts: "I earn almost as much as we spend." In his final resolution he has for his wife those scarcely practical or even humane words: "Oh, you will have to pinch and save a bit – then we shall get along. That gives me very little concern." Little concern for what she is to pinch and save from! Yet he is not at all an ascetic, indifferent to material comforts. In his first appearance he sounds quite complacent: "Ah, it is good to be sitting snug and warm here," with cigars and a drink, after a roast-beef supper. And in his last conversation with his brother he responds: "What a blessed feeling it is to know one is provided for!" To be provided with what the body needs is good to him, but to provide it, that gives him little concern. Is he dishonest, is he ready to sponge and abuse others? No, such a moral criticism of him would be hard to justify. Still, it remains uncontroverted that the material realities of life Dr. Stockmann values and devalues at the same time. This, as much as the other introduced conflicts and inconsistencies, is all in his way to be.

What do these illustrations show? For one thing they point to this definite conclusion: that Stockmann's character is outstanding and uncommon, harboring such contradictions within itself. But on the other hand, if the contradictory aspect is left aside for the moment, it can also be said that Stockmann very plainly shows himself as all too human. He moves through ordinary aspirations, he has to relie on brotherhood with his neighbors, he sees only a limited horizon and a partial view of truth, he enjoys the creature comforts of material realities. In no way does he stand above the level of social sorrows and personal perplexities of man: he is no Prometheus. And this in turn points to a more universally significant, if darker, conclusion. If such as Stockmann who see the shocks and shortages of human existence, still cannot tear themselves above them, where is the dream of eradicating them? If protest undermines itself when he who protests is human, where is the remedy? If salt itself is not salty enough, wherewith can it be salted? The limitation of visions, and its potential fanaticism and hostility; social organization, and its choking hold on spontaneity and initiative; leadership, and its enslavement of the led; demand for freedom, and incapacity to make use of it; the strength, security, and possible tyranny of majority rule; the elusiveness of impersonal and lasting truth to shortsighted and partial subjects; the indispensable material needs of the body growing into irreparable materialistic service to the body. All these "natural shocks" may thus be viewed as incurable, as wholly ingrained in the life of man, indeed as creating the stuff of which it is composed. This, admittedly not the complete nor the only picture, is nevertheless a true and universal picture of mankind, so inadequate, so disintegrating within that its cries must resound vainly in the wilderness. If there is truth in such a vision, then it must be admitted that Stockmann, before being a modern man, is a man; that his protest, far from being restricted to transitory and disposable features of nineteenth century's society, goes against all living of men with themselves; that to appreciate it more intimately, one must look not at the secular times of the present age but at the time of human existence.

In fact, one aspect of Stockmann's protest can only be inferred indirectly, and never studied in his words and actions. That is the very possibility of his putting forward an open protest. However correct his objections against the limitations and liabilities of "liberalism" may be, reflection can lead to those conditions and constitutions of human living where liberalism is either not yet or no longer actual, where the illusions of presuming men equal and being guided by the desires of the greatest number have been dispensed with. In such times, in such societies, the very opportunity for voicing a protest by one man, on his behalf or also on behalf of others, could never be given. This passing thought may suffice to recall again the human significance of protest, even if that protest be practically pointless, as with Prometheus, even if he who protests be not free of what he protests against, as with Stockmann. Sapienti satis.

In this sombre picture of mankind, transpiring through the protesting character of Thomas Stockmann, is there any positive trait? There is, but it is not accessible among the features of this world where Stockmann has been observed thus far: in his town, surrounded by his fellow-citizens, submerged in human society. It is revealed at the conclusion of Stockmann's tragic story, when he leaves behind this former world of his. The one integral, uncontradicted characteristic of man – indeed, his only property – is his persisting power to "be" none other than himself, his ability to dare remain faithful to his freedom, tied by nothing above his own conscience. Unfortunately, this property begins to shine for Stockmann as the source of strength in his existence only when he is already out of bounds of society. What kind of strength can be there involved, against what forces? Not any more against those social forces of his world which he is now dissociated from. An outcast claims: "I am the strongest man in the town," and corrects himself: "Strongest in the whole world." Because his town used to be his world; yet he has passed beyond it. His strength can avail him now only against what is in himself, his own temptations, ideas, choices, the germs from which another world may perhaps arise in his future. But there is none now in his present, no field for his unworldly strength. Does Stockmann glimpse now this truth that his character and destiny have been unwordly all along? He seems to, when his last words are "The strongest man is he who stands most alone." His strength obtains from his standing: standing for himself, standing out, standing free. On this strength a man can build a world around him. But the strength itself is shadowed by another property: to stand for himself is to stand at the foundations of a world, to stand there – alone.

Must this be so? The question is incomplete. There is no particular thing that must be there for everybody. Whatever is, depends on choice, and choice determines man to be this rather than that, thereby determining what will be there for him because he is this rather than that – himself. Events are such for Dr. Stockmann, since he is such as he is. Any man's tragic perspectives are neither requirements nor compulsions but openings of his existence in the world, the range of which is to be explored. For the understanding of the tragic story of Dr. Stockmann, a closer look must be taken at the roots of his character, in distinction to people around him in his world. But before that another interhuman phenomenon in that world calls for attention: it uncovers the ground of Stockmann's ultimate position, where he stands alone.

~

The light which has been so far thrown upon Stockmann is hardly flattering. Such a harsh scrutiny of his words and actions may appear to be moved by dissent rather than consent. This impression should be redressed. Because however human, wanting, self-divided, he emerges from this examination with his own character outstanding from a background, with issues, inclinations, ideas, proper to himself. What now about this background on which he stands out? It is human but not characterized, it is the town-world to which Stockmann appears to belong, it is the matrix in which his clashes and struggles are laid. The background to Stockmann's existence is the relation between the personal character and the crowd. Man against society; how many words have been spoken and written about this phenomenon, allegedly peculiar or at least peculiarly striking in the modern epoch? While Stockmann's life and vision, as already argued, is properly modern, its ground covers what is not exclusive nor even specifically different in modern times. As such, it presents an opportunity to enquire, on an incomparably vivid example, into this relation of man and the crowd, not merely transitory but enduring, old as much as new.

The crowd is here taken generically, as an envelopment to which each existing man can be related so or otherwise, but to which he cannot remain entirely unrelated. So understood, the crowd is of course not restricted to its definite examples such as the crowd at a meeting or at a parade, the crowd in peace or in wartime, the crowd of proletarians, civil servants, or taxpayers. However unlike, these are specific manifestations from what can be viewed as the same source. Nor is the crowd essentially constituted by the occasion of its gathering, the duration of its presence, the spatial contiguity of its members. To be in a crowd, men need not loiter touching elbows in the street; they can be in their homes or in a forest, separated not by inches but by miles, silent rather than shouting. What makes the relation of a man to the crowd is his way to be.

This must be elucidated. In order to do that, I shall describe in turn three of the factors present: the crowd as such, the men in the crowd, and the men outside it. These observations will be illustrated from the story, actions, and misfortunes of Dr. Stockmann, and the events he lived through, but not only in his literal encounter with the crowd at the town meeting, which, for this way of thinking, was no more than a specimen.

The crowd is in the background of individual actions such as Dr. Stockmann's. More precisely it should be said that the crowd is the background, the social setting of a man's world, the undifferentiated milieu of all the "others" taken together – which always remains other, the invisible elastic wall from which personal drives rebound, in which they often sink. As such, the crowd is a static entity, merely continuing to be there yet never here where you are: the crowd is always elsewhere, around, behind or ahead. You can move toward or away from or even amongst the crowd, but in moving you carry with you your own "here," and the crowd just stays. Its principal feature is inertia, since a move, a push, an action, is ever yours or his; "theirs" is the always uncertain re-action. When the crowd "does" anything, it is more strictly the men in it who do it, although they may not recognize themselves as the doers. So a drifting boat moves but aimlessly floating, its direction due to the haphazard but genuine steps of people on board, or else to the pounding of waves. Inertly the crowd resists novelty and burdens with its deadweight the fulmination of progress. Listen to the mayor who can well know what he is talking about: "The public does not require any new ideas. The public is best served by the good, old-established ideas it already has." That is, if it has any. The possession of ideas is contingent upon aspiration and interest, and such modes of individual movement and heat need not occur within that which is just there, impersonally. Incipient interests and diffused aspirations are all that can be looked for in the crowd as a whole. They barely suffice for the crowd to be aware of some events, weakly orienting itself and waiting for a push. Unidentified voices among those who come to hear Stockmann's public address: "I go to every public meeting, I do ... Tell me what is going on here tonight .. Who are we to back up in this? ... Watch Aslaksen and do as he does." Does this indicate trust in a certain leader who serves them in their love? No, the crowd is there only to support, not to trust, to follow, not to love. A possible change in its support can happen like the dislocation of a boat's balance by a barrel rolling across. It is a matter of push and pull, of whipping on the crowd so that it should not lose its momentum when rolling along. What is the lever to set the crowd in motion? Enlightenment, devotion, sacrifice? Hardly. The simplest lever is that of suspicion, in defense of its status quo, in resentment against any flash of novelty or brilliance, in assimilation to the lowest common denominator. "I say, what has come to the doctor? What are we to think of it? ... Have you ever noticed if the fellow drinks? ... I rather think he goes off his head sometimes ... Any madness in his family? ... No, it is nothing more than sheer malice, he wants to get even with somebody." Ignorance, lack of comprehension responding blindly, but to what? Drunkenness, lunacy, selfishness, those are the avenues of re-action to the puzzling, suspicious superiority of Stockmann. Can the crowd appreciate devotion? It would have to recognize where its interests lie; and that already lies beyond the receptivity of its dispersed power. Strongly pushed, demagogically warned against such curiosity, it obeys, since that agrees so well with its unwillingness to encounter anything novel and unknown to be coped with. Suspicious, it refuses information: "Don't talk about the baths! We won't hear you! None of that!" Yet, although Stockmann is not the man to achieve it, there are some chances of a change of support in the meeting: there is some initial applause for him, some confusion later, some amused laughter especially at his words critical of authority and prominent citizens; that sort of speech could turn the motion of the crowd, ever suspicious of those who claim to stand in front of it as its leaders. Because the balance of weight in the crowd is as precarious as in a boat on stormy waters. Without a pilot, the crowd is shaky, insecure. Its only safety lies in sheer size, in anonymous numbers. And that kind of strength is illusory since every chain is as resistant as the most fragile link in it, every boat stays afloat as long as its whole water-exposed surface has no break anywhere. Hence the inert servility to anyone who appears the strongest; because the concern of the crowd is only to remain unbroken, to float as an anonymous whole, to be there in "safe" bulk. Hence the inert timidity, as in the crowd of Theban elders, suspicious of all daring, so in the crowd pursuing Stockmann, which despite all its momentary hostility can only gather enough impetus to throw small stones at his house.[1] This is not to say that a crowd cannot be really dangerous and homicidal: but that only happens when a decided destructive intent is imparted to it by some leading individuals, or else when the collective insecurity of the crowd is so greatly disturbed and threatened that it thrashes out to break, often no matter whom.

What makes the crowd be as it is? Speaking generally, Stockmann provides a certain answer when he denies that "the crowd has the monopoly of broad-mindedness and morality and that vice and corruption and every kind of intellectual depravity are the result of culture." What he denies is the naive Rousseau-type of illusion that somehow the generality of mankind could be, or have been, more moral, deserving, not to say noble, in their "natural" vegetation, and that it is the more complex cultural transformations of social living which are at fault in degrading the crowd. No, such a pseudo-historical apology for the crowd's mode of being misconceives just that which it tries to account for in a short temporal perspective. The crowd and what it signifies is not a phenomenon of modern culture; it is as old as mankind. It is the unsafe, unresolved human being as such that is responsible for the crowd. To be sure, specific conditions can make for quality variations. This is what Stockmann visualizes when he continues: "That culture demoralizes is only an old falsehood that our forefathers believed in and we have inherited. No, it is ignorance, poverty, ugly conditions of life, that do the devil's work!" It is not the achievements of culture, of temporal changes in humanity, but its persistent lacks and perversions that can make specific examples of crowds particularly worthy of contempt. In other words, there can be qualitative differences, due to the menace of ignorance, poverty, ugliness, between a crowd of shivering, starving aborigines and a crowd of Athenian citizens, or between that and a crowd of automated laborers in the slums of a contemporary city. The arrow of history need not point toward improvement or deterioration of crowds through the ages. At any rate, for the initial grasp of the

---

[1] So in this confrontation, in midst of burning Rome: "He pushed his horse into the throng. All around, visible in the light of the burning, were upraised hands, armed with every manner of weapon, inflamed eyes, sweating faces, bellowing and foaming lips ... Grasping hands were stretched toward his horse's reins and toward him, but he rode further; cool, indifferent, contemptuous. At moments he struck the most insolent heads with his cane, as if clearing a road for himself in an ordinary crowd; and that confidence of his, that calmness, amazed the raging rabble. They recognized him at length, and numerous voices began to shout, – "Petronius! Arbiter Elegantiarum! Petronius!" – Sienkiewicz, *Quo Vadis*.

– 155 –

whole background of human activities the main target is not what the crowd is like but that it is a crowd. What makes the crowd be, as the undifferentiated others, as "they?" Whatever makes anything be, is a choice. But what choice is involved, and whose choice? The best light can be thrown onto this problem from enquiring into the constituence of the crowd. And that is – individual men, after all.

The men in the crowd. What is their way to be, their common ethos? Special attention will be given in approaching the existence of one such individual, in the next chapter: his name is Willy Loman. At this stage men of the crowd can only be spoken of in the plural, and that always means an uncertainly crowded description. If there is a word which can provide a clue to the conception of being of men in the crowd, it is: loss. Loss of himself by each member of it produces the selfless, driveless inertia of the crowd as a whole. How can such a losing choice or rather choice of loss occur in any man? To envisage that, one must remember that choice is not here treated as a conscious act of man, at least it need not be such and can still remain choice. Thus it would be vain and insufficient to try and find out for one man, then another and another, whether, when and how he has been aware of choosing to lose himself. The answers could be unmanageable or none at all. Not every individual retains, like Hamlet, his conscientious response to choice. Also one must not weight the scales in hastily assuming that the choice was his: perhaps he was chosen, determined not from within, to lose himself. But in that case, is it warranted at all to speak of choice of loss? Of choice man does not have full or safe knowledge; this was confessed at the outset of the whole exploration. Still, choice can be presumed as responsible for what is in existence, on the basis of what in it can be observed and known. What symptoms are there in the existence of individual men in the crowd, which would point to such a choice of loss?

The man in the crowd loses his self by giving it over to others, surrendering it to become common. Common property, one would say, if what is proper, own, his, could ever be common; rather it is the case that property of self becomes annihilated there. This is how men become common. Each one yields himself to all the others in toto, not just sharing with this or that other one. He remains subject: subject to their influence, an obedient subject, a receptive, manageable, loyal subject. Does this happen only in the slums of stupidity and superstition? Not according to Dr. Stockmann: "The kind of common people I mean are not only to be found low down in the social scale; they crawl and swarm all around us – even in the highest social positions. You have only to look at your own mayor ... He thinks what his superiors think and holds the same opinions as they. People who do that are common." The mayor himself does not get the chance to reply to these words; would he deny them? Immediately before, another crowd specimen, Hovstad, is in his speech very far from disclaiming such an attitude: he boasts of being common: "I lay no claim to any sort of distinction. I am the son of humble countryfolk, and I am proud that I come from common people." This is what a man has to say in the crowd, and this is what the crowd applauds. What a bankruptcy of existence: no claim to any distinction, to anything proper, uniquely his own, and pride in being just common! Someone may perhaps suggest that such words are only spoken to an anticipating audience, as here in the meeting; but this would be underestimating that loss which makes men think and act on this common pattern also when they are alone by themselves. Sometimes even more so then: without the comfort of surrounding others, dismayed by isolation, what would they do or think? Just "obviously" what anyone else would do in their place; there only is safety. And the predicament might not be so acute if, as Stockmann has it, they suited themselves to their superiors only. But this is how he could put it, he who is not a man of the crowd and therefore can discriminate for himself between superior and inferior. Discrimination demands a judging, aiming, longing self, not a self which is being lost, surrendered, and which is a constituent of inertia. The man in the crowd, yielding his selective powers, is open to all influence, inferior as much as superior. To him the danger lies precisely in being left to himself, isolated on his own, just himself as an individual – that is what he abandons, that is what he endeavors to shut out of his mind altogether. His vision becomes common, his thinking plural: not "I" and "he," but "we" and "they." To be "all-one" is disastrously unthinkable, always to be replaced by being "one of many." Hence his failure to discriminate between the influence, ideas, actions of this one superior individual and that one, inferior. Influences, forces, achievements are plural, everything that matters in the world is plural, finally he himself is – common, reducible to many, plural. Oneness of character must be lost. Therewith goes the capacity of moving and standing on one's own feet, leaving only the shaky balance of people who are in the same boat.

Is it conceivable that such phenomena in men "just happen," that they are not due to choice which determines them? To say that, one would not only admit casting about in hardly penetrated substrata of existence, but also would leave them in darkness. It may be a help to point out an alternative in this choice, other than common loss. Such an alternative was seen in Hamlet's conscientious in-dwelling into himself; more of it will be seen in Orestes. But the alternative situation of man can also be approached through what properly happens to Thomas Stockmann. This perspective must be gradually approached now.

If, for the man in the crowd, being one for himself is to be escaped, yielded, lost from mind, and plurality of the multitude is the imagined haven of power and security, then it is easy to see how to his imagination that power is endowed with a voice. The expression of that plural power is what is known as public opinion. It has no individual shape and must remain strictly anonymous, hence its voice can sound rather hazy and cryptic. But this does not put it in doubt for the man in the crowd; on the contrary, that disembodied voice, shrouded in the mystery of might, inspires him with insuperable awe. How could a mere finite one stand up against it? And thus takes place the formal ritual of prostration before the anonymous power of plurality. The day after the meeting, the news from his town-world which reaches Stockmann has no other form but this irritating, repetitious formula which passing from mouth to mouth could almost be used as a chant: one dares not oppose public opinion. Who does not invoke its protective charm, one after another? The glazier, the landlord, the school principal, the members of the baths' committee, the householders' association, the press, the leader of the majority, in short: the whole crowd. It is this phenomenon of consecutive – and thus individual – prostration before the voice of public opinion that points up a task in Stockmann's words that "the common people are nothing more than the raw material of which a people is made." A people, for him, would have a thousand voices, and not one mumbling distortion of a voice; because a people is composed of individual persons; that is the distinction he must have in mind, between a people and common people. The latter, the common lost men, are the raw material which should then be worked over with the aim toward a more finished, fine, or finite "product": a people, What working over can apply to this raw, undifferentiated conglomeration of material which is the crowd? Precisely the recovery from loss of finite limits, of finer awareness, of discriminating finish in place of common haze. To work over the men in the crowd is to pick them out of the crowd, to sharpen their vision so that they should appreciate distinctions of individuality, to raise them from prostration and to confront them with the bogus power of the multitude whose monstrous proportions are entirely due to obliterating additions of many single, finite, personal selves. A people can speak and dare only if it is composed, put together by existing individuals who dare to speak with their own voices. This task of working over the crowd's raw material, of proposing to each of its members the alternative of being himself just within his limits, is anything but easy. Its perspectives can frighten, stretching into an infinite future: because this task is nothing else but the reach of temporal progress.

To contrast the "safe" stability of being in the crowd against the dismaying alternative of being just oneself, it is now time to look at the mode of existence of men without the crowd, such as Stockmann himself. The individual who chooses himself as just one and stands on his own, must realize not only his unsafe position of all-oneness and hence aloneness, but also the natural negation of his background. He has to count with the suspicions and superstitions of those who are in the crowd and aim at his degradation into their common plural denominator, or else at his removal from their horizon. In such hostile surroundings he has to strive for a guiding vision of his own, for ideas which could assure his independence. Now the reason may dawn for the pull exercised on men who posit themselves against others by ideas. Ideas are logs for the building of an independent home in the wilderness, they can be tools for damming the spread of the crowd, and weapons for defending what is one's own. A man outside of the crowd can only rely on character in his own acts and vision in his ideas; in the un-owned sphere of events it can be quite proper for him to be ready for starvation, for stoning, for still worse outcomes. And yet he must be turned continually toward the future; it is out of the future that ideas may arrive to sweep over his present isolation, it is toward the future that every novelty, disturbing to the crowd, is addressed, expecting to be proved by time, to gain and work over those men lost in the present. Thus it is that individuals standing on their own bring about progress, they are its emissaries, "the fighters at the outposts" watching for tomorrow. Progress through time, properly grasped, can have no individual opponents. No one, thinking and striving for himself can be averse to novelty and transformation as such, since for himself he will always find lacks to be filled, disproportions to be emended, the drastic burden of his finitude to be alleviated. This is not to say that no serious disputes could arise among independent men about the details, the methods, the priorities in such striving; not, however, about progress as such. That is the reason why Stockmann dismisses as secondary in importance the adversity of older, slower, more prejudiced leaders. If they are capable of leading others, a fortiori of moving on their own, they are not genuine adversaries. Otherwise, if they are just chips off the structure of the crowd, which happened to be thrown on top, then their realm is entirely that of the past. "All these venerable relics of a dying school of thought are most admirably paving the way for their own extinction; they need no doctor's help to hasten their end ... It is not they who are most instrumental in poisoning our life ... not they who are the most dangerous enemies." The enemy of progress is no one, but only the plurality, "the compact majority," the crowd as such. Why? Because progress of mankind is nothing but the striving toward new independent existence for every one, the working over of the "raw material" into finished individuals ready for the future, the disintegration of the crowd's inertia of the present. Thus the crowd and those who bring progress are in antithesis; but while progress lasts, the crowd is immortal. Utopians dreaming of an inestimably future future, when all progress will have been accomplished, should decide whether that accomplishment can really be victorious, and that means whether the opposition to progress, the background of inter-human existence, the crowd, will ever be annihilated. Only then each man could find and be himself, all-one within and alone without.

Whatever the case may be with regard to what lies beyond a millennial horizon, life of the individual as one thus presents the alternative to losing oneself in plurality: to stay himself, alone within the temporal gravity of his ideas tending toward the future, faced with the tacit suspicious resistance of the social world around him in his present. Dr. Stockmann does not find himself alone, an outsider, only after the violent clash with his fellow-citizens at the meeting. He has been outside of their common life all along, and his inward strength of standing up for himself has been his outward weakness in the town. Perhaps it is now a little clearer why he could never be completely at home in this world of his native town, and how in the conflict tearing him, between belonging to the people around him and belonging to his own ideas, so many contradictions have accumulated in his character. His position is so precarious, because in the very same tendencies, thoughts, actions, he would sincerely wish to participate in the real life of the town-world, and also to preserve his idea-inspired independence. And also, because the world around him has precisely the nature of a town; and a town is just such a horizon on which the background of a crowd is most favorably raised. The town, the natural habitat of man, naturally furthers his loss in the crowd. Neither Prometheus raised above humanity, nor homeless Oedipus, neither Hamlet in his princely isolation, nor Faust storming through the universe, can be adequately characterized as town-dwellers. Stockmann, however, longs to belong to the town which is his native home; and yet, no less than they, he remains an outsider. The predicament of Hamlet afflicts him in another dimension, provided by the town crowd. While alone, standing for himself, he may appear strong and safe in his private sphere, completely devoted to ideas. But as soon as he decides to transform his ideas into deeds, he is immediately thrown into the whirl of conflicts due to the background wall presented by all the others around him, he is being sucked down into the crowd, and has seemingly insuperable disadvantage in his struggle for independence and progress. Then he may no longer be alone, but neither is he safe and strong. Only when the struggle in the public sphere appears conclusively lost, he recovers himself, and is again just one man, on his own.

It may be asked whether the phenomena described on the preceding pages are responsible for the tragic character of Stockmann. An affirmative answer would definitely take too much for granted. The relations indicated pertain to man's independence as oneself and to its possible loss. It would be presumptuous, however, to look for a clear demarcation line between where a man's self is his own and where it is no more than common – as will be still pointed out with regard to such men of the crowd as the mayor, Aslaksen, Hovstad. Also unjustified would be a positive assertion that all independent existence is tragic or that its loss must be, Even in the initial sense of "tragic," which amounts to a passage from good to bad fortune, it can hardly be maintained that every independent individual must suffer such. The reasons for the possibility, even perhaps the likelihood, of a crash have been outlined: what may await the man who stands alone against a crowd, who should not "wear his best trousers when going out to fight for freedom and truth." He must be ready for resentment, self-doubt, accusations of insanity or criminality, ostracism, punishment, death and forgottenness or damnation by all others. So wide are the vistas of social hell, where there is no longer an Evil One, but plenty of evil ones have stayed: in the crowd, inertly accepting the task of negation. But there is, as ever, no general inevitability of such infernal courses of events, since what must properly happen to one person need not happen to another in similar surroundings. And no events, not even those in hell, are tragic by themselves.

In order then to enquire into the tragic being of Thomas Stockmann, his character must be further brought into relief. Some observations of his own character have already been introduced, emphasizing the conflicts within himself, which relate to his staggering position, gravitating both toward his town without and toward his idea within. A "two-souled" character, Stockmann is in proper linear descendance from Faust; yet such hereditary resemblance is not sufficient to determine the proper disposition of his own existence. What is now required is a closer look at the color and mass of the idea dominating his relation to the world.

And that means finally coping with that shocking, injurious, seemingly alien label of "an enemy of the people." The vote at the meeting is for Stockmann much more than a passing incident easily dismissed as due to stupidity. "That hateful name – I can't get quit of it. It is sticking here in the pit of my stomach, eating into me like a corrosive acid. And no magnesia will remove it." Perhaps he could get rid of the corrosive effects of that name, if he were entirely clear in his innocence of which he is ostensibly so sure. But the poisonous staying power of the label is due to the fact that the devotion to his idea has driven him to qualify for it. And this, however much he may want to, Stockmann is too honest to forget beyond recall. Doctor Thomas Stockmann is an enemy of the people. Not simply because he has stood against the crowd. No, many may do that and be treated inimically by the common people, without innerly finding themselves to be such enemies. But Stockmann has gone further. He has spoken these words:

"My native town is so dear to me that I would rather ruin it than see it flourishing upon a lie ... What does the destruction of a community matter! All who live by lies ought to be exterminated like vermin! ... You will bring about such a state of things that the whole country will deserve to be ruined. And if things come to that pass, I shall say from the bottom of my heart: Let the whole country perish, let all these people be exterminated!"

On that follows the accusation. Is it improper? These words of Thomas Stockmann, shaking his whole world to its foundations, echo an ancient cry; Pereat mundus, fiat justitia. Desert, justice, truth, are here weighed in the balance of Stockmann's mind against nothing less and nothing more than the existence of men. And it is the abstract idea that prevails. In contraposition to that dis-ordering human benefactor, Prometheus, Stockmann finds people of less weight than principles.)Of what tragic significance the very posing of this contrast has been to Prometheus, has been considered. It will not be surprising if the contrast is no less tragic for Stockmann. While for the Titan the threat in defying order could be pregnant with anarchy, for this man serving the ideal order at all costs, the threat arising is fanaticism. It is the first trait of the fanatic mind that the order of his ideas can suffer no imposition, no compromise, no rivalry. Stockmann is a fanatic, if for him the living human reality must yield precedence to abstraction.(He is an enemy of the people not because he hates people, but because caring for them he sacrifices their existence to his idea.) Men may not tolerate that their being there, for themselves, should ever be taken as second to anything that emerges within that being, even an idea. In Stockmann's vision, however, this is exactly what must take place: men are less important than principles and values of order, they ought to exist only if they are good, just, truthful, otherwise they deserve to perish.) Order, value, idea is above human life: eternal essence precedes temporal existence.

What is the idea that has taken such complete possession of Thomas Stockmann? In his crucial words quoted above the main stress seems to be upon the destructive import of lies, and thus by implication upon the supreme merit of truth. But the dubious, inconsistent attitude of Stockmann toward truth has already been pointed out. The same man who here so despises absence of truth spoke earlier of truth's being perishable, marrowless, subject to individuals' approval. If truth were his central idea, could he ever express himself about it in such terms? Further, it may be noticed in those condemning words, what he finds to deserve annihilation is not the deficiency of lies for knowledge, but "living by lies" or "flourishing upon a lie." It is the relation of lies to activities of character, their part in men's ethos, that is being condemned. There is then reason for regarding as the central dominating force in Stockmann's life the ethical idea of duty. His first statement to follow the irrevocable outcry: "Let all people be exterminated!" and the subsequent frenzy of the crowd declaring him an enemy of the people, is this: "I have done my duty." This can mean: he has not failed to serve his duty – his deity or his idol. Because if it were to mean, more humanely, that he has rendered what was due, paid what he owed, then the question could not be repressed: to whom? And to that question there is no answer. Duty which can be served by a demand for the annihilation of all, is certainly no duty to man. It claims to be super-human and reaches beyond the world of human existence.[1] It cannot be said that Stockmann always wants it to be of such a transcendent nature, nor that he claims his devotion to it in a possessive, world-excluding fashion. As soon as he makes his critical discovery about the baths, he immediately discards any pretensions to personal recognition or reward for himself: "I have done nothing more than my duty." He treats his service as higher than his self. Even more explicitly, when he optimistically begins his town campaign despite the warning of his brother, he declares: "I shall have done my duty towards the public, towards the community." There is no conflict yet between the service of idea and the service of humanity. But one may well wonder whether it is still the same duty "towards the community" he has "done" at the conclusion of the meeting, where he has spoken not about the communal cause of the town but about the inferiority of common people. Clearly it cannot be the same. At this stage the idea of duty has become dissociated from human realities. The choice has been imposed on Dr. Stockmann, between what he sees as duty and what surrounds him in his world. It is the idea which is victorious. It is his existence which sustains a tragic defeat in that choice.

The choice between the world and the idea determines the future of Stockmann. That such a choice confronts him is the root of his tragedy. Then, on the altar of his idea he immolates his past, he is willing to sacrifice both his own and his family's material welfare with his "three big No's" to Morten Kiil. which are none too easy for him, in view of his respect for comforts and of his genuine affection for his dependents. In accordance with his manifesto of the night before, he must be ready to sacrifice much more – everything and everybody. Now that the problem is seen in black and white, in terms of wrong and right, of filth and purity, of stagnation and reform, the frame is set and rigid, no compromise or return admissible. The second, visionary Faustian soul has got rid of its more worldly counterpart and has spread wings to soar in quest of the ideal. Has it, really?

His devotion to duty is noble, admirable, infrangibly moral. For such an attitude reverence is due and often loudly expressed. But what is the role of such grand idealist thrust in the wavering situations

[1] A type of addict of transcendent duty is sketched in Rolland's *Jean-Christophe:* "Amalia did no more than practice Christophe's theories of duty ... She worked unceasingly, and wanted everybody to work as she did. Her work was never directed towards making herself and others happier; on the contrary. It almost seemed as though it was mainly intended to incommode everybody and to make life as disagreeable as possible so as to sanctify it."

of existence, what effect does it have in temporal striving, what guidance does it provide in men's everyday world, where enthusiasm is but a start of moving power? In order to place Thomas Stockmann in some comparable relation to other individuals in his world, and before passing to the final conclusions about his tragic ethos, a brief glance may be cast at the people amongst whom he lives. No other character is so much in the foreground of attention, no other ethical attitude is so clearly delineated, but a glimpse of the others can supply a sensible reference for comparison. Some of these others must be seen as men of the crowd, as individuals in the process of losing their proper selves. It must therefore be emphasized that such loss, earlier referred to, is but a phase of a man's way to be, in the course of life not something final, terminated, irrecoverable. About a man who reached a total condition of loss, nothing whatever could be said in singular terms – if he were no longer one.

There is, first, at the side of Dr. Stockmann, his wife Katherine, a not unusual model of female realism. She believes in an appropriate spread of human concerns, with greatest concentration in the circle immediately around. For her, duty begins at home. To her husband's declaration about duty towards the public, Katherine can straight away counterpose: "But towards your family, your own home? Do you think that is doing your duty towards those you have to provide for?" Stockmann gives her no answer. The limits of her moral realism also show in her wondering: "What is the use of having right on your side if you have not got might?" That which is right and due must for her be supported by adequate power of agency, must not be divorced from effectiveness. But when it comes to executing that which she sees as duty, she does not fail. Realizing that her husband's position becomes hopeless with the desertion of his supposed supporters, she nevertheless provides her willing and unwavering support: "I am going to stand by you, Thomas." This she does, it may be supposed, less because her husband is right than because it is her husband; but what is due to him from her, she renders fully.

Then there is Petra, his daughter. In her untried youth worshipping her father's image, she is perhaps formed most closely to resemble him. After him, she sees life contrasts in black and white, she is devoted to unadulterated truth, offended by its lack in educational practices and the duplicity of those responsible for adult media of communication. She condemns Hovstad for mixing with the service of a noble "cause" a personal sentiment. Her sentiment for duty makes her negate sentiment as such. But – one may wonder, what does Petra's future hold in store? Will she, past the dependent stage of inexperience, keep faith with her paternal heredity or will she, more likely, enveloped in the role of her sex, find it proper to follow her mother?

Of men in Stockmann's milieu, first to be mentioned, and quickly passed over, is Hovstad, the editor. He is at the lowest rung of the scale, by his own confession: "We are not worth much." The plural may be well noted, it is for him perfectly proper; so is his earlier cited statement, claiming no distinction but boasting of being common. The loss of a personal self is well advanced here. Lying face down into the wind of opportunity, trembling with cowardice, ever unwilling to stand up alone, resentfully dreaming of a common revolution but servile to any one who dares to speak up in a show of strength, Hovstad, along with millions of his fairly anonymous brethren, is useful to others. But only in the way all utensils are useful.

There is, next, Aslaksen who happens to be a printer and also serves as chairman of the householders' association. Again clearly a man of the multitude, yet of a different brand. He rather prides himself on never doing things, at any rate not ever undertaking any decisive acts or deep commitments. Despite this, he enjoys influence and leadership of a kind among the "compact majority." For the inert crowd, his timidity is a fitting symbol; he succeeds in being more average than the average individuals. This is what unites common people around him: their trust that he is incapable of uncommon moves. Afraid of the dark of the future, recoiling before crisis and violence, Aslaksen neither gropes nor thrusts himself forward. But thus hampered, he exploits his turtle character. He is aware that "a politician should never be too certain of anything," and the less impressive his activities, the safer he can feel. Therefore, in the local affairs of his town he is timid, but in "higher politics" of central government he feels he need not be, safe to snap at adversaries at sufficient distance, who will not even notice him. And so his way of living is harmonized faithfully around his idea of moderation, his commitment not to be committed. This shapes a character, not inspiring, not greatly efficacious, but still a character of his own. Except where it gravely matters, Aslaksen can be relied on.

By way of contrast, Captain Horster gives a suggestion of a man who is really free, but only because he has chosen to be a wanderer on the seas. With much of his time spent sailing, outside of his home town – which is in no way his world – Horster finds and accepts himself as an outsider. He knows his task, the art of running his ship; despite this, or precisely because of this, he is not interested in the art of political navigation, and leaves that task to the men able or at least willing to take the wheel. In his withdrawn role, he is no factor in the struggle of impersonal ideas and forces, which occupies the town world. And still his peripheral presence can be active on behalf of individuals suffering within; he can occasionally be helpful to them, as he is to Stockmann, his cause and his family. Thus in choosing independence and even homelessness, he retains his integrity and his power of being an agent.

A different specimen of this power of an isolated agent is presented in Morten Kiil. His is entirely the strength of a selfish badger fending off common curs. He knows he is alone on account of common envy of his wealth. But he claims to be "jealous of my name and reputation." His morals, of an extremely primitive nature, make him say to Stockmann: "I mean to live and die a clean man. You shall cleanse me, Thomas." How is that cleansing to be accomplished? By Stockmann's dementi of what he is convinced to be the truth concerning the effects of Kiil's business activities. This, like everything the badger needs and gets, is to be paid for, in Stockmann's family's being "provided for." Clean name for purchase, highest moral reputation for the highest cash bidder. Despite such primitive character, despite his social isolation, it cannot be denied that Morten Kiil wields power in the world of Stockmann's life, and is capable not only of affecting Stockmann's standing there, which is shown in his last encounter with representatives of the press and of the majority, but also of effecting far-going changes in the horizons and balances of the whole community.

Lastly, the individual closest to being the counter-partner of Thomas Stockmann in the world, who by a poignant throw of origins, happens to be not only his enemy but also his brother. The mayor and "master of the whole town" is in the eyes of the doctor a plebeian and common man, but judging by his words and acts he is certainly not the clearest example of a self lost into anonymity. More definitely than Aslaksen, he retains features of a character of his own: ambition, striving, activities proper for him, a view of what can and should happen to whom in the inter-personal flow of events. Peter Stockmann happens to be the brother of Thomas; but one cannot say that he just "happens" to be his adversary. The two make themselves opposed to each other in all ways they see and shape their lives. To the transcendent reach of the doctor's ethos of duty the mayor opposes a morality which is utilitarian but limited to the greatest benefit only in the shorter temporal perspectives. Thus in the affair of the baths, when Thomas maintains that silence would be not only wrong absolutely but also disadvantageous to the town's welfare in the further future, Peter can always retort: but what about the values of the coming present? If there were an objective method for the human mind to draw a balance between a certain though limited evil in the present and a greater though uncertain good in the future, then one could definitely say that one of the two brothers is wrong in his judgment. But such a balance must always be drawn by the mind of a particular person on whose existence it is incumbent to judge and to choose his way of living in time. One way is that of Thomas, but quite different is the way of Peter. As to the pure right or wrong involved, a man of Peter's brand may understand that as completely dependent on the concrete advantage or disadvantage in question. Because for Peter Stockmann abstraction of ideas is an alien perversion. He is no less ambitious, no less capable of wholehearted involvement than his brother; but these traits of character are fulfilled for him not in creation of thoughts but in their application to what is at hand. If Thomas sins in theory, the vice and virtue of Peter lie only in practice. And while Thomas gets to the point of divorcing his idea from life, Peter who may be idea-blind will never be unfaithful to his life. Hence his qualification for putting forward the diagnosis of his brother which has been cited at the outset. In that field, of "putting ideas into practical shape," the mayor is at home, there he is jealous, possessive, authoritarian. There he may lie, trick, malevolently pretend some "good will" – so in his interpretation of his brother's report as "merely imagination" – but he will have his way. He is not crude in his reaching for goals, either. Like Aslaksen, he is always for compromise and caution but also for persistence. With all in the crowd he wants to represent, he bows low to public opinion, but in the moment: he has won the insight that "public opinion is an extremely mutable thing." Without courageous independence to stand against it, he can crawl around it in the bushes between today, tomorrow and the day after, and surreptitiously inject transforming doses of his own intentions. If great objectives can be cumulatively attained by creeping up on them, then mayor Stockmann is capable of them. It is dubious whether he should ever be entitled to claim credit for any deed as "mine" and not rather "ours," since alone he would neither stand up nor move on. Still, greatness is sometimes ascribed to the common power of not rocking the boat.

What follows from these observations of the people around Dr. Stockmann? Only this. None of the observed characters, attitudes,

views of the world is sublime, none need evoke deep admiration. But
– it is not too much to say, equally, that none of them is inferior to
Stockmann's in "putting ideas into practical shape," none less effective
in the welding of vision with act, none less mindful of risk to fulfillment through time, and – none is more apt to induce tragic disaster.
What then must be said about the differing, the tragic character of
Stockmann in such a world? What is it that he sees and chooses that
prevents him from concretely enjoying his presence in the same world
with all these others?

Duty, truthfulness, nobility – it does not primarily matter how
one denominates what Dr. Stockmann is dedicated to. It is, whatever
its name, an idea. That it is abstract, drawn off the world of everyday
experience, is true but not extraordinary: intellectual abstraction
is a normal process in the human being. But to call it abstract
is not yet to characterize it sufficiently for the role it plays in
Stockmann's life. The idea is here not only drawn off the world
but actually drawn up against the world, in counter-position to
it. The light of the idea in its brilliance shows up the shadows
in all that lies around. The call of the idea contra-dicts the
noise of merely human voices. Thus the idea enters into contradiction
with what is there in life and a choice is imposed in disjunctive terms:
either – or. Either what is or what ought to be, either temporal existence or eternal order, either people or principles. Specifically, in
Stockmann's situation it means: either to effect some change in the
life of the town or to "have done my duty," either to involve himself
hopefully in the affairs of the crowd or to preserve the independent
purity of an outsider, either to "soil himself with filth" of political
actions or to stay "free" without touching or being touched. And on
the future horizon: either to have his family "provided for" at the cost
of "bowing his neck to the yoke" or to "have the right to look my sons
in the face when they are grown men," though they be clad in rags,
starving, or dead. One course is destructive for character through self-
hatred and contempt, the other deprives it of a point d'appui in the
world without which man cannot exist. Such is the extreme situation
into which the human being can be pressed by ideas.

Is there no exit? There always is when choice is possible, the knot
cut through, one course embraced decisively. For one thing, the choice
outlined above need not appear as pressing, or one of the paths may
only glimmer as a vague contingency. There can be people whose

devotion to ideas is equal to Stockmann's but who can spend their life building and dwelling in abstractions, regarding everyday's sensory surroundings as mere show, and never waking up to disappointment as the "scientist" Faust does. And there certainly can be plenty of people who cast themselves toward what is for them ordinary, ascertained reality, without suspicion of its inadequacy to possible ideas, successfully producing and handling certain things with certain other people, even, inmidst, losing themselves without missing any thing. Then there may be individuals for whom there is a conceivable contradiction between the world and the idea, but whose disposition is easily preconceived so that they pass each choice with hardly a jolt. But Thomas Stockmann is not like any of those. His way of holding to his ideas is such that the imposition of an either-or becomes inescapable; but while he reaches his choice, he does not resolve it. He comes to see that for him to stand up for his independence is to stand against all the others in the crowd, and that to witness and protest is to accuse and protest against. Yet much of what he protests against he carries right along within himself: the faults of leadership and organization, the appreciation of material comforts and family affection, the limited outlook on super-personal truth and personal independence. And he is not resolved to give up the community with others entirely, to cease from touching and interfering with their lives, to abandon the conviction that his town world is real and important. In the crucial, culminating phase of his action, at the meeting, the choice befalls him in silence when he is waiting for the opportunity to speak. In his speech he gives evidence of what he has chosen as primary, and to that he remains loyal: to his idea. Because speaking as he does, insulting, provoking, challenging, he reveals himself in such an aspect as cannot possibly be accepted or tolerated by the others. He shakes and undermines his whole world, his home to which he has wanted to belong. But his time goes on; and then? Has he cut his ties irreparably, does he accept a static stand outside and alone? By no means. He wavers already, facing his father-in-law's proposal; this he discards eventually. Then he rejects the possibility of leaving this town and country for the "solitude" of an American wilderness. He decides to strive for a further fight on the same "field of battle" and even to lower himself to an "experiment with curs"; an experiment which to his idea-possessed view cannot but be disappointing, a fight which in this world he cannot help losing. He has not torn himself away, he still longs for more time in the same world he has tried to shatter, he is impaled upon the horns of his choice. This is his misfortune, his inward break, this is what makes him TRAGIC. And this is due to the tragic power of his idea.

What idea should be conceived as tragic? More precisely, what status of an idea in a man's existence makes such existence tragic? Surely, it would be a gross distortion to predict a tragic destiny for all men devoted to ideas, although perhaps it is true that no man of no ideas can be properly tragic. Yet the outcome of these reflections on Dr. Stockmann is this. An idea is tragic, if it is no more than an idea torn off from its foundations in being and presumed to subsist as such. Then in a man's fixed contemplation of it, it shines with a purely reflected light yet of unchanging radiance, it is forever set in terms borrowed but invested imaginatively with splendor unseen in the fleeting flow; and it can effectively contra-dict whatever human time has to offer. The contradiction enters the man's existence and tears him apart, making it impossible for him to find himself whole in the world and yet impossible to be without the world. His protest draws him against and into a battling within, in which there is no enemy but himself and hence no victor ever. This windmill fight is tragic.

Thomas Stockmann is determined to serve duty, if it costs him his life. But he will never attain his duty in his existence, since there is no such fixed star within it; although many deeds, intentions, thoughts are "due" to his world, his partners in living, and to himself. He wages a campaign in the name of truth, as if truth were a goddess or an idol and he the select defender, as if it were above and not within his own being there; and so he despises the "false" altars of truth erected by other men. He complains that men make a "hodge-podge of right and wrong," without realizing that if right and wrong were not for men commingled in their task and pressing through their time, if they were laid out in clear patterns of super-temporal order, then life would be a fatal play of puppets pulled on strings, then risk, commitment, choice, would be out of the human question, then men could not stand out and exist. Such is the limited outline of Stockmann's vision, a vision alluring for him and yielding the temptation of superhuman purity and static perfection, but a vision which dazzlingly envelops his character and appropriates for him the label of the people's enemy. That he becomes the enemy of the people without whom he cannot exist, this is the tragedy of Thomas Stockmann.

CHAPTER VII

The Tragic Loss - Loman the Salesman

ARTHUR MILLER: DEATH OF A SALESMAN

Here is the experimentum crucis for tragedy: whether it could be properly conceived as a distant, aesthetic form of spectacle or must be searched for in the ground of what makes man be; whether, as some say, it had only a transient appeal to the human soul from by-gone ages, heroic and faith-full, or whether, appealing or not, it covers a horizon coeval with all of human time; whether or not it can be real after the death of princes, titans, prophets – and of God? – and still take hold in the life of one, "objectively" most insignificant of men.

For this "spectacle" you are about to attend, staging directions call for an approach for the actors to their audience; indeed, they could demand complete intermingling of them. For here comes a man who may be about to "perform" or just as well sit next to you. His name is Willy Loman. You must have seen him before, in stores, hotels, on the road, that man with such a simple, vacant face, and a childish, disarming smile. You have never noticed him? He is not very notice-able, that is true; he turns up too often and too close to you. But then perhaps you should start paying attention to him. Because, you see, he is not a true actor, nor merely a salesman. He can be your brother or mine. And he is lost.

All that is easily said, you can object. Why is he lost and where? And why should one pay any attention to what so ordinarily happens to such an ordinary man? Why? Perhaps just because of this. Be-cause the less extraordinarily this happens to Willy Loman, the more easily it may happen to you, it may be happening already. If you are not open to pity, surely you are open to fear on your own account. The loss in existence of Willy Loman might not strike you as signifi-cant enough to be called "tragic"; but if such were your loss, you might be prompt enough to demand the dubious dignity of that word. Loman is not lost in cosmic issues of empire like Prometheus, nor in a flight from criminal royalty like Oedipus; no one, except his contemptuous son, would see in him a prince, such as Hamlet, and no one would bother with a high wager on his destiny as on Faust's, nor even regard him as a dangerous enemy, such as Stockmann. He is unnoticeably lost because in a crowd of men just like him, in this everyday world. And how? A man may be losing himself in uncharted country the deeper, the less he pays heed that it is happening to him: lost but not aware of it. Are you so immunely sure that this is not your own position? Such a loss is of course irrecoverable without some find of luck, but it is not a particularly human event; animals stray in just such fashion. Then there may be an episodic phase of loss in a living adventure, but only trivial: easily recognized, easily repaired. And then there is the situation where a man is losing himself and anxiously knows it, but this is all he knows: the means of recovery being out of his hands, all he can cling to is his name, a low man's name, as clue to a hazy identity. As himself, he can always die. Yet even death may be only a supernumerary and obvious closure on a life which had already been consumed. Such a phenomenon of Loss, obliterating a man's way to be, can be tragic.

And this is precisely the way Willy Loman is losing himself: beyond recovery, in humanly signaling distress, with a bare consciousness persisting in his cry: "The woods are burning!" The burning woods are there, these tangled jungles otherwise known as civilized conquests of modern time, these combustible camps of men so long deemed secure and finally fostering fires on their own. They burn – nor are we out of them, you and I.

～

It is not difficult for sympathetic imagination to enter the world in which Loman lives. It is spaced wider than the modern town world of Thomas Stockmann; a town is not containing enough any more. This world, even for people like Willy Loman, has been quantitatively stretched out by planes and cars, advertising and communication networks, so that "all of New England" seems to be just a salesman's back yard. In turn, the salesman must be on the go; the stationary limitation to a home where he could belong undividedly has been displaced. This world of many homeless distances, challenging and also wearying, you can easily recognize as yours. However, to make sure that you share its dimensions with Loman, you have to limit it with a "roof," a heavy roof of leaden skies, or better still of gold and silver: to attach the straying glances upward but to prevent their breaking through toward escape. Because Loman's world is pressing down upon him, oppressing his dreams of no limits, impressing his experience and movement into a narrow place of business:

"The way they boxed us in here. Bricks and windows, windows and bricks. The street is lined with cars. There's not a breath of fresh air in the neighborhood. The grass don't grow any more, you can't raise a carrot in the back yard. They should've had a law against apartment houses. Remember those two beautiful elm trees out there? ... More and more I think of those days. This time of year it was lilac and wisteria. And then the peonies would come out, and the daffodils. What fragrance in this room!"

More and more, the fragrance of life stays for Willy only in the past. Crowded for breath now, he cannot see the sky: it has been built over. He can, or must, wander away into dream, and talk to himself, to that Willy who has been, hopeful and young but already fenced around. As his wife sees it: "Why shouln't he talk to himself? Why? When he has to go and borrow fifty dollars a week and pretend that it's his pay? ... What goes through a man's mind, driving seven hundred miles home without having earned a cent? ... And you tell me he has no character?" He has had a character, and is now rapidly abnegating it. His character, his way to appropriate life, is now turning in reverse, not owning but disowning: why should I "stand here the rest of my life ringing up a zero?" His self-reproach, his remembrance, his longings of the past have all been "boxed in" to accord with the stream-lines of career and success which he no longer awaits from the future. This is the roof over the world of Willy Loman, barring his imagination from a liberating swerve into another dimension. Here and now, whether he lives or dies, losing himself anyway, he turns his back upon his future and lets go of present reality into a dissolved haze where his dream and his past are one: this is his mode of loss, his own way for disowning his character. But all of this must take place on the flat surface of common material standards of living, measurable in social, business terms. Thus Loman has not had a chance for a long many years. The roof over his life, the impossibility of finding his escape path, antedates by far his present obvious self-loss. Because now he has been determined as just a salesman and is no longer any good as such; but the comradeship, the love, the poetry, which might have lain treasured for him in another future, and of which he sometimes only shows slight scars, have been suppressed stringently, just like an open look from his home toward the sky. That had been the restricting choice which determined Loman to become a salesman and to lose his way therein. Who bears responsibility for that critical, that destructive choice?

The crippled, suppressed character of Loman makes it understandable why you cannot expect too much of a protest from him, not too much awareness of what has been done to him, and not too much daring in expression. His protest can remind you of that of Oedipus: less an articulation than a gesture. The gesture is indeed ultimate. Is it not curious that of all the men seen here, who stood for protest, this humblest figure is the only one who carries out the decisive gesture against life, even more persistent in his deed than the deedful, storming Faust? His suicide is adopted in thoroughgoing contempt for this life in whose history "after all the highways, and the trains, and the appointments, and the years, you end up worth more dead than alive." This abnegating phrase is immediately objected to by his friend Charley: "Willy, nobody's worth nothin' dead." It may be open to question whether Charley is well qualified to object to Loman's words, since he, too, treats life as a quantity of business, only less unsuccessfully than Willy. But the main point to notice is not that someone else, if not Charley, could of course put forward this objection, but that there is a limited sense in which what Loman says is true beyond anyone's questioning: it is the business sense of life where the death of Loman is worth twenty thousand dollars, while his continued existence does not seem to be, in such quantified terms, worth anything to anybody. And it will not do for anyone to argue that such an assessment is insufficient and distorted, because, as already suggested, this is now the only assessment open to Loman himself. In the exclusively material dimensions of existence, which have been determining its course for him, this is an honest though bankrupt consequence. Having been made to plan his life in terms of quantifiable standards, Willy Loman is entitled to plan his death in those terms, too. To have a chance of discovering what for him is tragic, one must not cover up the boundaries of his vision of himself and his world.

The expressions of protest are rare and feeble in Loman's voice. But it would be unwarranted to disregard them therefore. Because if it is at all proper to think of Loman's life as a tragedy of loss, then some thought at least must be given to what has been lost already, and is not available now, as evidence. The phases of the moon must imply some possibility of a full moon's view: to see what is missing. Thus not the least of the missing properties of Loman's character is a full, resolute voice. Once it is raised in public, when he protests the record of his work to his employer: "You can't eat the orange and throw the peel away – a man is not a piece of fruit!" Yet this is just what he feels his life is being reduced to – an empty, discarded husk, with no title and no voice left. Because the very moment after raising this claim, Willy meekly, repentantly withdraws it: "My God, I was yelling at him! How could I!" That he finds himself no longer daring, no longer entitled to yell where yelling should be proper for him – that is what makes his fading voice tragic. He mutters still, when he is not overheard except by his phantoms of a fuller past, he reaches out for what is missing, aware that it is his own due: "A man can't go out the way he came in, Ben, a man has got to add up to something." Yet what an irony when these words, aspiring to existence, are found in his preparation for death. Not to go out empty – add up to something measurable – not nothing: a man's life is not nothing. Of such content is Willy conscious when he turns to face the nothingness of death. But granted that he still feels himself existing and wants to prevail over empty nothingness, where does he turn to exert this prevalence? To quantity, to measurable economic value to be left after him and thus in some way equate his missing life, to the amount of twenty thousand dollars. No other way for Loman to "remain," but this: to kill himself and die upon a guarantee of immortality in cash. Can greater failure of human chances be imagined, worse than this post-mortem quantification? What of death is elusive to business standards, just as little they can contain of life. But this already tragically eludes Willy Loman.

His protesting eloquence, as his whole life, is perhaps worth no more than that of most of his fellow humans. But neither should it be worth less, if it is so definitely of everyday order. This is what makes Loman a sign of common humanity – which may or may not deserve sympathy and attention: "I don't say he's a great man. Willy Loman never made a lot of money. His name was never in the paper. He's not the finest character that ever lived. But he's a human being, and a terrible thing is happening to him. So attention must be paid." That, understandably, his wife demands: not only of his sons to whom she speaks these words. Is she presumptuous in claiming attention for Willy? If she is, then no men ordinarily deserve attention from others, whatever may be the case with extraordinary occasions and extraordinary people. Because the case of Willy Loman is not at all singular, he is neither

great nor rich, neither famous nor noble, only human. What is said
of him can safely be spoken in the plural, not just of him, but of them
all, meaning the human race.[1] And this plurality also concerns the
"terrible things" which according to Linda are happening to her
husband. They are common, too, and could be commonly witnessed
– protested. But as with Loman, they may already be lost, to silence.
What terrible things are they?

Loman is a salesman. Is there any significance in it? Why, he could
be a driver, a railroad worker, an insurance clerk. There is no distinct
sign in his being a salesman, if by that one understands literally that
he spends his time in selling things. But one does not hear what kind
of things he is selling; and this suggests that perhaps his selling line
is not what matters for understanding him. No, Loman is a salesman
in the exquisite sense that he is a man for sale. He is selling, incidentally, stockings or textiles or cosmetics; but primarily he is selling –
as what salesman is not? – himself: his character, his smile, his winning ways, his confidence in others. The outward misfortune of his
story is that gradually there are fewer and fewer and then no takers.
Or so it appears. But is not the heart of his bankruptcy in that there
is less and less of him to be sold? That what he has in store is anything but inexhaustible and through this long history of selling is
finally emptied? If so, there must have been a buyer. In fact, Loman
can be imagined as a small-souled Faust who sells himself into evil but
without ever acting or contracting for such surrender, without even
being aware of his gradual possession. Naturally, such a high-spirited
or high-brow interpretation need not be strictly mediaeval. The devil
in question needs neither horns and tail nor tempting personal promises, and still he may be the same power of negation, corruptive and
destructive. His name, if a name be claimed, may be not Mephisto but
Mammon. Whenever and however he consolidates his possession of
Loman, its closure is certain when the clock stops for Willy: his death,
though self-inflicted, even self-aspired, is taken into the bargain by
him, for the sake of twenty thousand dollars. This bargain is struck
by the devil in his own kind. Where does he draw the sway he has over
the soul of Loman? The idea may at first appear surprising. The power
of evil in play here is nothing else but quantity. The rational category
of quantity, if you like, the foundation of mathematics and of all
measurable techniques of sciences; is this an evil? It is, when instead
of remaining an indifferent, subservient tool of natural expression for

---

[1] "If a single human being may be regarded as expendable, a hundred thousand
men are all but a lot of waste" – Beauvoir, *Les Bouches Inutiles*.

man it is transmuted into an impression upon his ethos. This happens when the fatal word: "quantum?" – "how much?" becomes a control of life, its only reliable counter, an imagination-stopping standard of its reality. To acquiesce in quantification of your vision, character and choice is to externalize for public auction that which is properly your own, to make your way to be exchangeable and common, to yield existence into negation: to sell your soul for nothing – which is the devil's own.

And is this method of loss somehow exclusive, private to Loman? No one living today can honestly maintain that. Loman is but a sign of what can be terrifying because universal. There is then scope for protest in his life, for protest which he is already too terrified, too lost to yell aloud. The protest is against multitudes' abdicating their conscience and their striving in favor of an interpersonal firm assessment and determination of themselves in the world. The protest, as observed in Loman's life, is against the system in which what is properly your own is equivalent to what you paid for, and where such "property" not surprisingly deserts you empty-handed. "Once in my life I would like to own something outright before it's broken! ... They time those things. They time them so when you finally paid for them, they're used up ... Figure it out. Work a lifetime to pay off a house. You finally own it, and there's nobody to live in it." The point of objection is of course not merely the transience of material things but the translation of what is man's own into their quantitative terms. Under such conditions, his friend can tell Willy: "The only thing you got in this world is what you can sell. And the funny thing is that you're a salesman, and you don't know that." Perhaps it is the single fortune and glory of Willy that this has not been his conception of reality, though millions of others will swear by it today. But in this final tired run, all he can answer is: "I've always tried to think otherwise, I guess." He does not try any more, he goes to sell his remnants for twenty thousand. This salesman's way of life is apparently too overwhelming, common, wide-spread. He falls, a victim to its call: the proper way to have and to hold must be to ask: how much?

Such people as Loman are hardly equipped to put up much opposition against this impressive creed. When years before his brother Ben asked Willy: "What are you building? Lay your hand on it. Where is it?" he could neither lay his hand on it, nor disbelieve this animal test of laying hands. His wife, an impractical woman of illusions, could then still ask an awkward question: "Why must everybody conquer the world?" What she implies is that there is some such universal demand, exercising pressure on everybody; she feels that pressure, too. So do her sons. Biff: "I've always made a point of not wasting my life, and everytime I come back here I know that all I've done is to waste my life." And Happy: "I don't know what the hell I'm workin' for." The pressure is to keep building something tangible, to work for its objective value, not to be "wasting" life, to conquer a world. But is it inapposite to wonder what world? No irrecoverable harm would result for men if it were a world which they could make their own, on their own; although even here a demand for conquest might appear oppressive. The world, however, alluded to by Loman's wife, is understood as common, objectively tangible and fixed in quanta. Thus the willingness to enter and work toward its conquest means an acceptance of its limiting "roof," of certain interpersonal and so best measurable criteria for contents and directions of existence. It is already a beginning loss. It easily induces such doubt, disorientation, incipient abnegation of one's own self, as shines above in the utterances of Biff and Happy. The world to be conquered by them as by their father is the world of serious business. After life has been "boxed into" such dimensions of quantity, it becomes assessable in solid categories of dollars and cents. After it has been accepted that whether one works for or wastes his life is to be decided by the test of laying hands, only a single track of success remains, material and measurable. Then it is unavoidable to "keep ringing up zeros," whether or not they are preceded by any other figures in the balance. Because as the quantitative series – of zeros? – is infinite, so interminable are dreams restricted to gain in its progression. When a house is successfully "owned," a mansion looks inviting, then a bigger acreage, a city block of "real property," and so on. There is no biggest number, and there is no end for an appropriation drive cast in quantitative terms. Faust knew that. What must be added is that the entry into such a world, shaped into a very long but very blind alley, is for an ordinary man a necessary matter of choice which will determine him. This choice may commonly be suppressed as to its significance, and it may be subject to greater and greater pressure as to its "obviousness," so that the alternative of refusal becomes all but impossible. If Willy Loman is in his ordinary destiny a sign of his times, then the protest ringing and fading around him concerns many more than just himself. It is a universal warning signal. The woods are burning.

It can be claimed in a hard-headed attitude that to describe money as the root of all evil is to indulge in a fanciful exaggeration, and to anthropomorphize it into diabolic shape is even more fantastic and narrow. And quite rightly. The spirit of quantitative values, however enthroned now, has after all been conjured or invented by men. To attack it alone is to attend to symptoms only. Men's interrelations of use introduce and underwrite the powers of "Mammon." The protest, then, of the life of Loman must witness and may attack those human interrelations. But they again are hypostatized into the idol of society, which was already encountered in men of the crowd around Thomas Stockmann. That anonymous force is presumed to be indispensable, invincible, capable of making and breaking any one human being. One's aloneness is its anathema: so Willy Loman must not be alone, must surround himself, out of his fright, with company even of phantoms, to be supported and guided from outside, never from inner solitude. The social network of power demands undivided devotion: so Willy's longings for individual, man-to-man "respect, and comradeship, and gratitude" must be degraded into morbid delusions from a past which never took place. The majesty of society is stern and unfeeling: so it is time for Willy to "grow up," and that means to give up the erratic sentimentality of liking others and wishing to be liked by them, so he must eradicate in himself and sterilize in his son the boyish temptations of enchantment by beauty, of trees and warm air, and sun, and animals, and spring-time. All respectable members of society must be engaged in business; for that it is not sufficient that they have work. Work can be chosen and carried on by you, as your own time-content, it can be changed, interrupted, cursed in favor of play. But business can never be purely your own affair, it can grant you no release, it unceasingly throws you into the world, to measure you against others as long as you live. To be in business is to be used if not abused in the exchange of little for much, of one for many. Business is service. It is the service of an anonymous, plural divinity as inscrutable and ruthless as Promethean Zeus. To live with society on the basis of business is to serve; and no other life is then available, only that whose standard is quantitatively efficient productivity. Making men into quanta, society pluralizes them: each is not to consider himself as all-one, each is to be used by and use others, but neither to know nor to trust them as such-or-such ones. "Never fight fair with strangers"; if that is a solid principle of business society – where are those who are not strangers here, when intimacy is frowned upon? When men are to consider themselves seriously as many, always many, and always in competition – which means "running together but against each other" – then there is no singular running track for any one, no genuine teaming or brotherly lending a hand to those whose strength gives out on the run; and no surcease from running. It does not matter how far you have reached, coolie, clerk, consultant, or company chairman: your service is ever in demand, hence your success is ever in question. When you want to stop, you can drop, by the way. Nor does it matter whether your true faith goes under the name of capitalism and you abhor the heresy of communism, or vice versa; both have their altars in the temple of social worship, erected on the ruins of the church of God. Your faith is not to reason why, your business is to serve and die. Society will go on and in its ordinary use substitute another zero for you. Its might is plural, multitudinous, quantified – ad infinitum. If the devil Mammon has charge of money, he is but a junior assistant in the ranks of the social pantheon. Did anyone say idolatry was dead?

It is in this world's temple with an oppressingly heavy roof that Willy Loman the salesman is offering himself, being taken and used and dispatched. His history is one of disintegration of that which supposedly cannot be divided: individual integrity, or being one and whole. At this stage it may already be appreciated that no aim at integrity can suffer quantification; what the latter means in Loman's life, still remains to be thought carefully. If such is his way to be in this world, it follows that his dis-integration means a lack of vision of his life as a whole with its end within itself. This cannot but produce a thoroughgoing sense of loss as to means, when the end is so veiled. Of this there are plenty of symptoms available, especially in his consultations with Ben, his alter ego, infused with all the superiority of an ego other than his own. When it is the question of choosing be-tween Alaska and Brooklyn: "Ben, am I right? Don't you think I'm right?" When it is the question of indicating some life ends to his sons, a task he cannot possibly cope with on his own: "Oh, Ben ... some-times I'm afraid that I'm not teaching them the right kind of – Ben, how should I teach them?" And what humiliation, what self-denying effort it must be for Willy, when he is driven to ask his friend's son, whom he always before disregarded: "Bernard ... what – what's the secret? How – how did you? Why didn't Biff ever catch on?" Ber-nard, still young though "successful," gives no answer. The answer might be that the secret of life – which is what Willy seems to be enquiring about – is that there is no secret. None, at any rate, that could be passed around or sold. The secret is that a man has to find his own ends and answers in supreme disregard of how they would possibly suit other aspirations of other men. How can Willy Loman ever arrive at such wholeminded self-direction? When in continuous exposure to quantitative care his integral thrust has lost its whole momentum, when signs multiply, to overwhelm his disbelief, that the external measured verdict: "no good" should be accepted and made his own, as it is accepted by Biff, then Loman as well as his sons must be lastly determined as sheep, blindly to follow, passively to obey, to be led – even into self-destruction.

And so the protest in the life of Loman must sound against the templar darkness of his world, a darkness if not made by man then by men deepened, blacked out with the veil of lost secrets, of mysteriously measured goals and accomplishments, a darkness in which a man can perceive the value of his own naked hand only when it grasps a shining suicidal weapon. This is the world where a man's affections are from above, from its roof, suppressed into such strange shapes as to impress whom he loves not with his life but with his funeral – because that is supposed to be "massive" with objective valuation of a crowd, that is supposed to make up a deadly balance for the lost existence. This is the world of Willy Loman from which the last word spoken in his requiem sounds odd, a lost, alienated word which has no ground there: "We are free ..." We are free, Linda claims, to console herself? To tie herself once more to her departed husband? To stress her bewilderment at his last act? Free. We are free – from care, from a material obligation, from a burden of quantity – and at the same time free from life, from objects of love, from a will to exist. "I can't understand it, Willy, I made the last payment on the house today. Today, dear. And there'll be nobody home. We're free and clear. We're free ..." This is all that Linda Loman understands by "free," all she can understand by it. Is this the great human idea of freedom, is this misery its last echo? Perhaps not: Orestes will claim otherwise. But the world of Loman with its banishment of ideas, with its distortion of the quality of life into externalized quantity, seems determined toward self-loss, and determining a self-negation of freedom. Is it not your world, though? Are you free to protest?

~

The dangerous situation of some one being in this world may appear as inescapable as to be fated. Belief in fate always acquires greater weight when the mass of things on the whole is considered, when the task set is generalizing the preponderance of ruling forces over a frail, finite figure of a man. To see that fate is not the only possibility of choice in Loman's world, one must look into the more intimate factors in his life, into his being with other individuals, his near and dear ones. This is indispensable for disclosing the main turn of his tragedy: it is the chosen personal relations which break him ultimately. And it is in his being with himself and with the ones around him that one may observe how Loman's tragic story does not simply "happen" but is of his own making, appropriated by him throughout.

The turning point of resolution in his events is by no means catastrophic, that is impressively, obviously striking. It occurs in the restaurant, after he has lost his business, realized the hopeless position of Biff and painfully relived the Boston encounter which led up to it. But the drop which overfills the vessel is his sons' desertion from the expected merry reunion, their "losing" him in an act of finished brutality. Then, giving a superfluous tip to the waiter, Loman utters the words of his decisive renunciation: "Here – here's some more, I don't need it any more." In only one way can he be free from the need of money, by not living to use it any more. His existence is lost finally, with the final loss of the sons he had lived for and refused to give up. From now on it is only the question of how to terminate it and to preserve the bare name – like Hamlet? – which is the only thing he still claims, minutes before his death: "I am not a dime a dozen! I am Willy Loman!" The name is to be preserved, the value rendered in that "you are Biff Loman" by his son's great impression at the funeral. But no more life for Willy.

If it is right to connect this death of the salesman with this personal outcome, it is necessary to approach closer to his life which determined such an end, to grasp what Loman has been doing to come out in this undoing. The tragic defect in his character is precisely what has been pointed to as his loss. More, however, has to be said to elucidate this loss of himself by way of disintegration, dis-placement in the world, dis-connection of beliefs and values. Here are examples of what happens in his words. "Be liked and you will never want. You take me, for instance. I never have to wait in line ... I go right through." And: "People don't seem to take to me. I know it when I walk in ... I don't know the reason for it, but they just pass me by. I'm not noticed." Or: "The trouble is he's lazy, goddamit! Biff is a lazy bum! ... And such a hard worker. There's one thing about Biff – he's not lazy." Practically in the same breath, with hardly a minute's lapse, Loman utters words attesting to an almost unbelievably contrary disconnection in his appraisals and beliefs. They are not strenuous contradictions such as those of Dr. Stockmann, where opposed tension dictates both directions with equal firmness. No, in Loman's con-

sciousness everything is weak and evanescent so that he really does
not know which he believes. This is the sense of loss, of drift, of dis-
connection; this plays havoc with his attitudes to himself and to all
present around. Obviously, no one could reasonably pose to Willy
the theoretically abstract question: what is truth and reality? But
not only is he incapable of thinking about such a question, he is also
deprived of the simpler practical, almost animal sense of what is true,
of concretely imagining what is for him real. It is this loss of something
expected as an ordinary human heritage that prevents him from living
in sincerity, that moves him toward dream pretense. For a man in
business as a salesman, which is his guiding belief, true or false but at
least conforming his behavior, that "business is bad, it's murderous"
or the addition "but not for me, of course"? For a father who wants
to teach his children, which is his primary tone strong enough to
influence them, his moral ambition: "I never in my life told him
anything but decent things" or his amoral vanity in them: "If somebody else took that ball there'd be an uproar," "You shoulda seen the
lumber they brought home ... I gave them hell, understand. But I
got a couple of fearless characters there"? For someone working hard
for measurable worldly success, which is genuine, his puzzlement
about Biff: "There's something I don't understand about it ... From
the age of seventeen nothing good ever happened to him" or his
earlier negligent presumption: "What're you talking about? With
scholarships to three universities they're gonna flunk him?" However loose and cast adrift, it is his way to be with himself and with
others that emerges as a continuous clue to his downfall, inevitable
not because fated but because proper to the man he has been. It was
said that the intimate loss in his family life is what breaks him; but
that loss was being carefully, though carelessly, prepared all along in
his own acts. One may wonder if his character ever does appropriate
his life, his experiences and beliefs, or fails to appropriate. But if
the latter is the case, is it any less his own chosen way to disown
reality, has he not paved himself his way to be and to act by precisely
failing to act, by losing actions' integrity and connectedness?

There can be no doubt about Loman's care for his family. It is
genuine, though not sincere. His wife and sons preoccupy his longings
and sorrows. When his friend Charley suggests, to relieve him, that
he had better "forget about" Biff, Willy has an unanswerable retort:
"Then what have I got to remember?" When he is fired by his employer and absurdly demands "good news" from his sons, his primary·
anxious motive is not worry about his own position, but that "the

woman has waited and the woman has suffered." Despite this, he is capable of deceiving his wife with casual females in unknown quantity. Despite this, it is his words and attitudes that lead to Biff's break-down under the gospel of personality and success, and result in Happy's cynical denial of him: "No, that's not my father. He's just a guy." In Loman's life arises an unexpected but clear human possibility of antagonism between love and truth. He loves his family. The objection someone might make that this is not true love, while perhaps quite correct, overlooks the fact that everyone can only love in his own inimitable fashion. And Willy's love is one which excludes being true. It is because of his being so wrapped in this love that he cannot be sincere nor permit sincerity toward himself. The normal mode of life in the Loman family becomes a net of reassuring lies told as a matter of course and of courtesy. Biff is the only one who repeatedly tries to cut himself out from it; gradually, no doubt, and not only after the climactic shock in the Boston hotel, he loses trust in his father preci-sely because he wants to be able to trust sincerely. And it is this escape of Biff toward truth about life and about the Lomans that Willy experiences as the deepest wound inflicted on his affectionate relations with his son.

As truth is a threat to Loman's break between love and sincerity, so reality is evaded in the break of his vision between dream and fruitful imagination. His dreams cluster around a blindly imitating formation of heroes to guide him, and for his non-avowed inferiority many can qualify as heroes. His father, almost unknown to him, was supposed to be a "great man," his brother Ben "was a genius, was success incarnate – the only man I ever met who knew the answers," even his old employer "was a prince, was a masterful man." Willy dreams of the past only to adore, not to be strengthened for his future. Having set his sights so high in indiscriminate dream-hero worship, he experi-ences as a bad let-down the return to present reality. His imagination does not bridge the gap, and rather ossified in his dreamland, it does not exert itself concretely to shape his place in living awake. It is this straight-jacketing of his imagination that makes it impossible for him properly to judge people and things around him in their reality. Thus he continuously snaps at his wife and rudely stops her from speaking, not so much from any contempt for her and her opinions as from a distorted need to assure himself of a proper place of importance in his home. Thus he continuously veers between despising and priding himself in his sons, unable to place them, especially Biff, in any perspectives proper to themselves rather than prefabricated on the model of his dream heroes. Thus he is, and even admits to, feeling "kind of temporary about myself"; he is disoriented and displaced in the time dimensions of his existence, completely under the temporal dominion of Care. Speaking of the past of his dreams, which might have been his true past, but also might not: "Oh, Ben, how do we get back to all the great times? Used to be so full of light ... And always some kind of good news coming up, always something nice coming up, ahead." Nice because still ahead, or expected as coming up because nice? Even his son Happy, not particularly perspicacious, characterizes him this way: "Dad is never so happy as when he's looking forward to something! ... And gradually it fades away and nobody's the worse. No content in what there is around him but a fixation in what may or may not come, may or may not have been – is this not the temporal subjection of man to Care? And with proper "not me" unconsciousness, blinded by Care, he accuses Biff: "Ah, you're counting your chickens again." In time and in the world, Loman has lost his place, his moorings, his sense of distance which requires a firm stance. In others, in his sons he condemns and criticizes just that which is his own property, for them not only inheritance but also infection from him. And at the same time, a displaced "little boat looking for a harbor," needing support, desperately turning to the least bit of what appears as terra firma, he depends on them: on the morning after his panic return home, he can only gather enough strength in himself to ask for a change in his working conditions, when he grasps some belief in the success of Biff's efforts and some warmth from the anticipation of a friendly dinner in town with his boys. No wonder that when instead of success only decisive disaster materializes for him and around him, when not warmth but a final freeze grips him in his sons' leaving him alone in the restaurant, his remaining resolution is to carry out what he half-heartedly attempted before, to locate himself irremovably in his past, to get to solid earth in his grave.

The outcomes, the events of this lost life can be surveyed crystallized in the epitaphs thrown on this insignificant grave by the only ones to attend the "massive" funeral, his sole friend Charley and the people through whom he lived and died, his family. From Charley, relatively unaffected though saddened by this death, comes the diagnosis which has already been characterized above: "Willy was a salesman"; his story is one of selling through time. Without any privileges or qualifications: "He don't put a bolt to a nut, he don't tell you the law or give you medicine"; he has to rely on selling himself, "riding on a smile and a shoeshine." His store empties when "they start not smiling back"; feeling his impending limits, "a salesman is got to dream." In the end, there is nothing left to him, only his dream, but it is the dream of his past.

And the family? Where does Willy leave them? Happy is critical and extravagant: "We would've helped him," so "he had no right to do that." Is Happy not the last man in the world with the right to say that? Of course, not in his own eyes; he pretends to be the heir; "I'm gonna show you and everybody else that Willy Loman did not die in vain. He had a good dream. It's the only dream you can have – to come out number-one man. He fought it out here, and this is where I'm gonna win it for him." Poor Happy, perhaps poorer than Willy: throwing himself under the business yoke of competitive numbers, blind to the Care which brought about his father's death. And lying, lying in his teeth: if he should be successful in "winning" a place, it would certainly be one for Happy and not for Willy. He speaks not from affection but from the set-back of spite. He is the heir of Loman, indeed, but the place he inherits is the worst one. Biff sees his father more sharply: "He had the wrong dreams. All, all wrong. He never knew who he was." But the sharp bite is one of truth; Biff does not claim superiority over Willy: "I know who I am," and that know-ledge which exploded on the suicidal night is nothing to rejoice in. Biff has been made to lose all respect for his father, "a fake," and for his own being as "nothing." Whether Loman were alive or dead, Biff would be lost to him; but perhaps thereby, despite his present self-crushing disposition, he might have a chance of not being lost himself and of reciprocating this pitiful love of his father, from a distance. Finally, Linda, staying faithful to Willy's lies to the end; her illusions are being buried with him: "Why didn't anybody come? ... Where are all the people he knew?" She is the one who would have needed a "massive" funeral for her husband. But there is no resentment in her. She just wants "a chance to say good-by," and finds it very difficult to part with him and with the life she had to live with him. "I don't understand it. Why did you ever do that? Help me, Willy, I can't cry. It seems to me that you're just on another trip. I keep expecting you. Willy, dear, I can't cry. Why did you do it?" Grief, and bewilderment, and desolation, all genuine. And just as in Willy's heart, love; but no truth, no vision of his mounting despair and loss. In close intimacy, living and loving side by side for years, Willy and Linda have yet never been together in truth. He dreamt his life, and was for his wife a dream, no more. It is hard for her to wake up from it, but she has to, alone. This is the requiem for Willy Loman the salesman.

What can be, then, concluded, from this view of Loman's life in closer perspective? That he has loved not wisely but too well? Too well for his own character and that of his loved ones. His break and fall impend in his choice of intentions, intentions too good to be true, intentions imaginatively too "free" to come to terms with some reality. He has lived and died in vain; and this frustration he owes to no one but himself. If a proof is demanded that Loman has been acting, and failing to act, on his own, and must be responsible for the sound of his requiem, then, as before, the answer is negative. But the destiny of his life – not of yours? – is so disposed that he could see he shaped it, if his vision were not lost. And if this consenting but unbiased view has brought you close to him, then you can see it, too. Then you can see that Loman's intimate misfortune is due to his being forced to choose his way between being liked and being "successful," between a complete involvement in the life of others and keeping an objective distance from them, between love and truth. His events point to such choice pressing him in his loss; whether it may be self-dependently assumed or imposed by the world, that is not easily decided: chosen. In taking Loman's character as it is, chosen, through the situations which are his own, some dark thoughts emerge, which may have human significance for you as well as for him. It can then be said that for men to grasp each other is to reach also for evil, that to look through the reality of another, to take his measure, is to abandon selecting the good in him. Recoiling from such prospects, it is possible or necessary to dream; but dreaming, an extension of vision which is one's own, should not be and yet through Care often is introduced and imposed upon others, then rebellion or self-abnegation may follow. And love? Love in this Faustian but constricted world is only a free grace, a gift, since no one deserves it as he is; and even as a gift it may be taken or rejected: timeo Danaos et dona ferentes. Love, once believed to be the moving power of reality, here shows up in failure as the link with conflicting realities of human being around you. It is a link with your images and dreams, with your good but only your good intentions. Love does not yield the truth of others, nor of yourself – if you know. Love remains as an escape for your choice, since truth may be frightening. But love can kill, too, and conflict can show the truth.

∾

Wherein consists the TRAGIC being of Willy Loman? In his loss. To collect the preceding trends toward this end, it may be advisable to answer now a question which might have accumulated the weight of doubt. If it is said that Loman is a man lost in the crowd of his world, and if that is to serve as conclusion, then it can be legitimately asked: in what way is Loman different from the anonymous membership of crowds, such as the Theban elders around Oedipus or the fellow-townsmen of Dr. Stockmann? Are men losing themselves in crowds throughout the history of humanity, those "others," are they all tragic? This question may only be understood in terms initially introduced: general, categorized, scientific knowledge of what or who is tragic is not to be claimed. To see the tragic, not detached observation of the world's events, but intimate involvement in existence is required. It follows that the word is to be used rather with regard to singular "you" or "me" than to "them" or even "us." This means you can not claim that "they," the unapproached others as others are or are not tragic: because you simply cannot know. No statistically valid conclusions have been or could be promised for such an exploration which must move through poetic intimacy with single existing characters. Thus, with regard to Willy Loman, the "dignity" of a tragic character can be claimed for him only through acquiring a sufficiently revealing and assimilating approach to him, attempted on the preceding pages. If you have given your consent there – then Loman can be seen tragically by you, because he exists for you, he stands out from the background of his world, even if his stance is staggering and stumbling, even if he sinks down, he sinks before your eyes which can appreciate what has been lost. Of crowds you could never maintain this. How do you intimately grasp a crowd? You might try to fix your eye upon some individuals in it, in the hope that in knowing their movements and apparent feelings, you would understand the crowd they represent. You could be justified in this, and still be wrong in what you conclude of the whole crowd.

But this argument by itself does not establish any more than the bare possibility of finding Loman tragic, in contrast to all the "others." In order to go further, it is necessary to look again at this phenomenon of loss. And first, lest again there be some lingering doubt, it should be said that while the word "loss" appears to be ambiguous, no play with this ambiguity has been exploited here. Loss may be understood as "loss of" something, a button, a book, also a house or a homeland. Loss may be, however, understood equally well as "loss in" something, a forest, a foreign place, also a study or a story. That these two meanings differ is clear; it is not clear whether and what connection may hold them interrelated. For the present purpose the following suggestion may suffice. When you lose, something you are the loser; but this means more than it seems to. It means not only an object missing but also your being at a loss, handicapped, constricted. You stay without not only that particular thing, which need not be important, but also without something you claimed for your own, hence you often prefer to search for what you miss, even hopelessly, rather than to "replace" it straight away. From this it could be argued that you never lose anything but what you are on your own; but the universality of such a view need not be pursued here. What about the other situation? Losing yourself in some worldly space or occupation, it is even more a case of your being not the loser but the lost one. It is your capacity for going on, your "bearings," your continuity in relation to the world, that is being lost. Again it could be argued that what you lose is only your motion, spatial or non-spatial. The root of meaning then, however it extends into all linguistic ramifications, is one kind of "loss," that of your own continued and connected temporal movement. It is this loss which has been observed in the life of Willy Loman.

But is such loss necessarily tragic? Once more: nothing is necessarily tragic for everyone. For Loman – his loss is what he protests and protests against. Here is perhaps a new factor: what makes Loman's protest tragic is not its quality, its objectives, its influence on him, but its mere continuous though fading presence: its existence in him. This is his cry: "The woods are burning!" He is as a human being fully aware of the oppressive heat, of flames pressing ever closer, of himself sinking suppressed. To the end he tries to maintain himself above the hot flood – witness his offended dignity in refusing to work for Charley, which you might find misplaced; to the end he asserts his name as a bare symbol of his being there: "I am Willy Loman, and you are Biff Loman! ... I always knew one way or another we were gonna make it, Biff and I!" But he realizes that his way must be "another," that of self-removal; in life, he does not "make it." In life, despite his protesting awareness, he is defeated, despite his cry, no rescue does reach him. The loss which he senses and which you can witness is radical: the loss of his self. And with regard to that, his suicide may be no more than an anticlimactic epiphenomenon, merely following after. As a gesture, it gives poignancy to his existence in protest, but it is not indispensable to the situation of loss. How is that possible? You may wonder: before he kills himself, Loman, his protesting voice, his living body, even his despair, it is all still there and still his; is this compatible with his being already lost?

In loss, he is not himself, he is not what he is. The description sounds absurd. Is it? Someone assured of its absurdity had better ascertain that he has not overlooked any problem in the transitive "is," referred to in the introduction. Is it all so clear how one "is" this, that, and the other? How one "is" right, or corrupted, or a Christian, or a man of business? How one "is" oneself and true? How one "is" preserved after death? And what negation may or must creep into such "is?" With regard to the "is" of loss, as displayed in Loman, this much can be said. The sense of loss, discovered here, is in its root temporal. A man can be "not yet" or "no more" what he is, since what he is needs be much more than the present. Orestes will deplore being "not yet" what he is: the heir of Agamemnon. Loman despairs in being "no more" what he is: a likable, successful salesman living on business expectations. This is how his existence has been determined by choice; but all human existence must be in a past as well as a future, to "be" anything at all in the present. Loman's loss "happens" to him from the future. from which follows his constriction in limits between the past and the present, the dream and the waking. He "is" no more the man living toward what is ahead, and yet through the power of Care he cannot "be" in any other way but through expectation and remembrance. He has lost himself in his time. But this loss has much to do with the determination of him as a salesman. Loman is selling himself. This is surrender, whether you believe in evil possession or not. This is the choice meaning: I am for sale, let the world take and assess me, I must "be" fixed, determined, measured I shall let "them" pay me in quanta. A finite human being who lets himself be quantitatively determined "is" only toward the stage when inevitably his time must have a stop. The loss of a future which could be inexhaustible as long as a man remained alive, is quite proper for this man whose future is not inexhaustible because measured in quanta of crowd values. Loman's loss is due to such a choice.

Would that be an escape for Oedipus fearing his own future self? Not as long as he remains on the flight-path by his own; in all his fear, Oedipus resolves to stay one with himself. Loman does not. He is willing to be measured by his sales; he lives not all-one but in and through the others, especially his family; he wants to be "objectively" right, to win support from the world, to accompany his heroes, rather than to be just himself. His own truth to himself lacking, that precondition is beyond him, where he could "not be false to any man."

With truth absent around him, with reality others could accept dissolving in time, he sinks, being more than ready to depart. Death just follows, as it will.

In such a human, humanly protested atrophy of the self not tragic? In the last analysis, your consent stands and falls together with your judgment of the world in which Willy Loman is lost and which can, if you choose it, display such remarkable signs of resemblance to your own world. It is a matter of entry under a roof, supposed to "cover" your insecurity. The meaning of that roof over your world is only a determination of "common" sense, a protection against going astray. It cautions you: in thoughts and words and deeds, do not go beyond what counts, and you will be accounted for. And yet, it is in this roofed-over world that Loman is losing himself, it is this world which exposes his own property for sale, this world which puts it beyond his frailty to avoid such determination. This choice of loss, was it his? Was it properly his own, if assumed under such massive pressure of the many others, could he stay one against the crowd and "to his own self be true?" That such a choice is possible and almost required in this world, may be for all who count themselves as living in it – tragic.

But if you agree thus far, ask yourself: is such loss accessible only today? Does it open in some amazing advance of man's modern history? Have there been no mute, unprotesting Lomans in older days, as far back as your mind can go? Perhaps the twentieth century makes tragic loss easier and more popular; it does not make it possible. The tragedy witnessed here is human, not merely modern. It does not depend for its essence on any thing recently discovered or conquered. More issues from this, for the sceptics: if you are doubtfully disposed toward seeing Willy Loman as a tragic character, while you admit that his story is not exclusively contemporary in its basic strains, should you not wonder what exactly has changed or been changed in the disposition of recent times? Perhaps the situation is such that clear attention to what is tragic now becomes dubious, out of date, hard to find, in fact that vision of tragedy is being lost, while what is tragic continues to characterize the human being, as ever. If such is the true situation of today, is that not tragic? Listen and look, carefully, around: perhaps the woods are burning.

CHAPTER VIII

The Tragic Liberation - Orestes of the Flies

JEAN-PAUL SARTRE: THE FLIES

"This emptiness, the shimmering air, that fierce sun overhead" – the great noon, the confluent climax of Promethean fires. Is it an end, a closure in the noon of death, this "sultry, windless noon, in which nothing stirs, nothing changes, nothing lives?" The stillness of choice becomes a time to end, to end a road, a vision, a faith; but not to end time. The night will fold down again, the night of despair, of fear, of violence. And after that, a new dawn will rise from twilight, the twilight – perhaps – for the gods, the dawn – perhaps – for new tragic striving.

A Great Year has rolled through the universe. The symphony of tragic movements, ringing in rich if somber expansions, dissonances, variations, now returns in its finale to the simple setting of its opening theme. It points the way toward re-discovery of the primal sources of tragedy. Here is again the classical world of Hellenic communities with their problems of rule for the polis, of "primitive myths" in their weight for man's life, of direct though terrifying relations to divinity dominating the natural order. Here is again a live concern for more than passing ideas and issues within the human being: freedom and death, creation and evil, solitude and time. Here is again a perspective reaching beyond man, searching "above" for an appointment of be-longing, of safety, of a path, finding existence in dis-appointment, and spreading into a defiant protest. The ancient cares and questions remain humanly fresh, while they are transposed in expression to accord with the contemporary world of man: they merge with and incorporate ideas and influences of Christian faith, of modern times, of scientific reason, of social power in the age of the common man. Yet in such merging the old yields into the new: the world in which Orestes

– 193 –

exists stretches beyond reason, Christianity, social dependence – it is post-modern. Transcending the flattened horizons on which modernity signifies a tragic loss of seriousness, this world makes available a depth in which the perennial questions of tragic being can be re-searched anew.

The world at noon: in balance between all yesterday and all to-morrow, in transience from fulfillment to demand, in resolution of his being for man, at his temporal crossroads. This world contains the flies of guilt, the light Athenian evenings, the bloody image of Zeus, the tutor's calm assurance, the suppressed pressure of Electra's dreams the cowed community in the Argive crowd; it also hides somewhere a task for Orestes, to be chosen amongst those facts: a path toward himself and toward others. This path he calls his freedom. But is it a fact like the other facts in this world, is it one of the available data of nature? No, it is not given by nature, not even to be given, but only to be taken away from nature, to be claimed, conquered, chosen in lonely emptiness. What is given is also sustained in natural order; but here only a struggle is to be expected where nature, far from sustaining tends toward re-traction of choice, re-voking the claim, re-assimilation of the estranged into the obvious, the unavoidable, the common. In this struggle Electra surrenders her self. Can Orestes continue inde-finitely on his self-chosen path? Can he be ever sure of himself, if all the ordinary safeguards of assurance, reason, faith, common judg-ment, are against him? Can his path lead to a terminus? All these are criteria of nature: continuity, assurance, determination; therefore they may not be taken for granted in his quest. And yet, not only does he approach to own it for himself but also extends this disowning from nature to all human being. Not in proving or teaching or com-manding but in the challenge of his protesting record emerges his strange call to freedom. Discontinuous, unassured, indeterminate, it must remain in suspense of self-demand. Nevertheless, this is what Orestes offers to this noon world in balance of times: a task, a promise, an opening into the future whence "all must begin anew" for the sake of man's LIBERATION.

～

Although the world's dimensions are for Orestes as vastly unlimited as for Prometheus or Faust, they have been largely emptied of their spiritual variety. Gone is the colorful presence of Olympians, gone the imposing multitudes of good angels and evil devils, gone the mythical population of woods and waters, gone the Earth Spirit. In this new vision, the rounded and bared earth has come to be possessed only by humans. Is not all divinity to go as well? In one sense, this Orestean struggle appears to be a simple continuation of modern times' positivist iconoclasm, removing all threats of mystery, aimed at securing for man the sole significance in his world. If this were all its sense, perhaps it would only strengthen this anti-tragic tendency where in the business of the world's conquest is lost all serious attention to the unconquered queries of any human existence and its destiny. That there is another, a deeper sense to the story of Orestes and the flies, may be remembered if it is seen that man's sole possession of earth could signify his solitude, that banishment of evil spirits need not uproot the origins of evil, that after the death of God the human being would still confront the challenge of mortal striving, of finite judgments, of self-constricting despair. Are not these avenues open to tragedy?

The old God still lives in this world. As old as the Promethean rebellion, his name is still Zeus. He is still "the king of gods, king of stones and stars, king of the waves of the sea." His will still rules over all the present natural universe in which men have their dwelling. And still, as with the Titan's prophecy, the king of gods does not dominate the future time, and anxiously knows it: "All this was foreknown. In the fullness of time a man was to come, to announce my decline." The fullness of time has approached, and hence man no longer dwells for Zeus in a corner of his universe, an insignificant weed, but looms large in the center of his preoccupation, a menace to his empire. In some ways the aging Tyrant of the Skies has not changed at all: "I love nobody – I've no use for love." Not love but fear is his instrument of dominion. Because ruling is the issue of the strange and terrible "godlike passion" for order, for ordering all according to the will of one. This passion, confesses that king of Argos, of whom Zeus admits: "You were made in my image," constitutes being "without love, without hope, even without lust." The passion for order crushes such dis-orderly elements. And it shuns, slanders, suppresses even more ruthlessly, something else.

One powerful presence is being lifted from the horizons of this universe, that power before which gods and men had to bow low: the concrescence of "That which Needs must be." Fate disappears, leaving behind but one divine secret – that man is free, that his necessity lies not in a fatal order but in a choice of his being. The secret is jealously, supernaturally preserved by Zeus, as the spark for a conflagration to reduce him to twilight. He knows that once man extends his groping way toward this secret, "once freedom lights its beacon in a man's heart, the gods are powerless against him." Why? Because then against all the divine and natural power, pressure and pain, he can raise the torch of Promethean defiance. Above all else, the ruling god of order must beware of the discovery of freedom.

As in the old days from Prometheus, so now from his heirs the haughty, unrelenting Zeus demands in return for his protecting favors just a little thing, "next to nothing, a mere trifle, what you can give most easily – a little penitence." This little is refused him by Orestes. This little is exacted by him from other men, in shape of self-negation, of disavowal of their thoughts and deeds as wrong, as improper, as not their own. This little is all that divides in the human being imposed order from chosen existence. It suffices. As long as their piety is vested firmly in abject fear of their grounding power, of what un-knowably makes them be and act, men can remain near to the heart of Zeus, or rather to the will of Zeus in its divine passion imposing law from beyond.

It is in the interest of his universal dominion that the natural order, prescribed by Zeus for men, must utilize their natural fear and rest upon fear's likely roots in guilt. "Fear and guilty consciences have a good savor in the nostrils of the gods." But the spread of guilt is more than just a satisfactory pattern selected by Zeus to serve his purposes of rule. It is an indirect inheritance or infection from his own source: the god himself is guilty, and guilty men belong to him. To perpetuate his law, he has appointed his anointed vassals to wield the scepters in his name: "A king is a god on earth, glorious and terrifying as a god." But the prominence of royalty, its glory and terror, is guilt. In the interest of divinely descended right, human rulers have to subdue their subjects, in the name of their overlord they have to commit themselves to overpowering violence, in impressing order they have to suppress freedom. Thus they become guilty in loyal procreation of the most ancient guilt, the divine crime – to "have made man mortal." Compared to that, all other crimes are petty, they just im-plement what is insuperably to come: "Once I had done that, what was left for you, poor human murderers, to do? To kill your victims? But they already had the seed of death in them; all you could do was to hasten its fruition by a year or two." The mortal being of men, as Hamlet felt, is the seed of their corruptibility, the alien barrier of their proper freedom. Perpetuation of the rule of Zeus, "god of flies and death," is for men identical with acceptance of guilt, of self-denial, of life overshadowed by its end. Even the overthrow of this god must bequeathe to a succeeding age a limitation: the liberated men can only affirm their freedom unto death.

But has the old Zeus remained quite the same as in the Titanic days of beginning, when heaven and earth were young and mankind in its birth? Has he not acquired some of the supernatural traits men have come to believe in the intervening Christian era? What is the relation of this latter-day divine survivor to the Lord of Faust and to his negation-waging opponents? Looking into these questions will immediately encounter some faith-provoking ambiguities. Because the deity seen here cannot be dissociated from sharing the characteristics of both good and evil.

Is it only a coincidence that Zeus takes the name of "fly-god" not from the Lord but from Mephistopheles? It could be; but it could also mean more, if Electra's contemptuous vision of him is proper: "You like them old, of course; the nearer they're to corpses, the more you love them ... You loathe youth and life. I, too, am bringing you offerings, while all the others are at prayers. Here they are: ashes from the hearth, peelings, scraps of offal crawling with maggots, a chunk of bread too filthy even for our pigs. But your darling flies will love it, won't they, Zeus?" The god of flies must be the god of death, like them he must be feeding on decay, like them he must find attractive offal, refuse, filth. If it be thought that hate distorts Electra's image of him, then Zeus' own words might be recalled. He says that the god-sent flies "are a symbol"; he finds a "worthy man" in that Argive who identifies himself with "a mass of rottenness" and willingly draws to himself the flies "teeming round, like carrion crows"; and he tells the tutor; "Much good they do you, your pink cheeks. For all your roses, my good man, you're no more than a sack of dung, like all those others, in the eyes of Zeus. Yes, though you may not guess it, you stink to heaven. These folk, at least, are wise in their generation; they know how bad they smell" – of mortality! Is it not clear that with all his interest in dying, decay, and destruction, Zeus can be quite properly seen as the spirit of negation, denying the worth of finite existence? Nor is this all. The god's super-natural "miracles" are here reduced to the level of tricks of a cheap magician who mumbles his deluding formulas to seduce the gullible, but who can be seen through as Faust sees through the lures of Mephisto. And what is more important, Zeus acknowledges his own role as that of a tempter, his means as deceitful, his task as leading men astray from themselves: "For a hundred thousand years I have been dancing a slow, dark ritual dance before men's eyes. Their eyes are so intent on me that they forget to look into themselves. If I forgot myself for a single moment, if I let their eyes turn away –" but he cuts his confession short, not to let out the secret of his end. Yet despite all the tempting might of his present supernatural rule Zeus fails here to subdue the human Orestes who discovers his own path, continuing and completing the Titan's rejection. Does the Promethean light or the seductive mirage of Zeus resemble more the role of Lucifer?

On the other hand, properly or not, the ruler of nature assumes also the attributes of the great Christian Lord, which the Promethean Zeus never did claim: the creation of man and of all, the praiseworthy justice of his enduring order, the law which everything naturally obeys, the goodness which is producing and sustaining all in being:

"Orestes, I created you, and I created all things. Now see! See those planets wheeling on their appointed ways, never swerving, never clashing. It was I who ordained their courses, according to the law of justice. Hear the music of the spheres, that vast, mineral hymn of praise, sounding and resounding to the limits of the firmament. It is my work that living things increase and multiply, each according to his kind. I have ordained that man shall always beget man, and dog give birth to dog. It is my work that the tides with their innumerable tongues creep up to lap the sand and draw back at the appointed hour. I make the plants grow, and my breath fans round the earth the yellow clouds of pollen. You are not in your own home, intruder; you are a foreign body in the world, like a splinter in flesh, or a poacher in his lordship's forest. For the world is good; I made it according to my will, and I am Goodness. But you, Orestes, you have done evil, the very rocks and stones cry out against you. The Good is everywhere, it is the coolness of the wellspring, the pith of the reed, the grain of flint, the weight of stone. Yes, you will find it even in the heart of fire and light; even your own body plays you false, for it abides perforce by my law. Good is everywhere, in you and about you; sweeping through you like a scythe, crushing you like a mountain. Like an ocean it buoys you up and rocks you to and fro, and it enabled the success of your evil plan, for it was in the brightness of the torches, the temper of your blade, the strength of your right arm. And that of which you are so vain, the Evil that you think is your creation, what is it but a reflection in a mocking mirror, a phantom thing that would have no being but for Goodness. No, Orestes, return to your saner self; the universe refutes you, you are a mite in the scheme of things. Return to Nature, Nature's thankless son."

Without hearing this self-defining divine speech, you could develop the easy, one-sided impression that the stand of Orestes is "obviously" right and that all straightforward, self-respecting men must align themselves with him in combatting the wiles of the death-dealing evil seducer. Without listening in hushed silence to the overpowering sweep of the God's universal claim, you could never be duly sensitive to the unique immensity of challenge confronting Orestes. Without attentively weighing all these words of Zeus, you would have to misunderstand how it is that behind them lies the accumulated support of common tradition, faith and rationality, how Orestes must appear alone and alienated, but also how he is able to withstand the persuasive pressure and to defy the massive sound of this call, hearing in it a supercilious echo of the human choice.

The choice for man is not at all straightforward; it is not like an obvious acceptance of good and rejection of evil; it is not even the quest to find the nature-radiating values. It is rather the self-demand of willingness to search the world in one's own dim light. The great, great Zeus offers peace, safety, gentleness to all the sheep in his fold – but at the cost of recognizing oneself as "his" sheep, at the cost of the human being's self-surrender, at the cost of service to the end of Zeus instead of risky striving for one's own path of liberation. Even if the God of nature is its Good; does this eliminate for choice-conscious man the possibility, the need, of seeking his good in his being? Even were it frail, feeble, "reflected only," yet sparked and warmed in one's own breath? If man's mortality may form divine guilt, his thirst for freedom may be due to divine blunder. Because now to the self-infringing call of Zeus: "I gave you freedom so that you might serve me," man has discovered a self-imposing reply: "Your whole universe is not enough to prove me wrong," you may be the ruling king of the universe you own – "but you are not the king of man" whom you may not own.

Thus the primary weight in human choice is neither relieved nor displaced by the conflicting ambiguities in the deity of this world. Whether Zeus may shepherd man toward Good or tempt him toward Evil, he remains an alien other from whom the human being may forever alienate itself, with whom it may never merge. Whether this be man's crowning glory or his condemning deficiency, it is due to the finite range of his own light which cannot exhaustively penetrate what is beyond him. It flickers when it guides or misguides him: "My mind is dark; I can no longer distinguish right from wrong."

Just so in the twi-light of the human time it may be impossible to distinguish the Lord from the devil.

But the time is trying. As it disquiets Zeus whose decline it may bring in its ebb, so it urges the men of this world in its critical tide. The Promethean choice has returned to earth: while menaced Zeus endeavors to pacify, postpone, prevent the spread of Orestes' claim to the Titanic heritage, mankind is pressed in the throes of choice, dimly, doubtfully awakening to the perspectives of an earth where no pretendent would succeed the rule of Zeus, an earth to be made free for all men alive. That such choice is present, that retrogressive and progressive inclinations are equally near, can be drawn from the view of contrasting horizons of Argos and Athens; the distance between them is spanned in the wandering search of the man Orestes.

The fuller, more immediate and real is the view of Argos: "Those blood-smeared walls, these swarms of flies, this reek of shambles and the stifling heat, these empty streets and yonder god with his gashed face, and all those creeping, half-human creatures beating their breasts in darkened rooms, and those shrieks, those hideous, blood-curdling shrieks" – that is the panorama in Argos of piety, populated by men in whom Zeus "can delight." Amongst the Argives, man-shunning in ignorance, suspicion and fear, "the only one who doesn't run away is a half-wit" who finds purely animal bliss while being bitten by the bloody flies. The others are more self-aware; they feel themselves to belong to the god of flies and death. They dare not stand proudly on their own feet, they cannot face in calm an enquiring stranger, nor can they bear to be left alone. The town of Argos extends a protecting roof over their crowd life, their community of guilt, their idolatry of self-loss. Is this Argos so remote in time and space, is it no more than a faded ancient vision – or is it possibly also a contemporary nightmare? Would a modern citizen such as Loman have to fee strange within the crowd of Argives, would he have grave difficulties in adopting their revered code in which one's own life is worth nothing, has to be carried on in self-apologetic service, and can only acquire a positive valuation from an outside power that can pay and repay all? Perhaps the Argives have one realistic advantage over the shallowed, conquest-driven, self-forgetful modern men: they know themselves throughout as mortal. Yet this advantage turns their life-knowledge into a mere anxiety of delay, when their main prayerful insight becomes: "Make us regret that we are not dead." Thus conscience does make cowards of them all, with vengeance: vengeance against their life which, moving toward nothing, is nothing worth; vengeance

from Argos to Athens cannot bypass the human facts of mortal nature, and its unpredictable Beyond; such a flight cannot be made too light, even for a "free" spirit. The Argive crowd is almost roused to rebellion by the gently inciting gestures and words of Electra, in her "dancing for joy, for peace among men, for happiness and life." Yet her peaceful, lightening attempt at salvation fails. Why? A crowd can often be moved by singular determination, though in its resistance it tends to return to balance. But the crowd of Argives is too heavy to be swayed into dancing lightly, too terrified to dare, too firmly stamped as property of the gods to incur their vengeful wrath by self-assertion: one sinister sign from Zeus crushes their conscience of choice. They are far, far away from Athens. Their road into another future must cross the demands of their deity, the dangers of death, the darkness of despair denying the light of any liberation.

Are such men as those imprisoned in Argos doomed? And are the Athenian free spirits safe? Neither can be the case, particularly if both visions present two sides of the same human being, a being aware of choice. The future is unbounded throughout all men's life. Zeus can challenge Athens, but Argives can awaken to the thought that they, too, are creatures of Prometheus. If the existence of Orestes means anything at this time, then the challenge and the awakening are drastically due – now. The human world has reached its noon.

Into this world of poised human contrasts, into this moment of balance between the god's preserving might and man's pressed search for a proper future, steps in Orestes, proclaiming his impious gospel of freedom. How many signs of kinship link him with tragic heroes of other worlds and times, in his acts, attitudes, and aims! Like his first ancestor, the Titan, he raises the possibility of defiance as salvation from tyranny, as the only unconquerable refuge from the overpowering, super-natural presence of Zeus; but at this time he may also claim to free Prometheus from his bonds. Like Thomas Stockmann, he is ready to accept social exile, sacrificing himself fort the sake of his fellow-citizens though against their present passions; he clings to his liberating idea but is willing to embrace all men within it. Like Willy Loman, he faces loss of everything he wants to possess, his paternal inheritance, his community with other humans, his only family love – Electra; and so deserted he finally has to remounce all love but to possess his self. Like king Oedipus, he is "bespoken" on his road, tied by his chosen belonging to his origins in his past; although he finds this tie in an anxious affirmation of his own and not in a determining decree of any superhuman fate. Like the prince of Denmark, he responds in his anxious conscience to the choice of offensive deeds thrust into his hands; but unlike Hamlet he lives to acknowledge and appropriate them decisively as constituent of his being in the world. And like the universal man Faust, he attains the insight that the human being is the human striving, that the conquest of freedom by daring is the only proper path through finite time, though it be beset by dangers not only natural but seeming divine. Will all these traits of resemblance to characters both ancient and modern perhaps suffice to guarantee the genuine status of Orestes as a tragic hero? If not, no matter; for he wears his tragic marks upon himself proudly and openly, to testify to the rebirth or re-formation of tragic character for these present times. If modernity has threatened to blind or distort man's vision of the tragic through surface smugness of scientific supremacy, through domesticating his destiny in the day-to-day drive of demanding distractions, through the conscience-calming creed of clear crowd conformity, here in the world of Orestes re-turns the concern for the sense of the human being, which re-opens the question of the tragic being.

By the classical Aristotelian criteria the story of Orestes becomes tragic through the complete overturn of his fortune and character in the action of one pregnant day. In the emptiness of a noon time Orestes grows up into tragedy. He passes out of the tranquil innocence of "a quiet little boy with happy, trustful eyes," and realizes it is for him "time to say farewell to all the lightness, the aery lightness that was mine – good-by to my youth." By choice he takes up the heavy man-load of action, which will make him a man amongst men, which will create a bond of blood between himself and the Argive community happening to be his by birth, made necessarily his by deed. There can be hardly any doubt about the "ordinarily" tragic aspects of this action, where to claim his blood he has to destroy his blood, where to establish his place in Argos he is to be refused and banished by Argos, where, emptily, in the attempt to flee his solitude he ends in flight and solitude. But, you may object, the story of the royal house of Atreus is obviously ancient and draws its awful fascination from "primitive myths"; its re-creation does not belong to, nor does it offer new significance for, this day and age – such warming up is far from reawakening the sense of tragedy. The considerations to follow will endeavor to answer this objection. They express the point of

view that if the dramatic events in Orestes' story are not contemporary, it is not events that make it tragic; that the world in which
this Orestes exists, in which he can do what he does and say what he
says, is by no means "obviously" ancient; that serious reflection on
the sense of the human being can still be primary and therefore
"primitive"; that the tragic significance of the Orestean message is
addressed also – particularly – to the present day.

The novel, non-classical aspects begin to emerge as soon as one asks
about the tragic "flaw" in the character of Orestes. Because this defect
of his, his offensive hybris, he insolently elevates as his source of
glory. More consciously than Oedipus, in justice or revenge he takes
life; like Oedipus, he acknowledges his sole responsibility for the deed
– but refuses to identify it as guilt: "I am no criminal, and you have
no power to make me atone for an act I don't regard as a crime."
Not at a mere magistrate are these words provocatively flung – at the
king of the gods! Pride then, perverted, unnatural pride, compared
to which the pride of Oedipus pales to subdued sense. Yet this pride
is seen by him as his free privilege; it is hostile to natural behavior,
but so is the whole aim of Orestes' striving; if it is perverted, against
what norm, what law can it be termed as such? In the face of the
overwhelming weight of law, divine, natural, social, this outcast
promises to admit "no other law but mine." When so an interhuman
frame of reference is lacking, or when the man in question even explicitly demands to be excluded from it, how can a defect be classified,
how can crime be contraposed to merit? Certainly, some externally
"objective" adverse verdict and sanction are always available: a
man can be judged and punished as criminal by powers outside him.
Yet such external powers may miss the heart of the problem of justice,
when they are powerless to make him recognize his act as improper,
and repent for it; when he continues to regard himself not as a criminal
but as a persecuted martyr, the task of justice has hardly been fulfilled. At any rate, what is in question here is not a judicial process but
a consenting approach to the existence of Orestes. For this purpose,
his unusual, incommensurable attitude forecasts frustration and misunderstanding, if the approach is made in harsh infringement of his
terms of judgment. And if these terms declare that crime and merit
are grounded not in the world but in the heart, then all "objective"
rights and wrongs vanish before individual sovereignty. Good and
evil are to be appropriated in each man's freedom from the time of
revolt against heaven.

It would be even hazardous to state whether or not he properly deserves what awaits him as his further destiny; because such a statement would involve ambiguity dependent on your evaluation of his whole sequence. His exile from Argos could be seen as punishment; and in this case you would have to say that it is an improper expression of gratitude of the Argives whom he has striven to liberate, or, also legitimately, that it quite properly condemns his heinous crime. But his departure from Argos could as well be regarded as his accomplishment; and in this case your judgment would decide whether his deed properly entitles him to glory in it, or is only vain violence improperly adopting a heroic posture. Orestes himself would certainly grant that these contingencies of valuing are all founded in your freedom of judgment and are therefore your own risk and resolve. Apart from this maze of free values, the affinity of the sequence could be considered as a span of hard facts, fore-known and fore-reached in choice. A true Promethean, Orestes clearly could call: "With firm resolve and knowledge I transgressed, nor now deny it." No optimist, he certainly could foresee the impact of shock in his action for Argos, his consequent dangers of direct reaction and repulsion by the crowd, and also the indirect long-term results of removing the flies from the city. The sequence shows then a proper necessity not of outward remittance by fate but of inward admittance by choice. Zeus himself acknowledges this inner thread of awareness and firmness through Orestes' steps – this is what makes them offensive against him: "He is thinking out his plan, coolly, methodically, cheerfully, What good to me is a care-free murder, a shameless, sedate crime, that lies light as thistledown on the murderer's conscience? – He'll go away with red hands and a clean heart." What Zeus desires in men is a break in their chosen sequence of events: thus he cherishes the murder of Agamemnon as "a crime that did not know itself, a crime in the antique mode, more like a cataclysm than an act of man," later yielding "a profit" to him in penitence, "for one dead man, twenty thousand living men wallowing." Thus he teasingly encourages resistance to his own orders in the soul of Aegistheus, anticipating that "it will add a spice to your surrender"; thus he triumphs in Electra's later repentance, self-annihilating her part in the killing of king and queen. But no such break is open to the crushing aim of Zeus in the actions of Orestes, where intent and deed, effect and memory fuse together into what he is and has been by choice.

To be human means for Orestes to build a free path through time in acts that are unswervingly one's own. Such a path alone will trace out an indentation in the resistant mass of nature, and attest one's presence to others. "Only yesterday I walked the earth haphazard; thousands of roads I tramped that brought me nowhere, for they were other men's roads. Yes, I tried them all; the haulers' tracks along the riverside, the mule-paths in the mountains, and the broad, flagged highways of the charioteers. But none of these was mine. Today I have one path only, and heaven knows where it leads. But it is my path ..." This path leads from the high isolation of his past down toward the common lot of Argive citizens, to whom he wants to belong in their future. It marks his search of his own being.

He starts out as a non-entity, "a mere shadow of a man," displaced but hardly a displacement. "Why, an old, mangy dog, warming himself at the hearth, and struggling to his feet with a little whimper to welcome his master home – why, that dog has more memories than I! At least he recognizes his master. His master. But what can I call mine?" Without anything to appropriate as his, without any investment in memories, without "the solid passions of the living," love, hate, which call for giving of the self – he has no self to give. He is as yet free in one sense, perhaps in the abnegating sense heard in the requiem on Willy Loman; free of the presence and pressure in time, "free as the strands torn by the wind from spiders' webs," free of the full thrust of standing out into the world – of existing. Yet strangely, it is from this "freedom" that his liberating path originates. From the negative void of his time and the absence of his wandering dispersal through it, emerges the quest for being in time with others, "as one man of men" in the Faustian disposition. Orestes discovers that "there is another way" to own freedom.

The other way requires not clear detachment but dwelling commitment, not sublimating tensions but solving tasks, not veering vacancy but involving identity in time – once you have "staked your life on a single throw of the dice." Tending your life as a solid stake rather than a strange show is not only the way of repentance – as Clytemnestra sees it; it is also the way of resolution, for Orestes. It may mean, as it does in her case, a realization of dragging a dead weight through one's history, and a vain, struggling effort to disown it, dreaming of the shadow of innocence. But it can also mean a conscious effort to assume and respond to the full weight of one's past, realizing it not as dead but as life-giving. The Argive way to be claims Orestes; it loads his lightness of a non-attached, non-tragic Athenian free spirit with the historical burden of Aegistheus, Clythemnestra, Electra. To Argos belongs his past. Instead of dissociating himself from it, as the Athenian tutor would have him do, he wants to locate himself on this ground. Like Oedipus after the failure of his escape, Orestes discovers that the human being ever exceeds its present in striving which can only attain its future from its past. Dis-covering his way toward his self, he finds that he has been but is not yet the heir of Agamemnon. His time out of joint is to become his life, filling his emptiness. Is any avoidance possible for him? Certainly, if his history is not outwardly necessitated. Orestes could abstain from action and absent himself silently from Argos, now and forever. Yet this "could" properly points to the inward hold of choice on the human being. Because that abs-tention would diffuse his tending toward his own destiny, that a-voidance would reopen that void of his presence to the world, which he misses as ab-sence of a temporal sense. Orestes "could" not be himself then, as he feels he is not himself when arriving in his home town as a stranger. His temporal identity is staked upon such choice.

How is it that Orestes feels dispossessed of his own being, not entitled to call any things of the world around him "mine?" It is because the appropriating content of "mine" is lacking unless reflecting in "yours," unless conquered from "theirs," unless distributable into "ours." A man does not exist in the world, unless he exists with, against or toward other men. Zeus rightly warns Orestes that his light, uncommitted "innocence makes a gulf" between him and his burden-committed fellow-citizens; although the intent of this warning may not be right: that this gulf could not and should not be bridged. Orestes knows his displaced distance from his past search: "I wander from city to city, a stranger to all others and to myself, and the cities close again behind me like the waters of a pool. If I leave Argos, what trace of my coming will remain?" He has displaced no thing elsewhere; in what way should he feel that he properly displaces a place in Argos, that he engraves a trace there, that he disturbs, affects, ties himself with anyone, if no one feels his presence, no one judges or responds to it? In what sense is Argos his city? "These folk are no concern of mine. I have not seen one of their children come into the world, nor been present at their daughters' weddings; I don't share their remorse, I don't even know a single one of them by name. That bearded fellow was right; a king should share his subjects' memories." For this king's son, to come into his own means to invade that standing order which excludes him, to cast his weight upon the alien waters so that they should yield and be channeled by him, even though with time they could obliterate his imprint. It is not only a question of his memories; these might be stolen or imagined. It is rather a demand to share, knowingly, all the days' heat, the evenings' cool dusk in Argos, to watch its people watching him in his rooms, at his door, within his palace, or at their houses, in their places of pleasure or grief. Still, it is not a receptive collection of similar impressions that matters. His need is to capture a part of the others' life, to provoke their reactions, to impose his presence inevitably upon their witnessing awareness, even through a purchasing hold of that guilt which is theirs. Then, only then, would he stay in their world, would inject himself into their unconscious rejection, would be acknowledged: the way we live is Orestes' doing. Then he could grasp that alien Argos as "ours," hence also "his." To be in Argos, he must have it have him; and for that, he must do for it – what? "If there were something I could do, something to give me the freedom of the city; if, even by a crime, I could acquire their memories, their hopes and fears, and fill with these the void within me, yes, even if I had to kill my own mother –"

Orestes is not a criminal type, if there be such. His thoughts and inclinations do not naturally and smoothly turn in a homicidal direction; nor does he take lightly the murderous alternative. He is a displaced royal heir, like Hamlet; but what primarily prompts him to act is not a compulsion "to set right" the wrong order of succession in the state; and it is not, either, a crown pretendent's ambition. His more modest but more undeviating ambition is to be: to become someone, to fill "the void within" with his proper history, to acquire the witness of his existence in others. The essential features of how he is to be, while not immaterial, are not pretentious at all. "Try to understand. I want to be a man who belongs to some place, a man among comrades. Only consider. Even the slave bent beneath his load, dropping with fatigue and staring dully at the ground a foot in front of him – why, even that poor slave can say he's in his town, as a tree is in a forest, or a leaf upon the tree. Argos is all around him, warm, compact, and comforting ... I'd gladly be that slave and enjoy that feeling of drawing the city round me like a blanket and curling myself up in it." He is ready for any fortunes or misfortunes to dwell in his place. He is ready to risk his life and to part with his "property" for it: "My sword can serve the city, and I have gold to help the needy." But he is told, and comes to believe, that in none of these capacities would he ever accomplish his purpose of belonging. Electra tells him that; do her words inform or misinform him? She has long dreamt of his arrival; so she certainly does not want him to depart with empty hands. Yet her dreams have been vindictive; so perhaps she does not want him to stay – with clean hands. Aside from her desires then, what is the outlook for him? It may not be true that, were he to stay in some service in Argos, he would remain "a hundred years a stranger"; it may be that he would anonymously get mixed into the crowd and successfully lose himself as one of many in its background. Would that do for him? Would he gain a doubtless conviction that Argos was his? Would he sincerely appropriate the Argives' ethos of self-denial? Would he become a true son of Agamemnon? Would he "fill the void within" to be – himself? A positive answer to any of these questions is very, very dubious. Walking on crowded paths does not make them one's own.

The result is Orestes' resolve to move on the offensive lines first pointed to by Electra: "An evil thing is conquered only by another evil thing, and only violence can save." The harsh shape of this belief can not and need not be smoothed over; but it deserves to be visualized in all conscience. Electra herself descends to this drastic depth only after the failure of her more high-minded attempt to convert Argos by liberating words, by a light flight of joy in life; and that attempt fails through the direct interference of Zeus. There is then a possible implication that it is only the law of Zeus that demands violence, that balancing evil with evil belongs only to the "piety" of vengeance, that if and when men become free, these dragging bonds might drop away in their movements. Looked at in the perspective of Orestes' decision, however, such a hope is dimmed down. Because although Orestes discards the natural or eternal law over his deeds, although he declares himself free against Zeus, yet he finds it necessary to perpetuate evil and to identify himself in violence. Zeus foresees such unavoidable predicament, telling the king that when the gods withdraw their rule "it's a matter between man and man, and it is for other men, and for them only, to let him go his gait, or to throttle him." This human choice shows the unstable, suspended balancing of justice; it shows the continuance of violence ingrained in judgment and punishment; it shows that in freedom one man's good always may or must be another man's evil.

But the resolve of Orestes, while self-seeking, is not self-insistent. It emerges from his chosen idea that his freedom is responsible for both his good and his evil; it is addressed, however, toward the freedom of others. The resolve toward an interhuman balance is not privately self-enclosed as only an idea; although open to the prospect of continuance of evil, it is also open to the prospect of mutual responsibility in expiation. Orestes wants to belong to Argos, wants

Argos to belong to him. By his anxious resolution, the Argives' guilty way to be is to enter his existence in his own horrifying deed; but his deed is to enter into their way to be to destroy their guilt. Thus the intertwined responsibility becomes undivorceable. Orestes' belief in deliverance through violence is yet a belief in deliverance. He will be entitled to tell the Argives: "It was for your sake that I killed. ... Now I am of your kind, my subjects; there is a bond of blood between us, and I have earned my kingship over you." He will have earned it not only by his acceptance of a heavy weight upon his conscience but also by his renunciation of earlier longings to have the air of Argos around him, to walk through his doors into his palace, to gather his own peaceful memories in his city. He must go away, "a king without a kingdom," if he is to take the flies away from Argos. With himself, he removes the deadly self-suppression in repentance, from those he loves as his people. They, who had a silent knowing share in the crime against Agamemnon, have none in his son's crime; they can, when the balance has been struck in blood, straighten out their bowed shoulders and resume some dignity in existing, delivered by him. The initial presence of Orestes in Argos amounts to an absence; his future absence may continue to pass in his city as his presence, on record.

Is this a fulfillment of the void within his self? Perhaps, but only perhaps. His future evolves toward another shadow of negation. He delivers the Argives, letting them stand up to exist, only if he assumes their burden in his being. He does so, decisively. Decisevely, he promises to take to himself the guilt flies, not to breed them but to "wring their necks"; to turn to nothing the shadows that darkened in Argos any light of its life. Decisively, after the deed he reaffirms the full anguish in recalling his matricide, not trying to deny it; decisively, he confronts the authority of Zeus: "I regret nothing." So he can go on decisively, "with a clean heart," as long as his conscience responds to the deed as proper. But – with a sensitive memory, in brooding isolation, through outward if not inward emptiness of indefinite wandering – how definite should be the firmness of his self-affirmation? How long, before as Clytemnestra felt, he might break into himself: "It wasn't I, it could not have been I, who did that?" How assured could be his future that he would never, like Electra, abnegate himself, in vain unmaking his past, making it passed in vain? Orestes has fulfilled his quest; properly or not, he has unquestionably reached the human being. And precisely therefore, like Faust's, his destiny extends open to ambiguity, his fulfillment re-

mains undetermined through his time, all the property and im-
property of his existence is tragically questionable.

How do these sympathetic explorations throughout Orestes'; why,
whence and whither, affect a conclusion upon his ethos? If consent
is given to his vision and character, it seems to demand that his killing
of Aegistheus and Clytemnestra, be seen as proper for him. Does this
constitute a justification of such murderous actions? This mode of
posing the question discloses a radical misunderstanding. A consenting approach to a human being means an unprejudiced effort to
appreciate and appraise as closely as can be, but neither to accuse
nor to excuse. The preceding considerations were intended to show how
it is that Orestes intimately needs his resolve to kill and not to repent
for killing. This need originates in his choice to liberate himself and
others; it is from this origin of his own being that his path through
his actions appears as proper. Yet precisely this origin in choice does
not permit development into the limits of constraining conclusion.
In other words, Orestes' call to subjective human freedom shatters
the terms of any objective justification fixing the worth of the human
being, foreclosing further fluidity of judgments, for or against. In his
or anyone's existence, the proper factual formations should be observed for proper understanding: action and reaction, crime and punishment, merit and glory; these belong to the balancing sense of
human justice. But where the forms fit, how the values are therein
discovered, what choice in judging is still available and required –
such queries are not to be universally determinable, if striving for
freedom is more than a fiction. Orestes' liberating claim thus leaves a
wide but dark horizon for illusion, erring, regression, failure, offense
– and this uncertainly free horizon can forever contain disclosures of
tragedy.

~

Once more, as in the previous perspectives, the theme of tragic
protest will be sounded through the dimensions of this latter-day
world of Orestes. And once again, as in the boundless Faustian
perspective, a horizon for light may record that man's protesting
stand, even if tragic, is not wholly a night-born issue of negation.
Yet at first, the Orestean perspective, with all its disappointment,
denial, debasement, may present the position of men in existence as
unduly dark; particularly so, if it is noticed that here the Promethean
protest against men's mortality seems to be mixed and coupled with
Hamlet's traits of protest against men's life as no more than a cala-

mity. It will be necessary, then, to consider both of these two pro-testing modes in turn.

The protest against death is sharp in form of a meta-physical accusation against the God who made men mortal. His gifts of nature, of the whole universal physis, do not properly suffice to obliterate that "first crime." The inadequacy is shown not only through the re-bellious eyes of Orestes: toward this oppressively mortal human con-dition three different attitudes are indicated.

There is first the common stand of Argives, not standing but staggering. The crowd of Argos know themselves as mortal and attest this knowledge. The abyss of death, immediately close to them in anything past, in any felt loss, in the finality of any deeds and mis-deeds, overpowers their life. These common men can not and will not raise their sights beyond their nature to challenge at least by question; but that which is unreachably beyond them does reach into their present nature to challenge and undermine its worth and reality. Life which is annihilable is worthy of annihilation; only death cannot be annihilated, death therefore "is" more real than life. What is deadly must be super-natural; the deity to be served and worshipped is the "god of flies and death." The flies are his symbols: they suck blood out of life, they bite into conscience to prompt regrets and regressions, they provoke hatred, disgust, abnegation. The flies seek death and decay; they draw men to desire death and to debase life as no more than decay. Such an inversion of the protesting response to death turns in this common lot of Argives into self-surrender, no more tragic than the lot of sheep. Beyond question, the nihilistic Argive "religion" corresponds to the aims of the spirit of vengeance and negation, the one who does "prefer eternal emptiness."

The contrasting alternative is the Athenian attitude of irreligious humanist confidence. It is epitomized in the words of the philosophical tutor from Athens: "There's nothing else but men." Here the reason-ing efforts to humanize the world are immured in reductive self-insistence. This makes their spirit modern. If there is nothing but men, then meta-physical protest has no outward point: there is no one to protest against. God is nothing, men's relations to the super-natural are left behind on the level of primitive myths, and death is not ac-cessible, being only where men are not. Life can be lived in the light of nature, whether enjoyable or only endurable: whatever and how-ever men may evaluate, they must always evaluate from within their existence. Hence it cannot even be said that death "is" an evil. Reason cannot handle that which is responsible for death; therefore, as irrational, death "is" unreal, and questions about its origin are pseudo-questions. Only within finite, sensible limits can occur human experience, judgment, explanation; outside these, death "is" absurd. This confident Athenian tendency to explain away death seems intended to uproot the possibility of complaining against it. But perhaps it is rooted just in what it moves to uproot. What else would give such power to this movement reducing all to finite and accessible terms, if not an untermed anxiety against the infinite, and inaccessible? The flies bear no danger here, being natural and destructible; but the god of flies, as nothing, is not destructible. Death is silenced; but its silence may be louder than the voice of reason. Tragedy can be forgotten; but forgetfulness need not be liberating. This atheistically positive rationality of Athens – at least as visualized here – is vulnerably human. It endeavors to ignore the negative aspect of the finite human being, not to protest against it; thereby, it cannot radically grasp its own post-Faustian quest.

Orestes, the native son of Argos, was brought up in Athens, and returns home as a stranger. The realm of death he finds appalling; it offends his Athenian confidence in life. But to look down upon it with his tutor's superior indifference would be to cut in advance any possible bond with these cowering Argives; yet amongst them his own blood had flown in the past. Neither horrified self-abnegation nor irresponsible self-insistence are open to him. Confronted with only alien directions of choice, he cannot easily discover his way to exist; when he does, it expresses his tragic protest against death. Orestes makes himself come to terms with the flow of mortal blood and even with the god of flies and death – but not to serve in these terms. He does not immure himself blindly against the inscrutable deity, the self-regression in guilt, the violence of nature, the negative presence of death in human life; he lets them be, when he stands up for liberation. His deed for Argos, that is to give him "the freedom of the city" and to liberate its citizens, is his most needed gesture of protest against death overpowering them; but in very serious irony, that very deed turns him toward death. If he were later trying to regret and forget it, would it not seem to him due to his confident, overconfident assumption of freedom over nature? If he were later to regress and embrace his burden of guilt from Argos, would it not be due to the former lightness of his free spirit from Athens? It appears that Orestes may have to accept what he rejects, undergoing what he strives to overcome: Argos and Athens, God and freedom, existence

The Tragic Loss - Loman the Salesman

This play is the experimentum crucis for tragedy. Willie is not really an actor, only a salesman that is lost, Willy is loosing himself beyond recovery.

and death, none of these may be unambiguously posited or negated by him. Such a way to be may be properly tragic.

The primary roots of Orestes' protest are Promethean. It is a protest against that power in present and finite nature, which constricts human mortals to the staggering status of useless weeds, whose being or non-being could "make no difference." It is a protest against the nightly might of old Zeus, subjecting the human being, dimming the light of life. With this attitude, Orestes belongs to Argos and is religiously bound even though only to dissolve the bonds. His hatred for death dominating his city rises to challenge the deity of death. Man's mortality, whether absurd, accursed or accepted, forms the frame of the factual situation for his existence; it will not be obliterated. But it is not the ground for his valuing or devaluing existence, and especially not for a prostrated obliteration of his self. The god responsible for death visits with vengeance any man rising to liberate his life. But to persist in vengeance against him would return man to his knees, impotent against impenetrable might. The bonds of Argive religion can be loosened not by pretending they are no threat but by letting be death and deity, where they may belong: beyond man's life. Thus Orestes can tell Zeus: "As for me, I do not hate you. What have I to do with you, or you with me? We shall glide past each other, like ships in a river, without touching." He no longer "hates the hater," as Prometheus did. He does not aim at the overthrow of Zeus' rule for the sake of a better successor; he aims at no rule in the liberation of man. For this exclusively human turn, his spirit has been made free in Athens. In his protest against death, man has to attest his proper temporal existence.

Through this attitude, the Orestean hold on life obtains shape, light and worth, although it is by no means a pure joy. Orestes' aspirations toward life basically stem from Athens; they are, however, violently jolted in his view of Argos. It is here that he comes to realize a human road to freedom, and correspondingly to regard life as "a matter between man and man." But what he discovers of these interhuman relations is sufficiently dark to dispose him critically into Hamlet's mood: "Man delights not me." His protest against life is articulated only in his meta-physical demand for freedom against nature; but it is expressed from many sources in the social world around him, not very different from those oppressing Stockmann and Loman.

It is men who mutually distort themselves in childhood and youth, praising no "want to be born," "ashamed of growing up," being alive only by a "fault," if not their own fault; from such distortions of the

seeds in shame, fear and guilt, what fruits can be expected in ma-
turity? It is the same men who become obsessed equally by their
avoidance of and longing for events of horror, straining "forward to
seeing for once a violent death," entertained by the flow of blood,
cowering under yet eagerly insisting on punishment. It is men who
oppress one another with rule and order, playing "a god on earth,"
yet finding only sinful "sacrilege" in reckless joy of living. It is men
who develop a need both to be served and to serve; men who struggle
for might yet desire to be confirmed by "their right" more securely
than by mere "my right"; men who war amongst themselves in order
"to live at peace"; men who claim to rearrange their world by conquest but who agree to have their own striving and dreaming interpreted more "really" and properly from outside, ready to own or to
disown themselves on request. It is, above everything else, men
themselves who identify all these features as elements of their god-
given or fate-determined nature. Seeing men as such, it can be appreciated how Orestes' protest against life becomes a protest against
nature. He finds it necessary to negate any positive human nature
in order to be able to posit any human freedom.

What is nature? It is in the original sense "what is to be born":
whatever is due to come, whatever time has to bring, whatever in the
Promethean words "Needs must be." It is then perhaps not at all
ruled by Zeus, if Zeus has been so long anxiously guarding his dominion
against it. It can be understood as the emerging power of being as
such, in which are grounded powers of all beings, even divine. But if
it is so understood, how could it be ever negated? To understand at
all, man must be able to question being. If anything "is" for him
genuinely questionable, then there "is" for him choice. And then
whatever is can be thought of in at least two ways – as chosen or as
choosing to be or not to be. The former thoughts have to descend
toward the origin of whatever is chosen and comes to be; in this
supportless search, they can and often do seemingly specify this
origin as necessity or fate or super-natural beyond. This way of thinking finds nature, the totality of what is to be, needs de-terminate
before or beneath its own being; choice then, if not relinquished, is
removed beyond approach in time. But there remains the other way
to think, where what is may also choose, appropriate, participate in
its being; its ground need not be restrained beyond. Then nature can
be conceived as coming to bear as well as to be born, be-coming,
temporally de-termining itself. It is not due here to ask how this
approach to nature can affect its totality. But this much can be

asserted: it is the latter, choosing way to be that Orestes calls the human being to participate in; it is the former grasp of fate-determined nature that he strives to transcend. He discards as improper Zeus' claims to have given man a nature or to have given him to nature, because he believes that man has to stand up before any nature as alien to appropriate it, and that to rest in any given nature as an excuse for his existence is to expropriate himself. This is what he calls his freedom, and this "means exile," means groping through time "foreign to myself," means existing in his world but "outside nature, against nature, without excuse, beyond remedy, except what remedy I find within myself." With this he negates the super-natural determination of human ways by any deity: "For I, Zeus, am a man, and every man must find out his own way." This is the Orestean choice of choosing to be human.

From the denial of a positive, given nature issues Orestes' message to the men around him, to whom he wants to belong: "The folk of Argos are my folk. I must open their eyes ... They're free." The perspective of freedom is what lights the light in their darkness protested by him. The power of choosing loosens the bonds of their religious impotence. It enables them to protest for, not against their life, to appropriate, not to abnegate their hold in being there, to seek, if not to find, the human "path that is true and fit." Does it, then, deliver them from evil?

The dis-covery of freedom dis-poses men's lives into their own hands; it changes their relation to "natural" facts. But it does not change their factual situation in itself. It opens the possibility of selecting their aims and of resolutely pursuing them; but it does not render men omnipotent. It yields up to them their attitude toward time and death; but it does not transcend human mortality. It gives them responsibility for whatever should be to them good or evil; but it does not make them good. Men's way to move on is not built for them, and therefore they have to build it on the ground made available. Orestes himself longs to dispel the vengeful rule of Zeus over Argos, yet the only means he finds to establish his presence there is to enter Zeus' own world with a deed of blood, of horror, of vengeance. It is up to him to do it or not to do it, at a price; it is up to him to do it with such intentions or others, in his conscience; it is up to him to exploit the deed for selfish gain or for the sake of delivering the Argives from the spirit of vengeance, by removal of himself and the flies. But it is not up to him to alter the factual face of what he does: he kills his own mother and her husband. Again, it is up to men of Argos to acclaim or to attack Orestes; they can find his act good and they can also, not unexpectably, identify it as evil. No men can ever expect a deliverance from evil, if evil like good is founded in their own free judgment of facts.

And there are other shadows to subdue the glow of Orestes' "victory" over nature, to darken the bright, seductive appeal of a free life. "What do I care for happiness?" – exclaims Orestes. Whether he cares for it or not, he can know that in absence of any objective norms of perfection the subjective status of a man's happiness must remain questionably in flow. Guilt, horror, vengeance, provide men's lives with self-diverting, preoccupying contents, even if they revert what is proper in such lives toward negation. Not without reason, Zeus demands: "What could you give them in exchange? Good digestions, the gray monotony of provincial life, and the boredom – ah, the soul-destroying boredom – of long days of mild content." The boredom can be a shaded clue to emptiness: because to be in a situation where nothing is taken for granted and everything is to be done with one's own hands can make freedom feel like an empty suspense in time. So suspended, a human being, finding his all up to him, can also find himself not up to it and, like Electra, clamor and pray for an escape from freedom, for given nature, order, determination, for the full solidity of a thing enslaved. The empty gift of freedom can be "a sad one, of loneliness and shame," unveiling human "lives as they are, foul and futile, a barren boon," aptly passing the threshold of despair. This free fill-claiming void of existing "on the far side of despair" is revealed to Orestes at his time of self-identification, through anxiety surrounding the solitude of conscience in choice: "What a change has come on everything, and, oh, how far away you seem! Until now I felt something warm and living round me, like a friendly presence. That something has just died. What emptiness! What endless emptiness, as far as eye can reach! Night is coming on. The air is getting chilly, isn't it? But what was it – what was it that died just now?'" It was his youth, comfortably relying on universal order, his familiar part of a sheep inmidst of Zeus' fold, his warm and waiting content of a given life – his "nature." On the ruins of all home-like places, of providential belongings, of social safety structures, a man striving for freedom may encounter alone his tragic being.[1]

---

[1] "Freedom is not a reward or a decoration that is celebrated with champagne. Nor yet a gift, a box of dainties designed to make you lick your chops. Oh, no! It's a chore, on the contrary, and a long-distance race, quite solitary and very exhausting. No champagne, no friends raising their glasses as they look at you affectionately.

Such is the properly human way, for which Orestes protests. His protest can be seen as tragic, because it neither breaks the bonds of what prompts it primarily – death, nor can it abolish the factual limitations on what it claims to appropriate – nature. If it does open novel horizons of life for men – for these the protest is sounded – in their depths much may be promised but nothing provided. The protest of Orestes does not accomplish anything, though it paves the way for human accomplishment. But is not this characteristic of all protest explored here, from Prometheus on? Is it not due to the fact that he who protests is "merely" a witness inscribing himself into man's record in the world? If the protest strains toward more, to produce, to effect, to transform – and breaks in this strain – is not this inward break what makes it tragic?

And yet, through this span of human history, it should not be said that nothing has changed since the opening of Promethean time. The spanning lines dis-cover the coming to be of the human being. The stages on the way showed Oedipus standing out from the human kind as a single man responding to his fearful destiny; Hamlet doubtful of his being yet holding to it in his conscience; Faust striving to embrace his earth with all its weal and woe; Stockmann grasping a dangerous devotion to ideas but finding himself in aloneness; Loman staggering under the threat of common loss yet persisting in his cry of warning. The way traversed, winding up and down, can hardly present a steady climbing progress; but it re-presents outlines of a history. Its final stage breaks off toward the future with Orestes starting out from Argos; and the record he carries forward with him corresponds to the past way's culminating point: the end of the Faustian search in the dis-covery of freedom. At that point Faust died; from this point Orestes begins to step forth on the same way, on men's "patient way – towards ourselves." The point has the character of crossroads: in one direction lies the human being's anonymous loss in the universal background of a crowd, in the other direction stretches the ground for daring movement to earn one's own identity from day to day, from demand to deed. from despair to decision – choosing to be; human, mortal and free. If this way is now open and in light, and if neither natural nor super-natural power can cover, close or crush it, then the prophecy of the Titan is fulfilled and his protest is not vain. But the choice at the crossroads is not straight-

Alone in a forbidding room, alone in the prisoner's box before the judges, and alone to decide in face of oneself or in the face of other's judgment ... Don't wait for the Last Judgment. It takes place every day." Camus, *The Fall*.

forward, smooth or simple; the ease of regression, the soothing security of self-surrender, the lures of the lord of flies and negation, are all too humanly present. And the time of men's world is noon.

~

Much has already been suggested on the preceding pages with regard to the Orestean liberation. It remains now to take it up into the central focus and to ask final questions about its import. They should finally clear the ground on which this human liberation is conceivable as TRAGIC.

The first question may seem a matter of name only but involves more. Why should the term "liberation" be used instead of the simpler word "freedom," most readily present in Orestes' own speech? The reason has just been alluded to in the question: because what the word signifies may be neither simple nor readily present but remain in question through time. It is not a state or a stage but a way; it "is" not at all unless being made, earned, chosen. The description of it in terms of the past is insufficient: "Yesterday ... freedom crashed down on me and swept me off my feet." This freedom of yesterday, which struck down Orestes, is extended by him to Electra: "Her suffering comes from within, and only she can rid herself of it. For she is free." And yet, today this freedom is being denied, struck off, rejected within – by Electra herself. Nor is his past freedom available to Orestes, only an illusory recall, when he has to call upon himself to stand against the imposing stature of Zeus challenging him with the might of all nature. The freedom of yesterday has consumed itself overnight into dead remains; if it is to be, it has to be reborn – now. It cannot be "naturally" continued. But how is Orestes free right now, in the present? Is he, as Zeus taunts him, any different from "a prisoner in fetters, a slave nailed to the cross," when he shelters in the temple, "cowering between the legs of a protecting god?" Is he free not to be a murderer, not to be sought as prey by the avenging crowd, not to be surrounded by the swarm of the flies-Furies? Certainly not: in his factual state he is imprisoned. And he accepts being compared to a prisoner, still asserting his freedom. Why? Because that freedom is no more than an opening out of the present, a demand upon himself alone, a choice. As a prisoner may resolve to seek his escape, so may Orestes strive to obliterate his image as a murderer, to subdue the crowd, to drown the vengeful Furies in the depths of his conscience. His freedom then is to be born toward the future, well-coming to himself, overcoming his state, be-coming new. But can such freedom be as a matter of fact predicated of his, or anyone's, tomorrow? Something to come is no thing today, it may be anything yet. Orestes' freedom "is" neither stronger nor weaker than Electra's; and so the previous doubts reappear – his tomorrow like her today may be one of regression, renegation, repentance. No freedom can emerge tomorrow, if its seeds are not sown today. The warning of the dying king resounds seriously: "Beware of the flies, Orestes, beware of the flies. All is not over." All cannot ever be over, while a man exists; and his freedom is ever yet to be earned.

Is freedom nothing, then? It can yield no appearance as anything naturally obtaining, obtained, or obtainable. It cannot be given in the nature of things or men. It is not "there" in the world. But unless the previous visions of the human being up to Orestes are entirely discarded – can any man responsibly hazard that? – it is the making of the human world. Its vision is not fulfilled throughout all the fullness of natural facts, because it is only an emptiness within the human being, demanding to be filled. A demand is not a statement of a state, it is a question of a quest to be. It is not to be found in the past, in the present, or in the future; it is to be searched for through the suspense between them, to be de-veloped anew by each self-determining gesture of resolve. Wherever it "is," it may be questionable for the human being; wherever it "is not," the human being may quest for it. Freedom can not be "in" existence, founding it temporally. appropriating it in daily choice. "He only earns his freedom and his life who takes them every day by storm." A man's freedom is no thing, no fact, no entity; it is "only" a human way of being – liberated.

The next question concerns the setting of this liberating way. What does it move away from or toward? At superficial glance, it could appear clearly that Orestes raises a loud cry of revolt against heaven, aiming at the liberation of man from the super-natural power of Zeus. But taken as the main thread of his striving, this cannot be adequate, if, as previously suggested, Orestes' speech lets be the deity, on its own. "What have I to do with you, or you with me? ... You are God and I am free; each of us is alone." He does not thrust his freedom against Zeus; he maintains it in spite of and in the face of Zeus. God is for him another entity alone; and his freedom, which is not an entity, need not be locked in struggle with God. It cannot be Orestes' end to liberate himself and men from God, since such an end is indeterminable. If God is the ruler of nature, he is more than man's grasp could destroy; if he is nothing, he is less than man could grasp.

Whether a deity has created man, persists as a question; but it is not a question that man has re-created more than one deity to serve. If Zeus is no more than an imaginative reflection from primitive myths, then like primitive dreams and pains and fears of man's imagination, he is there for him on the factual face of nature, and can be disregarded but not destroyed. But Zeus is more than an element of nature: he epitomizes the super-natural Beyond. Orestes certainly will not claim to have removed all Beyond from the human being. On the contrary, his claim is for human striving beyond nature, beyond the present, beyond the near and given: "Beyond the rivers and mountains are an Orestes and an Electra waiting for us, and we must make our patient way towards them." This way beyond is not chosen in Orestes' conscience as a way towards God, whom he disregards. Yet is it straying any further than the regardless apostasy of Faust? Orestes' faith is neither theistic nor atheistic. It is a faith resolved on the being of man, and dissolving the religious bonds in which the intrusion of another, devil or god, constricts that being into nothing. But it is a faith asking for man's Beyond of destiny. In his search of himself, man reaches "the undiscover'd country, from whose bourn no traveller returns." That country may and may not be divine.

From this point can also be viewed liberation with regard to death. No dream of immortality disturbs the vision of Orestes. Framing the situation of his existence, Orestes must let death be. His Argive blood and body not only tells him he is mortal but also turns his deeds toward death; his Athenian free spirit confidently insists upon life while he is living. He removes the overpowering weight of death from the human conscience, but in his thirst for temporal identity he moves eagerly ahead into his destiny, ahead toward his own death. Yet these two, while tied, are not identical: man's only liberation from his death as non-being can be sought in attesting the destiny of his being.

In a parallel sense, there is and is not a possibility of liberation from evil. A Zoroastrian construction of the universe, in which man finds himself on the battlefield between the forces of good and evil, alien both to each other and to him, is here certainly torn down. Man's discovery of freedom re-covers all values appropriate to him as valuable only by him; so owned, good and evil approach each other, intermingled in the human conscience. In their balanced status, however, they become inseparable: if choice is genuine, both alternatives have to be. But then, in free suspense, how can they ever be distinguished? A strange re-turn of the Platonic vision arises here. That which you resolve, project, posit, cannot be your evil; your evil can only rest in what you dissolve, reject, negate. Both must be available, if you do choose; and since your choice is not omnipotent, what you disclaim may claim you back in time. Yet in the valuing void of choice, your pursuit of good is your pursuit of being; and your liberation from evil is only as successful as your overcoming of what, for you, is not to be.

Here is then a clue for the understanding of Orestean liberation, a guide through its confusing aspects of for and against, of approach and escape. It calls the human being to liberate itself from its own nothingness. It assaults whatever diminishes and constricts your striving properly to be in your world. It does not destroy what you take as divine; but it defies what takes you over into self-debasing service. It does not suppress the barriers of your finite being; but it impresses your title to call your time your own. It does not transform your life toward perfection; but it informs your power to build a path. The liberating vision understands that to exist is not to kneel down but to stand out; pro-testing such existence cannot do anything for you, but it can enable you to earn a property in what you do by your choice.

If Orestes' liberation demands a way of over-coming the negative emptiness in human life, then the last question remains: what negation must be under-gone on this way beyond one's own denial? The previous aspects need not be elaborated any more. To become free means not to serve: not to be a servant of any deity, not to subserve life under death, not to enter the service of any values but chosen. But this discloses a further paradoxical risk – of becoming a servant of the chosen way. The cut through the paradox may be resolved for yourself in negating the difference between you and your way in your world, in striving to be, as Orestes does: "Neither slave nor master. I am my freedom." This resolution of yours, however, is not accessible to anyone but yourself. Your freedom can never be established in that world on which you have a hold but in which you are thrown together with others. They may judge you as Orestes as no more than a condemned sinner, an instrument of vengeance, a destroyer of life, a "determined" criminal. Their presence is more immediate with you than that of a God or of death; and they may deny you in what you claim. But to deny their presence in their judgment is to deny their freedom – can you do that? Orestes does not; he wants to belong to them, he wants men's world around him as "our" free world. Thus he has to undergo this breach of negation between belonging to himself in his freedom and belonging to others sharing in his human being.

– 223 –

The predicament of Stockmann lies on his way. His promise of liberating progress must aim at the demise of the present life of the crowd;
his faith in the human being must defy the human kind of nature; he
must call for men against men, alone. Stronger than Stockmann, he
subdues his "subjects" to give them a gift that cannot be given: their
freedom. Then he "vanishes forever" – but men stay behind. While
they "owe" their freedom to his liberating protest, the destiny of his
freedom is shared in their hands. They may resent his impudent light
strength; they may "naturally" recoil from his violence against their
order; they may find themselves irremediably bound in their ad-
diction to service. And then they will "determine" him as an alien
intruder, his message as impious and improper for them. They will
refuse to respond to this responsibility which he has passed to them.
His vision of the human world sharing in freedom will seem like an
illusion; his call will fade away with time, like the warning cry of
Willy Loman; the burden of resolution he undergoes for their sake
will go under, like a burning meteor in the cold waters of the human
sea. His protest for them will have been tragic in vain.

But who are really "they?" The ancient, primitive Argives? You
can hardly believe that, unless the world of Orestes has been displayed
for you as no more than a spectacle. No – my reader – "they" in this
question are you and I. It is your "real," present world that Orestes
addresses from his time which you may find remote or very close:
that – is up to you. Perhaps, however, you will acknowledge the
relevance of this last question here. In this staggering world of the
twentieth century, in which evil is familiarly shrugged off, from which
a super-natural God has receded, which deems itself conqueringly
immortal – is it not here, in this humanized world that the destiny of
freedom may belong? Here, in your ears sound the words of Orestes,
and you have the privilege of mis-hearing and mis-understanding him.
For your existence here you, as a man, have the last judgment, and
you can reject the Orestean liberation as pointless, irrational, offensive.
That will be the final negation of Orestes' tragic being: if you no longer
see it as tragic.

Why is the question of tragedy appropriate now, at this time?
Precisely because man has been for centuries struggling to liberate
himself from God, from fears of death, from meta-physical evil, and
now has discovered the dubious service of his own being or nothingness. He finds no place to dwell but to displace, no human sharing but
competing, no time to live but to kill time, no destiny but death.
Continuation of man's existence on earth is not just factually in doubt

for this age. The self-made light is apt to surrender to darkness; the insuppressible striving which humanized the world turns to serve dehumanizing it; a last noon can unnoticeably cede to the dawnless night of self-destruction, loss and despair. At this time it is proper to heed a call from "the far side of despair," even though it sounds in self-questioning protest, even though it demands the power to face tragic existence – standing up, even though all it promises is being and choosing to be human:

"It is not night; a new day is dawning. We are free ... All must begin anew."

CHAPTER IX

The Tragic Protest

The lights have burned down. The characters have passed. The stories have been enacted on record. Does the history moving through such characters leave a light upon the tragic dimensions of the human being? Or does one have to leave the men tragically involved in their individuality, with a consenting but constrained silence? Between these alternatives is formed what now can be said on the pages to follow.

This chapter is by far the most difficult for its writer, since it demands the gathering of disparate threads into a firmer fabric clothing some questionable and elusive shapes of thought. And for the same reason it must remain the most difficult for its reader. However, I shall endeavor to stage gradually the descent into depth of difficulties, through the sections to follow; each of these is to portray some level of the concluding insights, though none, not even the last one, need be regarded as terminal. Thus whoever you are, my reader, you are entirely free to conclude this exploration of tragic being at whatever stage you decide to be adequate for yourself. For the author, the exploration will be conclusively adequate only if its final word passes into further reflection.

∿

What may be expected at the goal of this imaginative journey? What is its reach of accomplishment? Perhaps its stations were properly illumined, perhaps the passage was view-provoking, perhaps the passed lights are sufficient unto themselves, even if the end hides in darkness. But the journey has been undertaken not only to move but to move somewhere; and quite legitimately the question may be pressed: what fund of learning has been gained in regard to the tragic protest? In one sense it is true that what has been learned here tells how some men – Shakespeare, Aeschylus, Ibsen – have found what is tragic, and how they have recorded their witness of this in words. Does it mean, though, that the results are simply biographical, and even dubiously so, since they render no more than an image of feelings? Yes and no. If you consider yourself absolved from such involvements in existence, if this image of feelings has no more than flashed on some receiving screen of your awareness, then that is all the acknowledgment these tragic illustrations can ever provide for you. But it need not be all. What other men have felt need not be regarded as stored forever in the privacy of their minds' camera obscura. Despite the popularity of opposite views, feeling is not primarily a mode of seclusion but of reaching toward and orienting oneself in the large world felt in its abundance of textures and flavors. Whether there is any unfeeling knowledge of anything in this world, may be doubted; what is more pertinent here, however, is that there are no unknowing feelings. This means that in all feeling there is available some kind of knowledge. A neglected kind that requires a special effort of expression in words to penetrate toward other men in the world; this is not easy and can often fail. But if it is admissible to your mind and if you can visualize it as the aim of poetic communication, then you are open to the claim that such knowledge has been gained in the preceding approaches to tragic existence. How can this "knowledge" be elucidated, though? Is it not an abuse of the term to apply it to what may be only one's self-consciousness of feeling locked within bounds of one's own existence, and as self-made or self-making – barring possession by any other self?

Not to be expected in the results of this exploration is any scientifically categorized formulation providing the definitive answer about tragedy. At the outset already all pretense to found a "science of the tragic" has been disclaimed. To those who cannot make themselves believe that there are human questions of knowledge which are not scientifically accessible, the present discourse would and should remain meaningless. To put it more strongly: it would be a tragic error to manipulate such questions in scientific terms. Whoever conceives himself as a scientist could well laugh at such an attempt; although his laughter might eventually resound against him. What has been introduced in the preceding chapters? Clearly nothing capable of serving for an inductive generalization. An examination of seven isolated "cases" can be dismissed as both an arbitrary and a ridiculously small sample. Further, the reaches of this examination are not given as any kind of verifiable data. On the contrary, instead of working toward data which could be publicly interchangeable and susceptible of verification by anyone, some sort of unique intimacy has been urged. And also, the ostensible purpose in examining these cases has been not the collecting of facts, events, or even unequivocal statements, but rather the appreciation of single subjects' ways of holding some facts, of appropriating events to happen, of evolving visions questionable in meaning. What procedure could be less scientific, less objective, less capable of confirmation and assessment by significant quantity?

The scientist who could say all this would be perfectly sanctioned in saying it on the ground of the scientific spirit. Yet it can be and has already been maintained that the human being is not identifiable in the scientific spirit; that the manipulation of it in interchangeable cases serves only the continuity of anonymous crowds; that the tendency toward impersonal quantification accounts for loss of personal character in life; that the "positive" negation of anything beyond the given nature of events is a tragically self-forgetful feature of the present time. Some other position then, some other aim, some other ground must be attained if this exploration is to conclude with meaning; and if it learns something, some other sense of knowledge. What could it be?

Much depends on how modernly preconceived are the criteria for the term "knowledge." If the title to this word is established by securing impersonal, quantitative, unequivocal data, then this exploration gains no such title. But someone demanding such criteria might well consider how much of what used to be "known" he has to exclude. To put it simply: did men have no knowledge before Descartes, Galileo, Bacon, or for that matter before Aristotle, Democritus, Pythagoras? Because if they did, then knowledge is not a monopoly product of a rationally determined science but rather an irrevocable privilege or burden of the human being as such. Plain, plebeian, primitive individuals, as long as they are human, "primitively" know at least this: that they are there, for a time, and not alone but in a world. What their existence means, what destinies their time conceals, what contents their world provides, of all that they may have no knowledge; yet irrepressibly their imagination inclines them to grasp for it. So they reach to know suffering, ambition, friendship; and so they come to know what illness means, without studying medicine, in their own or their intimates' closely moving afflictions; and so they claim and cherish the acquaintance with beauty, while remaining aesthetically illiterate; and so they assume and appreciate even awareness of greatness, if their time gives them but a sample of it in a man or event. Thus "primitively" learning to know, I hazard to suggest, have been also you and I. Unless you "knew" by concrete witness in your own existence what it is to be ill, to have friends, to encounter beauty, how could you ever learn to recognize these by a learned description? To this order of knowing, undetermined yet undeniable, self-questioning hence self-involving, perhaps scientifically inadequate but imaginatively intimate, this exploration would contribute some light on what it means for the human being to be tragic.

On this way of knowing, the light-forming images of tragic feeling afford you the only possible access to what is tragic, unless you already know it on your own. But even if you do, as many may, this intimate knowledge of yours is likely to be mute. Because to express outwardly what you inwardly own, to abstract into terms what is primitively concrete, to speak of feeling that gathers in silence, is the unique distinction and demand of poets. The poets therefore were asked to speak here, to find protesting words in tragic predicaments they have known. And you were asked to listen to those words in friendly consent, as if sitting at the bedside of someone close to you: to learn about that "illness" which is called tragedy, to shape an image of it for your own existence. If this attempt at intimacy succeeded, then you have come to know the tragic, through less inflexible pattern but more indelible appropriation than what you ever know through science. Unless the enterprise of poets is forever doomed to failure, it endows you with imaginative knowledge, less concealingly your own than that of direct acquaintance but more outspokenly belonging than that of indirect description.

My contribution in regard to your encounter with the tragic poets has been throughout the mise-en-scène: intimating the world's frame in which such words are spoken, such feelings tied, such acts imposed; inviting your imagination to immerse itself in deeper dimensions of vision, character, choice, constituting those individuals existent here in your scope; introducing the order of speech so as to elicit the thrust of its protest, so as to stress its hold on men's tragic being. At no time has it been my intention to interpose myself between you and Oedipus or Loman or Faust; if what I suggested they say to you sounded in any way improper, perhaps your grasp of their ethos was closer than mine. Yet I have asked you to take part in this imaginative journey for my purpose; in my arrangement you have learned what now you know about tragic protest. Perhaps you do not want to dis-cover any further reflections of what is involved in KNOWLEDGE so acquired – if so, farewell; but if you do, bear with me.

~

First of all, it is advisable to reflect upon the sense of such search for the tragic in individuals, its right, its reason, its result. Might it not be objected that such an approach is too selective, that it does not allow for consideration of tragedies of nations or epochs, that it paves the way for indiscriminate hero-worship and risks losing itself in the subjective quicksand of the merely pathetic? These objections must certainly not be disregarded; but the proper mode of dealing with them will become clearer when some rays of light from the preceding illustrations are made to shine in focus.

The individual approach to tragic heroes not only harmonizes with but is necessitated by the striving for an imaginatively intimate knowledge of tragic being. Whether this statement seems too easily plausible or prejudicially implausible, quite a lot depends on looking closer into what it says. It connects with my introductory statement that the aim of my exploration is directed not to the aesthetic surface of what is composed as tragedy, not to the public appearance of tragic events, but toward the underlying roots of what is tragic. What does that mean? An illustration might help, of ordinarily familiar persistence. When you genuinely desire to know another human being, you can not rest with the common currency of verbal constructions – "I love you, I want to be with you always, for you I could do any-thing"; nor are you satisfied with the ambiguous pattern of acts and gestures – he or she meets you every second day, is exuberant or pensive in your company, accomodates your wishes or is critical of your conduct. You realize that the same words and movements do not have the same weight in every being, that talk of "love" or "doing anything" can result in just conversation or in a commitment, that quantity of time spent together can be just bearable or blissful, that demure or dominating behavior can arise from a despising as well as from a devoted attitude. Throughout, you long for a grasp of meaning beneath surface appearances, for knowledge of what this human being is in itself. Even if the reaching for such knowledge could be de-spondently understood as interminable, nothing less is the goal of intimacy: the grasp of being, not of seeming, acting, wording. Such, too, is the conductive tendency of this exploration.

Of course, it is true that the objective under discussion is that of tragic being – not essentially identical with individual tragic beings. But within the finite horizons of the human mind – unlike those of the Faustian Lord – a grasp of being involves a limitation of scope. No man can claim to know a nation intimately, as he knows a friend; although his friends may serve him as models for his ideas of nations. When an imaginatively concrete grasp of being is striven for, the approach must be from and to the human being, and any genuine intimacy in this approach must endeavor to penetrate through the mask of words and acts, through the common layer of what is publicly shared, in search of that which is proper and unique. In the preceding encounters with tragic heroes this necessity was reflected throughout.

A proper VISION of existence was assumed in each individual: a way of his own to see, project, imagine, schematize, understand the truth of his being in the world. It is clear that to shape and to express this vision he must make use of linguistically common counters or categories; but it is his being that responds in his use of them. For instance, it can be truly and vacuously said that the concept of ambition may be exemplified in Oedipus, Hamlet, Faust, Stockmann, Orestes. Yet could anyone familiar with these men suggest that the term "ambition" has for them the same weight and worth – apart from the content of what they are ambitious for? Oedipus' desperate hold in his royal refuge, Hamlet's isolation in his time out of joint, Faust's embrace of humanity with all its weal and woe, Stockmann's misanthropic purification of his town, Orestes' longing to fill the void within – do these constitute the common meaning of human ambition? Or, just to cite some other examples, is there more community or contrast in the significance of "love" for Loman and for Faust, in the devotion to an "idea" shown by Stockmann and by Orestes, in the revolt against "temporality" of Prometheus and of Hamlet? Certainly these terms cannot be taken as commonly interchangeable among the world visions of individual characters. On the other hand, one cannot maintain that there is no common core of sense among them; because then any discourse correlating them would be to no purpose, if every word should cameleon-like change its sense entirely from one usage to another. An all-human matrix of speech has to serve the articulation of disparate visions, to become humanly meaningful. But how to draw from this matrix, how to bend and stylize it, how to depart from it even, these questions pertain to varied living styles of each genuinely unique human self. Of greater importance even is this: the more indifferent, neutral, non-challenging a vast number of words may be, the more stereotyped remains their usage; while on the contrary, those words which are for an individual more significant because in them he wants to sign his own ethos, those are the ones in which a common universal meaning must not be expected. There need be no variations in meaning, and no disputes about them, with regard to uniform terms of mathematics or logic; but there are and must be such variations with regard to such terms as "love," "conscience," "fear," "freedom." In these, the challenging import for individuals amounts to their self-involvement, self-shaping, self-interpretation. For that reason, an attempt at intimate grasp of being of such individuals must enter into their self-expressing vision and weigh their words not for what they mean – but for what they mean in their speech.

Parallel to this is the necessity to appreciate CHARACTER, not in reference to uniform descriptions of objective behavior, which are at best outward and unsafe clues, but in consenting approach to what such behavior may issue from and what it may yield to the agent. Behaviorally speaking, there is likeness between the acts of Hamlet and Orestes, both avenging the murderous deaths of their fathers, or between those of Faust and Loman, both preparing a self-willed termination of their lives, or between Prometheus and Stockmann, both refusing to bow to the present order of their world. Yet how far from a proper understanding of these men would be someone who systematically pigeonholed their characters under such labels as: "vindictive," "suicidal," "subversive!" The understanding absent in such objectively legitimate procedure may only be attainable from a deeper awareness of what human character is. Character is not the total outcome of what a man does in his activities; rather, it is the sense in what he appropriates by his acting. "One and the same" natural and social world gives and obtains a unique proper impress in each individual's being; it is his own impress of the world into which he exists. Vengeance, suicide, rebellion may be thrust upon a man, decisively evolved by another, occur incidentally to one, absorb someone else's whole energy, claim proud justification in this man, regret and hesitancy in that one; and such or other modes of holding any of one's actions are as unlimited as human imagination can carry them. Again, therefore, it must be stressed: to know what a man is in his existence, it will never suffice to observe what he does and compare it with what others do, seemingly alike with him.

More necessary even is such tentative, not objectively obvious approach with regard to what in the human being is darker, deeper, yet more determinant than either vision or character: CHOICE. Neither language nor behavior can there provide safe and sufficient evidence. On the contrary, that may obscure sympathetic access, as when from their words and acts, Oedipus is "explained" as fate-driven, or Loman "accounted for" as a determinate product of certain social forces. Such ex-planations never reach the tragic plane of existence, such accounts dis-count what in the human life is unlike the forced rolling of a stone. If on the other hand the guiding insight is the one adopted here: that choice underlies everything in being and man responds to choice in that awareness of being which is his own – then it should be seen that to know man as himself it is required to respect his choice of being, proper to him and possibly to none other. That this is the hardest and most groping stage of the exploring way, does not make it any less indispensable. In this stage, if not before, must fall away the outer considerations of aesthetic surface, dramatic structure, publicly interchangeable events, to leave in question only the essential search for what determines the human being as tragic. The common categories and criteria, indispensable in verbal expressing of vision, still legitimate in the understanding of character from acts, become quite irrelevant at this level. Choice is not a category, nor is it classi-fiable in common categories or concepts. Choice is concretely unique, in the chooser as in the chosen: to be this, to become – to do – to transform this as mine – as in being for me, concerning me rather than anyone since no one else can be, or choose for, myself; such is the half-articulate realization of choice in a human awareness. General considerations, kinds of things, similarities of circumstance, these may be of relevance for deliberation but not a substitute for choice. Consequently, appreciation of choice must be not conceptualized but lived; and appreciation of choice in others can be accessible only to an imaginative grasp of them as others, of how they are in their individual being.

This is then the compelling right and reason for the adopted mode of exploration: that for a human being tragedy is always his tragedy, submerged within whatever makes him be himself, below the outer shell of his words and deeds which are not uniquely his but attribu-table to similar others. Thus tragedy cannot be shared nor transferred from one man to another, like an office or a set of clothes; although this does not mean that men around him may not be sucked into the whirl of his tragedy, to feel with and for him. Because the word "tragedy" has a foundation in being, not just in verbalizing, appearance, activity; and tragic ethos must be explored in that hold on being which envelops any man in his own existence. To avoid abstraction, knowledge of tragic being can gain access only through concrete tragic beings.

The result of this way of approaching tragedy is partly negative, as already observed; it does not and never will yield a scientific formulation, easily managed for determinate objects; it gives only unsystematized. "guessing" applications. And this result is in agreement with the loose and variable linguistic usage of the word "tragedy"; only perhaps now the vagaries of usage can be explained. There are possibilities of very liberal against very sparing applications of the term: for some people any setback or sad feeling deserves to be called "tragic," while others may find no justification for that term in seemingly more serious experiences. In line with what has been asserted on these pages such vague fluctuations are to be expected. Because, to be ultimately strict, to know when and how a man's existence becomes tragic, you have to be that man; failing this, you must have intimately consenting access to him. But in the majority of cases, you have no intimacy, hence no knowledge, and what remains is imaginative guesswork. Outward appearances, incidental expressions and actions do not suffice to determine presence or absence of tragedy: a genuinely tragic character may appear to you silent and immobile, while another's turbulence of cries and motions may be a contemptible fraud. Amongst witnesses, then, some warm sympathy can lead to exaggerated frequency of "tragedies," while some stern notion of justice can forbid such squandering of words. The uncertainty of what, among men, is or is not tragic corresponds to the indefinite bounds of their knowledge of one another. Yet in this predicament it is not scientific knowledge that can offer help but only imagination.

This reference to fluctuating, chaotic scope of use of the word "tragic" is not intended to rest in flux and chaos. It describes undeniable events; but it must also point toward the source from which such events eventuate. Does it now mean that anything anywhere can be called "tragic" with equal legitimacy? It does not; otherwise surely this whole enquiry would be completely pointless. Its negative result is, on the contrary, pointed to a much more questionable positive claim to be pursued: that any understanding of tragedy, limited to the consideration of events, experiences, entities in human existence must remain inconclusive.

All the approaches to individual human subjects through the several

chapters were not meant to establish any kind of triumph of subjectivism over objectivism. The preceding remarks should have made clear
how an "objective" examination would miss the point tragically, if it
sought to determine tragedy in human objects or in the objects of
their objective speech and behavior: because the objectivity of such
objects always depends upon the subjectivity of the subjects for whom
they come into question. But after this conclusion something harder,
more paradoxical, still has to be attempted: a project of objectifying
such subjectivity. If this succeeds, then not chaotic whimsy but knowledge may be claimed for the result. And yet this project can rely
"only" upon the aid of IMAGINATION. At the outset already a suggestion has been made, provisionally, that the "tragic" may be only a
mold of human imagination, with some reserve regarding the strength
of "only." Now this suggestion can and should be returned to. The
term "only" must now be read not in a deprecatory but in an eliminative sense. If it is a matter of going beyond the objective sphere of
events, experiences, entities, what else but imagination could serve as
guideline? Imagination, as Kant conceived it, provides the roots of
both perceiving and understanding; imagination must be presupposed
as responsible for all science, religion, poetry; imagination spreads out
the horizon on which any entities are to appear. What is the horizon?
It is the horizon of being.

The reliance upon imagination must disregard the widespread prejudice for which it is equivalent to fancy. Those who recognize a primitive insight in Pascal's: "The heart has its own reasons beyond the
knowledge of reason" may perhaps appreciate an equally primitive
claim: imagination has its own order beyond the factual orders of
objects. To proceed by aid of imagination, while necessitating an
imaginative subject, does not throw the gates open to a flux of
subjectivism in which everything flows. To be sure, imagination
recognizes no boundaries between reality and appearance, between
facts and fictions. But this need not make imagination disorderly,
arbitrary or capricious. The order to determine the directions and
dimensions of a human subject's imagination differs from irrelevant
fancy in that it can be objectified both "outwardly" – what properly
belongs to the imagination of this subject, and "inwardly" – how the
imaginative subject is himself subject to being. Both of these ordering
lines have to be understood as temporal. To illustrate these undoubted-
ly difficult projections: thinking of Willy Loman as a "prince" is not
imaginative but fanciful, both because what he can mean to others is
due precisely to his "unprincely" ethos, and because the whole being

of "principalities" is quite removed from the milieu of his historical existence. Or again, it is not a legitimate exercise of imagination to "identify" oneself with Prometheus, both because the scope of the Titan's mind in his awareness of pain or pity is other than human, and because the being proper to a man's imagination is never immortal. By contrast, imagination sets no bar against a man's dispositions to fear one's own future self with Oedipus, to strive on behalf of all men with Faust, to yield oneself to the splendor of an abstract idea with Stockmann. Yet these are, and indeed must remain, only general hints, when phrased with regard to mankind at large. How close you can yourself come to know and feel some tragic ethos, that is precisely what cannot be predicted, because it eventuates from who you are, you, a unique subject, and how you are in your temporal being. It can be said that there is an order of man's imagination but not what that order is for a man.

Another way of suggesting this imaginative order, as it affects tragic being, consists in viewing imagination as the reach toward POSSIBILITY. This accords well with its indifference toward distinctions of reality against fiction, and also with the undeniable wealth of imagination in youth compared with its scarcity in old age of men, for whom little remains possible. But it must be well noted that possibility is not here understood in the sterile "logical" sense, where it is synonymous with abstract absence of self-contradiction. When it is said that imagination reaches toward possible being, and it is always a concrete subject's imagination, then what it has to encompass is being possible for that subject. The lack of such reference accounts for the vacuity of unowned hence improper "logical" possibilities. On the other hand, to speak of "real" possibilities or of possibilities of "reality" seems to carry the flavor of either misunderstanding or begging the question. Perhaps for the moment it might suffice to suggest that possibility is not a description or a mode of classifying entities, to distinguish them from real ones or from those which are forbidden by the law of contradiction. Now there "are" no entities other than those which "really" are there; and some of these might not be free from self-contradictions, either. What else can be said, then? That possibility is relevant only to the horizon of being on which entities emerge, and that such a horizon is available to every human awareness, But this, of course, is quite obscure. How does a human being reach toward what is possible? What does "possible" mean?

Looking toward the origins of the word in Latin one faces "posse, potest, potestas," and this points to potency, power, capacity, competence. The same affinity obtains in the French word "pouvoir." But the German "möglich" points in a different direction, through "mögen" and "mag sein," the English "maybe"; here the connection is almost with "likeable," the possible signifying that which likes to be or lets itself be like-ly. And still another strand of associations arises, if one links the equivalence of "maybe" with "perhaps"; what is possible, can be, is that which maybe is, which is perhaps to be, which can happen through "hap" or "mishap" and so is due to fortune or misfortune. "Perhaps," in Italian "forse," derives from the same root as "fortune," and that is the Latin "fors" – one's lot, allotted in a proper destiny. Thus these different strands of verbal origins in Western thought yield a schema of the possible as what is within some power, what is likeable or like-ly, what is allotted to hap-pen properly. Is this schematic derivation self-coherent? There is no reason to deny it, provided that possibility is understood as possible being for a subject. Then a certain order arises from these etymological criteria, the order to which imagination is devoted. Then what is available as possible in being for you means "externally" who you may become, what you may have power or competence to encounter, to cope with, to acquire, and "internally" how you may become that, what within your ethos may be like-ly, adaptable, concrescent in growth of time. Both of these "possibilizing" directions obtain through the proper temporality allotted in the hap-pening or mishap-pening of your existence – your finite destiny in being. The boundaries of this order – objective in that they are neither chaotic nor fanciful – only your imagination explores. Does it yield knowledge? It does, if the ancient maxim: "Know yourself!" has sense. Because this is the primitive order of knowing yourself, your possible being.

It is in this way and in no other that you have come or can come to know your own affinity with the tragic being of man. This is what the tragic figures in the preceding chapters have been acquainting you with, poetically. If their presentation here has been proper, if it has illumined in sufficient intimacy how their being is tragic, then the self-knowing task can be left to your imagination. It means reaching in your self-awareness toward such questions: What of this may be mine? Is Hamlet's conscience like-ly for me? Would I struggle against the power of negation like Faust? Might the cost of liberating my identity be as high as for Orestes? Or, perhaps the chosen hap-pening of my existence is already so turned toward self-loss that I cannot seriously heed the warning cry of Willy Loman? And – how do I view the time of my possibility, my future, am I ready to find my own lot even as Oedipus did? Needless to say, these are only examples which could be multiplied indefinitely, on the basis of just the seven tragic illustrations examined; and these in turn never claimed to be in any sense exhaustive. Further reaches of what is involved in the tragic being of these seven men have yet to be explored. But I believe that the above explanations already do provide an answer to those who wonder why the "subjective" access is considered appropriate in an attempt to gain knowledge of tragedy and what kind of possible "objective" knowledge is here indicated. A subject's approaches to the tragic are variable yet objectively ordered, as are the outlines of visibility from a far-sighted to a short-sighted viewer; only the differences are more self-involving and not susceptible to an easy adjustment by means of uniformalizing spectacles.

From these elucidations it is possible to turn to the earlier mentioned objections against this "subjective" treatment of tragedy. Three such easily raised objections were alluded to: that in the selective approaches to individual subjects no room is provided for considering tragedies involving more than single individuals; that such treatment is onesided in encouraging immature romancing of hero-worship; that in its regard for private feeling and disregard of public fact it is apt to confuse the tragic with the pathetic. An attempt must be made to answer such understandable criticisms.

Perhaps the simplest answer can be offered to the last of these objections. To consider the relation of the tragic to the pathetic it may be helpful to recall the longer introductory discussion of the difference between the tragic and the dramatic. The essential point, equally pertinent here, is how in affirming that a certain story or action is dramatic or is tragic, the claim and weight of the word "is" does not remain the same. That which "is" dramatic may be legitimately so found due to the formal configuration of events; but such a criterion is insufficient for calling something tragic. The general problem, only touched upon here, emerges from the rich variability of ways, scopes and senses in which some A is truly B, particularly when such A is a human being. On these pages it has been claimed that when a human existence is truly tragic, this is not ever entirely due to entities, events, experience involved in that existence; this claim will be supported further. And consequently it has been granted that one man's knowledge of another's tragedy cannot be scientifically objective or rationally certain, but has to rest in an imaginative grasp of the other's being. The role of feeling then is undeniable; and to this extent the awareness of what is pathetic may be parallel. Yet there is a clear difference. Is it not a fact that you would never describe yourself as pathetic, while you could very well so describe another person? This may be partly due to a somewhat disparaging connotation of the word: someone or something is merely pathetic, wretchedly, piteously, almost contemptibly pathetic; your selfloving pride could not admit that of yourself. But this disclaiming connotation is the result rather than the source of the word's meaning. What produces it is the admission of distance, of separation, of unlikeness between you and the one you find pathetic. Again, people thrown together into some sorrow or struggle would not experience themselves as pathetic; but an outside observer could find them so. What sounds in the word "pathetic" is the felt otherness of the other being, admitting incidental contrasts rather than essential community, even though it is open to compassion. The lot of animals of other species is sometimes found pathetic – not tragic. And so the distance between you and the pathetic human may cause you, perhaps wishfully, to dis-claim his unenviable lot as almost beyond your human kind: you never could change places with him. This does not point to selfishness; an accomplished egoist would be of all people least qualified to find anything pathetic. Those susceptible to it reach out toward the pathetic in feeling – indeed, in no other way, as the source of the word "pathos" indicates – but it is an unterminable, dis-satisfied, goal-less feeling. Consent in a human community is lacking; and hence, as will be observed later, there is no participation in protest. To summarize: when you find that something "is" pathetic, its being touches you more inwardly than when you say something "is" dramatic; and yet it fails to envelop you in its possibility as tragic being does – that always may be yours. Mere pathos provokes no likely power in man. This absence of the human community in the pathetic withholds from it such imaginative significance as the tragic yields for understanding the existence of man as such; therefore also the question of "knowledge" of pathos is of a different order than that of knowing tragedy.

The second objection arises from the attention devoted here to the "tragic hero" and thus raises the problem of heroes and heroic life. Yet this attention need not be connected with any hero-worship, because it is not really addressed to the heroic element at all. The import of this remark may be brought into focus, if I first express my basic disagreement with Nietzsche's phrase: "Around the hero everything turns into tragedy." This phrase may bear truth only when applied to the tragic hero – and he is not identical with the hero as such. The heroic life proper is not tragic. What is "heroic?" The word, from its mythical origins, carries indubitably the sense of some distinction; and in such sense its scope can spread to include tragic heroes. Yet that is only a spread, not an identity of source. Originally, the hero is distinguished as a demi-god, as elected and elevated by the divine, as transcending in his life the ordinary limitations of the human, and thus worthy of worship and emulation. The heroic being signifies fullness of accomplishment. It is with this, often amoral, significance that heroes have acquired their prominence in humanity's historical thought, through ancient myths and sagas, through classical tales of formative conquest, through dreamy legends of mediaeval striving: Heracles, Aeneas and Siegfried, Alexander, Caesar and Charlemagne, Arthur, Roland and Parcival. Around such heroes nothing need turn into tragedy. The only quasi-tragic feature of their real or fictitious life would be their death; but that only ties their bond with the worshipful humanity, emphasizing possible greatness in mortality – and the mythical imagination often tries to circumnavigate this deadly rock through its attempts at apotheosis, immortalizing its heroes. The following of heroes, whether naively starry-eyed or ambitiously meditated, never intends to follow them into tragic existence, only into conquering the glorious wholeness of the almost-gods. How is it, then, that there are, nevertheless, unforgotten and challenging tragic heroes? They do abound through all those older sources of inspiration, whatever their status in man's newer history: against a Heracles rises an Orpheus, great Caesar faces his Brutus, triumphant Parcival has a strong rival in death-seeking Tristan. As already suggested, the tragic heroes also dwell in human memory through their distinction. Only this distinction is toto coelo different from that just elaborated; it is almost antithetical. There is in the tragic hero no fullness of accomplishment, no glorious semi-divinity, consequently also no worth for emulation. The tragic hero need have no followers. The aura around him, turning all into tragedy, is a danger zone in which his voice of protest sounds warning men that what is his may be theirs too. His appeal is a challenge and a provocation – but not an allurement. He speaks of such deeper solitude, such unhealing breach, such questionable destiny, as can never belong to the wholeness of a conquering hero. Whence, then, derives his hold on the human imagination? To put it simply, from the questioning ambivalence of the human being, interested alike in distinctive success and distinctive failure, capable of fascination by both wholesome grace and horrifying deformity, torn in pursuit of destiny between fulfillment and annihilation: all this emerges as like-ly in hap or mishap for the human existent. The power of possibility extends his imagination toward being and nothing. Thus the human tragic hero is not properly a hero who somehow encounters tragedy – he is a tragic being and thereby becomes a hero for the imagination. His heroic title is given in metaphorical courtesy. Previously the sense of the pathetic was suggested to contain some distance, unreached separation, almost recoil; now in the contrary sense the properly heroic can be said to contain some devotion, incipient imitation and following. And that which is tragic provokes neither recoil nor imitation, neither contempt nor worship, it need neither alienate nor invite. It remains there through history as possible, not in the indifference of logical possibility, though, but as possibly your own. Your attitude to it can consequently be identified as that primary feeling Descartes called "admiration," taking hold of your imagination without either attraction or repulsion, yet taking hold of you in being there. But this is very different from emulation. Such admiration and consenting pursuit of humanly possible tragic being should have no connection in anyone's mind with the individual vagaries and onesided excesses of hero worship.

The last kind of criticism, visualized earlier, concerns not the connections and effects but the scope itself of the individual understanding of tragedy. No doubt it can invoke in its support various available modes of speech in which one may say that a certain era of humanity is tragic, that tragedy obtains in the destinies of a family, a class or a whole people. If the tenor of this exploration is accepted as proper, if indeed that which is tragic involves mainly or wholly the individual human being, then what becomes of those modes of speech? Are they ruled out as illegitimate – and if so, with what justification? Is it not rather the case that the "subjective" approach is illegitimately narrow and cannot do justice to the meaning of tragedy? The difficulty is genuine and rests deeper than the arbitrary use of words. To deal with it, I must partly anticipate reflections still to follow, and my answer may not sound quite plausible until later.

If you conceive for the moment that tragedy is "like" an illness, an analogy results for further understanding. Because while you may rightly wish to say that a family or a whole town is in the grip of some illness, you will probably grant that their being so depends on the illness of individual members, that diagnosis and treatment must start with single persons to cope with the super-personal phenomenon. It is not at all illegitimate to think of illness without interest in individuals – sociologists, health officers, community planners have to think of it in that way – yet such thinking can never rest in its terms and must tie in with the direct encounter with illness, present between a physician and a patient. There is nothing arbitrary about this single direction for use of such a concept as illness: a community can be ill only if its citizens are ill – while it is plainly false that individuals can be ill only if their community is ill. What is thus said must reflect knowledge of that feature of the human world, called "illness"; the feature originates individually and its knowledge is of a different, more tenuous and abstracted order in going beyond individual persons. It is not claimed here that all features of human life have the same origins and directions. Plato, for instance, may be right in thinking of a reciprocity in the concept of justice: a perfectly just man must live in a just society and a perfectly just society must be composed of just men. Or again, there are various notions important for contemporary researches, which seem to reflect human features originating socially: equalizing or accumulation of wealth, technological advancement or backwardness; these can only be known in a larger, often statistical frame, and they are directed toward individual citizens only in a secondary order. Correspondingly, tenuous results would obtain for them in strictly individual approaches.

What is in question, then, is the reason why tragedy should be "likened" to an illness rather than to one of these other interhuman features. This reason, while not yet fully elaborated, has already been indicated more than once. It has been stressed that the tragic is not determinable through public experiences and events; that it involves a man in what he is and not just in what he says and does in relation to many others; that its proper knowledge emerges either in one's own existence or through an intimacy in being of the same order: from one whole self to another. Such knowledge, like the knowledge of friendship or of beauty, cannot be conceived as socially originated. Of essence is the shared being of an equal order, that can envelop the same possibilities and thus provoke the imagination. To illustrate this, rather fancifully: a nation might perhaps have some feeling for another nation's tragedy, since they are equal in being. What this could mean, is of course unclear, because you or I cannot really speak on behalf of nations. But you or I, being men, can feel and know the tragic being of other men in direct encounter. If such knowledge exerts your imagination from how an Oedipus or a Loman exists toward how you may exist, then it cannot originate from superpersonal sources. Rather, the colloquial application of the word "tragic" to times or peoples is in a liquid language the result of a vague, guessing extension of usage. As mentioned earlier, depending on your temperamental inclinations you may tend to speak of a man or his story as tragic without really knowing him; in a similar way, you may hazard the name of tragedy in reference to a historical period in the life of some human community, in particular if you have a closer awareness of t.agic existence in some of its members. There is nothing on these pages to rule out such modes of speech, since what is undertaken here is not a reform of words but an exploration of what underlies them. If the exploration is proper, then it remains true that to speak of tragedy apart from the tragic human being has only secondary sense, not ever substantiated in knowledge.

These are my initial comments on doubts an difficulties arising more or less immediately from the scope of the preceding chapters. I have attempted to summarize how and why I hope some gains had been accomplished through those individual approaches toward a deeper understanding of the tragic. I shall now try to move into the darker zones of such understanding.

~

The reflections to follow, still reflecting the light of the preceding seven illustrations, will deal mainly with such questions as: how there can be a history of men's tragic being, what is expressed through it, and why this expression is formed into tragic protest.

To begin with, there are some preliminary considerations relating to the treatment of tragic heroes approached, in their varying remoteness. My attitude to them has been throughout, as it had to be, HISTORICAL. But this does not mean merely that they were called upon in their chronological order of emergence, from the inconceivably distant Titan to the paradoxically contemporary Orestes. Nor does it simply mean that they were addressed in their relevant climate of consciousness, Oedipus among his gods and oracles, Hamlet with his post-mediaeval, not so fervid Christianity, Stockmann in his spirit of social advancement. Least of all does it mean that they were regarded as staying in a dead and unavailable past, whose interest now is quaint and antiquarian. A consciously historical attitude means primarily that these men of former and recent time are regarded as essentially expressing the history of existence so that without them men of the twentieth century, such as you and I, could not be what they are. It means that this present and their past belong to one history of the human being. It also means, on these very historical grounds, that their remoteness can and need be reduced in a con-senting ap-proach.

Such an ap-proach is imaginative. And while it was observed early that the inexorable bond of time and space extending over all reality does not equally bind human imagination which can bend and transcend it, this does not render the thrust of imagination altogether atemporal. Although the factual distances of some 2500 years from Oedipus as compared to some 500 years from Hamlet are void of meaning for the imagination of men for whom the former may stand closer than the latter, this only changes but does not eliminate time in human history. Any participation in such history is only possible on the temporal horizon. The order of your imagination, that distinguishes it from fancy, is temporal. That means: how you find and grasp and know the tragic, either in that Prometheus whose creature you are or in your neglected brother Willy Loman, how their existence strikes you as like-ly for your power per-haps, thus possibly also yours, all this emerges only for the time in which you live. Your tragic heroes swim in the stream of your history, away or toward you; but you do not watch them standing on a firm, dry rock – you are yourself submerged in the same stream which also carries a future, theirs and yours. The tragic possibility of each human being, sustained in his imagination, is temporal.

This is why the proper understanding of tragedy, in the sense envisaged here, has to be historical. And this is why the tragic men ap-proached before were treated in a corresponding mood and manner. It was announced prior to any contacts with the tragic figures, as a necessary adapting of the Aristotelian foundations for serious concern with them. Aristotle's considerations for them and the very positions of these tragic heroes were to be actualized, brought up to date and into this time. This does not and must not license tampering distortion. Prometheus was not to be shrunk into human dimensions; and indeed, in compliance with this demand of historical honesty some intimate hold on his essence had to be renounced, precisely because that essence includes immortality and foreknowledge. Faust was not to be viewed as a contemporary frustrated intellectual turning to a career of corruption and of international political adventures; it was his dissatisfaction with his kind of knowledge and his despairing acceptance of gothic devils that had to be stressed. In brief, the "updating" adaptations are certainly not equivalent to masquerading remote figures in modern dress. Yet while their distance was respected, the significance of these figures had to be turned into the temporal angle of present vision, in order to emphasize how they belong to the history of the present time and of today's man. Thus I took the liberty of comparing Prometheus to Adam or Lucifer; this comparison, obviously inappropriate to the Hellenic world of myth, is appropriate to the present consciousness reflecting on its possible genesis. Thus I spoke of Faust's criteria for knowledge as forming the prototype of modern science; this again does not belong to the period where only magic could satisfy such criteria, but it belongs to the present, space-flying, atom-bursting age which comes to weigh the conquests and comforts of scientism with its risks and responsibilities.

What is involved in this treatment? Nothing less than the truth that all life-affecting and formative meaning is temporal. When Caesar crossed the Rubicon, perhaps he alone in his genius could dimly foresee the significance of this event in the subsequent existence of millions in Rome, Europe, the Western world; and perhaps even he could not – but now a schoolboy can. When men began to roll round objects as wheels, when they found themselves counting, when they visualized the roundness of earth, although they had immediate joy and use for the discovered knowledge, they had no inkling of such eventuating interdependence as between ideas of circularity and straightness and the process of calculation. When they take place, physical or mental events just happen; but in the human world they do not happen as complete, self-contained occurrences, they radiate around their possible energy of meaning. To speak of human history is not to speak of merely one thing happening after another, but of an emergent appropriation of meaning brought into light by other men in time. And this is inevitable: there is no such thing as an insignificant historical action, because an action becomes historical through its significance. That significance, however, is not abstract or absolute; from its remoteness it holds by acting upon and involving human beings in their awareness then – or now.

And therefore my reflections now with regard to tragic history of men must reflect it from and into the time they are undertaken, your time also, this latter half of the twentieth century. For you and me, acknowledged or not, Loman must be anonymously close in the quantified crowd of this age unmanning the common man. For you and me, the mythical Orestes must become contemporary, as a regicide descendant from the waves of revolutions, as a subjectivist well schooled in the thought of Descartes, Hume and Kierkegaard, as a self-seeker in the era of displaced persons and displaced personality. For you and me, tragic men of the preceding past must have something to say about those germs of tragedy which the present time fails to discover and observe around – carrying them already well within.

History is men's per-vading occupation of time. It stays in a never stable, never static and never statable awareness of the present world. It searches self-consciously for its own sources from the past world of preceding men, of men who have passed through existence before and who have passed on some traces active in this present search. It passes on, in a parallel way, the present presentiment of eventual future, of what is to come out of these sources and this search. The traces of the past, being already present, may easily be missed in a search for what seems by-gone and long ago. Equally, the present pre-paration of the future may be elusive for the awareness pre-occupied with what is fluent and influent in it now. Nevertheless, although not noticed, the past pre-ceding and the future pre-paring are active throughout the existence of man preoccupied with himself. Such is his hold in time; and if it were different, man would have no history.

There are, of course, different modes and aspects of history: geographical influences upon human habitations and migrations, struggles and conquests of social power, spread and decay of languages and customs, transformations wrought by original ideas, creeds and discoveries. Pursued in separate channels of investigation, these various histories must construct various relations of events. Yet according to the judgment reiterated here, that events are no more than outcomes, histories of events stay on the surface without grasping the root of what comes out here or there, so or otherwise. What is that root? The human being – the human relation to being. So understood, the various "histories" are not thoroughly different or separate, if they all in their specific ways pertain to – and could not fail to concern – the HISTORY OF THE HUMAN BEING. But in a day of specialized knowledge to speak of any merging of channels in some "super-history" is hazardous. Also, the question could be raised whether there is any access to, any way of conceiving, the history of the human being, which would not be a history of particular human events. To answer: first, no merging of channels is in question but rather an indication of what they are channels for; second, there is a possible access and more than one way to conceive this fundamental history; third, one of such ways has been suggested on the pages of this exploration. But not to take it for granted, another such way may be first pointed to: the grasp of the whole of human history in the Christian conception of it, in terms of creation – fall – redemption – resurrection – eternal destiny. It is not claimed here that these

Christian concepts are either proper or improper; but it is claimed that this way of grasping history is more radical than any history of empire, of culture, of economic systems. There are particular beings involved in it, the Creator, Adam, the Tempter, Christ, and there are references to events and situations, paradise, the eating of the apple, crucifixion, the day of judgment, hell and heaven. Yet it is not their obtaining actuality that matters: Adam might have had an orange or transgressed without partaking of food, Christ might have been stoned to death or imprisoned for long years. Would that have changed their historical significance for Christianity? I think not. Because that significance is rooted elsewhere: in conceiving man's possible relation to being – in life and death, with and against God, in human time and divine eternity. The possibility must be in question – not necessarily accepted – for any man, each man must be open to it as like-ly in his power, through his participation in temporal hap or mishap. That is why events do not matter there as events; surely, for a Christian redemption, temptation, eternal destiny are hap-pening even now and to him? Compared to his transcendent terms of rest in being, even tremendous events like the Roman empire, the great migrations, the forming of modern society, the industrial revolution, are without exception only symptomatic and superficial. There is then a way of gaining access to human history, of conceiving it beyond the specialized pursuits of what actually happened, then or now. The faithful Christian would maintain that his is the only way. But is it?

The presence of other religious schemes of history, such as Judaism or Islam, seems to refute this exclusive claim; there are also secular attempts suggesting a grasp of history in a more radical way, as in the thought of Hegel, of Marx, of Darwin. Such a plurality, implausible to those who fervently believe in only one truth, can be perhaps justified by recalling that while the roots of historical events lie in the human hold on being, that hold need not be visualized as unequivocal and simple. On the contrary, its complex possibility issues in the difficulties of determining man, in the residua of his subjectivity, in the uniqueness of his destinies. The history of men's relations to God, to any absolute, to mankind, is not just repetition; that would destroy it as history. Rather, it is emergence from and toward the unknown that demands to be known. It is the questionable that provides abundance of space for thought, for belief, for the imagination.

It is then only one line of questioning the possible history of the human being that is explored here: the line of that relation to being which is tragic. And even that line is only an out-line. It thrusts out, for further reflection, passages and turns of existence no less tragic than the acts on record here, though perhaps there are no others more decisively illuminating the image of tragedy. The out-line, not complete, possibly never complete, nevertheless lines out a history. How is it a history? Like the Christian way of conceiving man, the tragic history is neither a series of isolated and incidental happenings, nor a straight rise toward expected greater fullness in some necessary progress; it winds and turns and branches off and seemingly loses itself and, reflecting the living shape of man in time, is unpredictable. Like the Christian history, it starts from pre-human origins to project the becoming of the human being; fulfilling the Promethean heritage, it reaches its critical stages whence man's own determination casts light and shade toward the now; and having shown its sources, it confronts the present human age with the noon question of a possible end or yet beginning. Like the Christian terms of grasping existence, the tragic ones are possible for every man. But this history in its own approach to the human being is not the Christian one; it involves the Christian message as it involves the Hellenic awakening and the modern predicament; its terms, however, must be alien and partly contrary to the Christian concepts, since they have to record how even Christian hope can turn into tragic being.

Historical records are preserved in various form: in geographical boundaries, in national communities, in customs and practices of daily maintenance of living. The record, the very happening of human tragic history stays alive in an even more exquisitely human way: in SPEECH. Ways of securing survival and procreation, flocking together of like individuals, their locations and migrations, all of these symptoms of existence are not in any exclusive sense human; speech is. Not as communication or emotional outlet: other living beings accomplish that too; their "speech" in crying, in begging, in pointing, in announcing, ties them to something available within or without, pain, joy, danger, food, effort. Speech in the human being can command and demand and deny that which was and may be and is not there: it is temporal in its full extent inaccessible to any other beings. Perhaps therefore human speech is primarily not informative but interrogative: it questions even where it does not expect answers, it queries alike what is there or nowhere or not yet or no more, it undermines itself about its own appropriateness and reference and derivation, it searches throughout for the unspoken, but possible in being. Speech is the ex-pression of the human quest in the world, of man's pursuit of himself – of history.

It would be difficult to deny some tie between the well understood uniqueness of man's speech and the way the human being exists. But a detailed consideration of this tie is clearly beyond the present task. Still, while it would be an oversimplification to claim that all human speech is tragic, there are indications that the weighty significance of speech for man, in both its achievements and its deficiencies, is not independent from the questionable sense, explored here, in which the human being appropriates tragic possibilities. And this is the ground on which this exploration turns toward the tragic meaning of speech ex-pressing itself in protest.

That speech records individual queries and attitudes to existence, is obvious. What is claimed here, however, is less obvious: that the ground from which some men's words are expressed concerns all men, that it claims allegiance or provokes defiance from you, shaping your life's ambitions or pressing you into despond – that without such words having been possible in history you would not be who you are. If you are a reflective man, you reflect your own history in speech, and even if you never heard some particular word or phrase, you still respond with others to their actual or legendary expression, to their possibility which is yours in the world where you do not exist alone. What are some of such words? Here are examples, from varying regions of human history: An unexamined life is not worth living. There is no god but God. Give me liberty or give me death! The king can do no wrong. Property is theft. He who desires to save his soul must lose it. Man is the measure of all things. Life is a tale told by an idiot, full of sound and fury, signifying nothing. You have nothing to lose but your chains. There is a time to live and a time to die. I have sworn eternal hostility against every form of tyranny over the mind of man.

To say that such expressions are important is not to say much. It is harder and more proper to say why they are important, how it is that while some of such phrases may strike you as admirable and others as repulsive, you can hardly shrug them off in cold indifference. This is because what they ex-press is like-ly in your power to think, because they speak of how you have grown to feel about your world and your part in it and your humanity, because they move from the pre-ceding past of others toward pre-paring your mind's possibilities of truth. Such words as these, sounding in you through home, school, church, study, converse, have not merely formed your cultural tradition: that contains plenty of trivialities, too. But they, or rather some of them, appropriated by you, have come to be your past and therefore your future; they out-line how you can think and feel and act – how you are, though yourself, inmidst of the history of the human being. Which of these expressions are properly also your own, only you know; that some of them are, you cannot honestly deny.

And if, indeed, man's history in speech involves you shaping your search of your own human being, then again you cannot be purely indifferent to such non-trivial ex-pressions of others' being: O Earth – O Sky – ye see this anguish and this wrong! To be or not to be, that is the question. If ever I say to the passing moment: Linger a while, thou art so fair ... These out-line the tragic history in speech of protest.

In the approaches to the tragic heroes the foreground impression might have arisen that what is heard in their protest amounts to no more than vehement rejection and revolt; although the "testifying" role of their protest was indicated repeatedly. This ambivalence of protest in its for and against had been stressed already in its intro-duction, with the warning that protest against is more apt to be heard. Now it is proper to reflect more radically on what is spoken in protest; and this is inseparable from the larger query: what is speech?

The reference of speech to particular experiences, events, entities, need not be mentioned; it is sufficiently emphasized in its contempo-rary understanding. It can also be taken as known that speech is ever an individual man's speech and that he adopts it for himself from others who effect his human growth. But all this does not elucidate what speech is originally, as in the first man who ever spoke or, if speech is more than mechanical repetition, what it is in any man who has something genuinely his own to say. In this regard, what matters first is a sort of adaptation, an open questing, a listening conscious-ness; not yet an attention to some thing but a hold in being there with all things, in a way, in a constellation that projects together, con-crescent, asking to be called. There can be awareness of an unnamed relation among entities, an object unlike the known ones, a mood that pervades all experiencing right now, a happening unattended to. In any case, not to be overlooked is the whole horizon available to the awareness, the back-ground from which something is put forward: ex-pressed into speech. This horizon cannot be looked over, surveyed in its wholeness, except by omniscience; yet it must be looked into, sounded by man whose pressing otherwise is no ex-pressing, whose speech otherwise is ground-less. When the grounding horizon is over-looked, re-pressed, forgotten, as it is apt to be, the property of what speech speaks of is not established, even for the speaker. His speech must find roots antedating what he is about to ex-press. Yet he exists: he stands out from a background and he has to move on it through time, has to per-sist, to per-form his future, to feel and act and appropriate a hold on his coming to be. What he finds and calls out in speech is then per-tinent to his way of per-vading time, his ethos. And although this is so often over-looked, the significance of speech, its signing, marking, forming role for man can be wholly re-membered when it is derived from its ground, when its demand belongs not to beings ex-pressed but to the horizon on which they emerge – the horizon of being as such. His proper speech is for each man his EX-PRESSED HOLD IN BEING: in his human being.

Speech is man's power to anchor himself in being, his security, his record, his witness, prior to his manipulation of entities. Geographical or social changes effected by them would be no traces of any men's existence, if it were not for their record in speech: so there are no such traces of other living beings, ob-literated. And yet this human power is ever a quest; it would not be so in a non-temporal realm, where the anchor could stay firm. Man's being in time yields as much hold as withdrawal, allows finding and therein directs searching. What is attested now by immediate witness may soon be lost from sight, passed by, opposed; the witness comes to be de-tested. In absence of security, or more precisely when any security absents itself, feelings grow dark and divided; clinging-to cannot be identical with reaching-toward. One against the other provoke dispute and discord, driving in violence. The world, the human occupation in it can be thoroughly de-tested. Speech thus naturally acquires the potential ambiguity of protest.

Protest for and against: paradoxically turning to and away, assent and dissent, participation and rejection. What is ex-pressed in it, the source of the paradox, is man's relation to being. Not his grasp and support in entities, not his use and abuse of things; these are there, so or otherwise, ever available and so often without avail. But being as such? To be had, held firmly, en-joyed, called out, recorded; it must be so for any being human. At the "same" time – not to be had, impalpable, missed, empty, gone by; it cannot be wholly absent for any human being, yet it absents itself. Despairing of the security of his anchor, man can willingly tear it out; yet it is not easily determined whether he then chooses to break away from being or is chosen to be broken away. His search is tiring, his movement demands rest; but it dawns upon him that his existence is to chase time unto the end, pursue and be pursued, prepare a well-come stay to which he may not get himself – only BE-COMING. The awareness that in human time being is not warranted but only through be-coming is the ground of protest. It is ex-pressed in defiance of finite time, by Prometheus; in distancing fear of that to which he may be coming, by Oedipus; in conscientious doubt of whether it is well-come to be, by Hamlet; in striving for time to stop and show itself as more than nothing, by Faust; in a leap toward a well-founded, not time-worn idea, by Stockmann; in loss of the pursued except for the pursuit, by Loman; in questing liberation from being of nature, still thirsting after free self-made being, by Orestes. Protest, such as has been explored in these men, is always speech, is always awareness of being in the world – tested, attested even in such a slight hold on named presence as in the cry: "The woods are burning!" Protest is looking into the pre-ceding ground of what it calls out, as in Faust's unceasing gallop through the world, refusing denial of traces of his earthly days. Protest is pre-paring the horizon of what man is coming to, though it be an unknown country of no return, though it be nothing – there is being in the coming to it. Protest in despond, in finding all entities of no avail, yet arises on the ground of being available to man: narrowed, shaken, risky, unfulfilled – but not nothing.

If it is thought that here a confusion of thought takes place in that the two metaphysical terms of "being" and "becoming" are dispensed loosely, then the answer must be that this is an indispensable historical feature of human thought. Being without becoming only subsists in a transcendent idea irrelevant to existence. Becoming without being persists abstracted and deprived of any ground. For specialized cognitive purposes they have a technical sense: becoming of entities, their movement and change, their production and destruction, is of necessary use to physics, while being in idea, static and non-temporal, is exploited in logic. But neither of these is in question here. For primary thought endeavoring to ex-press some truth in the existence of man, not just as a physical object nor as a logical mind, for meta-physical thought the con-fusion of being and becoming is and has been of essence through time. Such con-fusion means con-ceiving together: man's joyful hold on being in his becoming and man's be-coming desperate in withdrawal of being; it does not mean their identity. On the contrary, the efforts to ex-press their difference are those which have been here understood by the name of protest.

Man thinks that he is there and feels how he is there in the world. He also acts, seemingly; but his actions are throughout addressed to and performed upon the entities of his world. Can he act upon or en-act himself into his being? Movements and gestures only attain other things or people. His only other mode of acting is speech, when genuine – creative. But speech is a quest, not an end. And therefore it remains unanswered, whether the Logos of speech shall be also conceived as Deed, whether man's spoken record can be en-acted beyond denial, whether his awareness that he is to be coming does reach into making him be. His protest expresses these questions, its significance is due to this historical quest through time. As the human being pervades a way between hold and withdrawal, so the human protest pertains to both presenting a witness for and dissenting against. Nor is it exclusively a matter of man's chosen action, but also of passion: he who actively affirms and en-joys, the witness for, is not thereby assured of a hold on being but can feel drastically its withdrawal, and he who actively rejects can be passionately held in his rejection. The absenting of being is not dependent upon or equivalent to man's negation or position. Perhaps if it were, the human being could not become tragic. When searching historically for truth of his own existence and ex-pressing this in protest, man per-vades the medium of time in which being and becoming must be con-fused. There is, fundamentally, only ONE TRAGEDY FOR MAN – THAT OF TIME.

It is protest that out-lines this dubious way of man's temporal tragedy. Earlier, it was suggested that the tragic should be distinguished from that which is either pathetic or heroic. Pathetic would be the "story" of ruthless sheep-slaughter, also in human shape: where men are blown down in mishap's violence, and meekly submit, and neither resist nor show signs of awareness that fatal cruelty annihilates them. In protest they have to stand up and be human; protest ex-presses their vision aspiring to combat, to break their own breach, to respond and en-act themselves. When they pass down acting, they come to be tragic; even annihilated, they had not yielded to nothingness but witnessed their human being in speech. This the mere patients of pathos could not reach; while on the other hand, the fullsome heroes seem not to need it. In their reliance on entities, in their dominance over events, heroic speech is more imperative than interrogative; they find, even when they do not search, they break without feeling the breach, through them things happen with no mishap and so they are convinced of acting, in no need of en-acting themselves. Not all action is protest, not all speech becomes tragic. Protest ex-presses response to what eludes the conquering grasp, ex-presses loss of what is bespoken as to be held, ex-presses liberation which is neither submission nor triumph. By hap the hero rides the adventuring waves, above questioning that he is – is happy; by mishap the pathetic victim rolls on to his end, below questioning that he becomes nothing. The tragic character protests, aware of hap with mishap, when on the temporal horizon he conceives being in his becoming.

In this con-fusion, the tragic protest must not be identified with either praise or plaint; what it ex-presses is neither joy nor despair. To approach the tragic human being through protest is to avoid two kinds of onesidedness in its understanding. On one side is the un-relieved gloom of those views which mingle tragedy with terror, which count its impressive strength in numbers of its victims, which despoil life of all but suffering and thus must end it in despair. From this angle of view tragedy cannot be anything uniquely realized or expressed in human existence, since not only man is susceptible to terror, to suffering and death; nor is there much outlook for sense in such mishappening, any more than in the crushing sweep of an ava-lanche. On the other side there is the unrealistic perversity of those who refuse to see the tragic hero as anything but joyful and tri-umphant, even against his own acknowledgment of failure and pain; such persons take tragedy for a crutch in their own want of support and assurance, as though it provided easy answers rather than pro-voking questions; they mistakenly assume that those who do not lay down arms are thereby guaranteed a victory; they greedily clutch at fragments of joy scattered over the surface of tragic history, as if this were all, and all were well in their world, and they could be uplifted, entertained and relieved all at once. Through such a view tragedy be-comes all too human, entitling every joker who ever coped with some obstacle to his own satisfaction to claim the role of a tragic hero; and the sense of the tragic, seen as issuing in wholesome if scornful cheer, becomes just comedy. If these two attitudes, oversimplified no doubt, can be termed pessimist and optimist, then it should be clear that the present exploration of tragic protest corresponds to neither of them; and if these reflections are proper to it, the tragic protest justifies no pessimism or optimism. Despair may sound in it, yet when voiced it is not wholly desperate – as it would be, remaining mute and impotent even of expression. Joy may sound in it, yet such en-joyment is only gained in strength despite its own losses – it is not joy that makes the voice tragic. The tragic protest speaks not in a devil's denial, not in a god's acceptance, but in demand of a human being to which "No" and "Yes" are both available. It is human in its search; it is tragic in yielding no ultimate find; it is protest in finding itself only in the search it testifies. It ex-presses no dispossession in a void, no possession in fullness, but Ap-propriation of being in time.

This protesting "ap-propriation" should be understood first as ad-herence, ad-justment, ad-equation: turning toward a horizon that is there, available, to be brought into focus but not into existence out of nothing. This horizon in the human subject is not his subjectivity – arbitrary, manipulable, relative – but his subjection to being: the only horizon to which, as human, he ever belongs. But further, the appropriation is making proper, making just, equable, good: actively entering into, building an accommodation, announcing its fitting place and name. This taking of property cannot be ever determined as accomplished, it can be succeeding or breaking but not successful or broken – because the horizon of the human being lies in time, even if it were immortal time: incipit tragoedia. And thirdly, the appropriation indicates claiming as one's own, struggling for exclusive grasp, clasping and sheltering even the fragile and trivial when private, intimate, unique. This is where subjectivity comes into play, where only imagination is a guide, where possibility corresponds to each individual on his own – and thus some men's appropriation of being is expressed in their own tragic protest.

It may be noticed that such appropriation – the making of human being proper and intimate – is the root of poetic expression, in the original Hellenic sense. To say that all speech is thus in its sources poetic, need not evoke any drastic disagreement. But there are further suggestions here, such as that all poetry has at least deep tragic affinities; to elaborate this in detail is not necessary here, especially in view of likely objections from those who would not part from formal criteria of poetry – lyric, epic, comic, satiric, heroic – all seemingly alien to the tragic and, might be added, to the spirit of poetry; but suffice it to point to Horace, Tasso, Cervantes, Swift, Hugo, Heine, Baudelaire, Kafka. Also, if speech is understood fundamentally, as man's questing mode of taking hold in being, then it can be suggested that in the poetry of protest speech comes into its own. Speech can be superfluous, formalized, abused; it can merely "appropriate" shallow experiences, useless entities; it can forget its sources and speak in the indifferent, automatic mood, having nothing to say. This is not so when speech poetically makes protest. There it is not only useful but indispensable, because nothing else avails; there, whatever its form, it has to say that which the speaker longs to record of himself; there it is rooted centrally in the human position, proper to the man who is more than his extreme passing phases of joy and despair – because the impotence of despair cannot reach any strength of expression, and the abundance of joy needs none.

Therefore a drastic diagnosis can be addressed to such an age as the present. Where boasts are raised of having overcome primitive pity and fear of tragedy, where human life is measured up to mechanical, streamlined standards of success determined in objective quantity, where the might and mystery of the future means no more than scientific prediction of events, there tragic protest is absented. But this absenting may also signify the silencing of poetry, the drying up of sources for genuine speech, the blocking of man's search for his own destiny. If such absenting were final, it would mean the end of history of the human being: the end should be no less imaginable than the beginning.

This last claim needs still to be amplified with reference to such human history as has developed here in terms of tragic protest. It has been said that protest is the ex-pression of what makes man's tragic being. This of course does not exclude the contingency of a tragic silence – though there are different kinds of silence and the silence of a Hamlet should not be equated with that of a stone or of a god, neither with the silence of a Caesar nor of a wretched idiot. Yet it does exclude access to it, or any imaginative knowledge of tragedy when it remains unexpressed. It has also been said that tragedy emerges from man's per-vading search of being in time, and therefore must be historical. Now it is necessary to tie in these reflections by at least a summary glance at the out-line of history of the human being, recorded in tragic protest. Each of the men ap-proached before has his own tragic history, and these have been already illumined as far as time and capacity permitted. But since human being in the world means more than individual subjectivity, an attempt is required to show how tragic history in its time sequence not only concerns such individuals themselves but also per-vades through them from one to the other, from a beginning into a future, and thus also toward you and me.

This radical vision of history begins in the mythical empty dawn of gods and titans, where men were not and none were human records. This was yet the beginning, because the ground, the back-ground of human being was there: man-kind. Thrown into life by non-human source, these crowds had no human being yet: "Little-doing ... blind tribes ... as shapes in dreams they moved ..." Like any men in dream, they had no hold on their selves, experiencing yet seeing no order or time in what happened and thus hardly capable of acting, of making things happen. Somewhere, somewhen an opening was made for their entry into being human: the Promethean firing grasp of time in a defiant leap over its flow and order, in a dis-ordering breach of natural necessity. Whatever the ways of myth on which mankind reached this opening, it now started pre-paring their quest for temporal ap-pointments in awareness that they are be-coming; it made possible pointing out and pre-serving entities or events, hence hope with its dis-appointments and fear with its over-coming. Only on this back-ground one could expect a man to stand out from the crowd – his name might be Oedipus – with an inkling of self, with a pre-sentiment of what is like-ly to happen or mis-happen and of what deeds or mis-deeds might be proper to himself. From this future-bound self he could screen himself in fear and search through the world for his own location; yet when time brought the "two" into identity, he would have the power to over-come his fear and to acknowledge his human existence. Man was then born through his being in time, protested when ap-propriated. Is it an accident that to the same horizon of dates and places belongs the time-bound thought of Heraclitus, the time-defying thought of Plato?

Objectively measured, there is a long interval between these opening phases of tragic history and its subsequent ones. Nor is this interval immaterial, because it is filled with the rise and reign of the greatest non-tragic human hope: the Christian "good tidings." Christianity cannot accommodate tragedy, not only because for it to put in question man's triumph in salvation would be to deny itself, not only because it sees the defiant and self-relying word of human protest as both impious and superfluous in view of its exclusive reliance on the word of God's promise, but also because it hopefully relocates the proper human being beyond its world into divine eternity, so that man's hold here or its withdrawal, sought or denied, in joy or despair, becomes insubstantial: it is "only" temporal being. On the other hand, in exploration of tragic being Christianity must not be disregarded as alien, because its seeds germinate in men's search of themselves, sometimes soothing, sometimes aggravating their tragedy. Even when its social dominance over the mass of man-kind has weakened, its message continues to appeal subjectively with the task of pre-serving the soul or self. Such appeal contributes both to the Cartesian conception of self-conscious subjectivity and also to the self-tormenting yet self-true conscience of someone like Hamlet. But this conscience is no longer mediaevally sustained by transcendent hope; its secularized concern is not with eternity but with time imposing the question "to be or not to be." It is as impious in its absolute claim to responsibility over the whole man, even in his impotence, as the "pride" of

Oedipus whose preceding quest it resumes. The heritage of tragedy is again to know and to own one's being, to frustrate or be frustrated by time's becoming, yet to ap-propriate at least a "wounded name" in existence. Man lives again coming to grips with his temporality. His next step, pre-paring his modern self, is to cast himself onto the waves of time to conquer them by active striving. The "crown of humanity," the mastery over "this earth" and all its nature, the Promethean refusal to bow even before eternity, these are the challenges to the might of Faust; only in these can he find himself coming into his own being. The searching movement, the preservation in deeds are pre-cedent from Oedipus, the exaltation of subjectivity overleaping the world from Hamlet, the buoyant hope, though a new one, descends from Christianity – perhaps its dis-appointnents, too. Faust's mighty ambitions correspond historically to the possibility thought by Kant of man's powerfully judging rather than meekly studying nature, of taking time itself as no more than the human form for intuition of being. Only if thus time and nature lie in the power of man, can he grasp himself as one whom being becomes to make things happen, as one who creatively en-acts a world for men alone. Yet from this world and from this humanist combat the Christian Lord is far, far away, only the mediaeval phantom of evil haunts through it still; the non-human power of time confronts Faust in the shape of Care; and when his "gallop through the world" runs to its finish, he realizes that the con-fusion of being with becoming is less a conquest than a quest of life.

The post-Faustian horizon has widened greatly, so greatly that it is like-ly to over-come the sustaining strength of the self alone. There is, now, "nothing but men." The human being they now ap-propriate would not be theirs without such prototypes in history as Faust, Hamlet, Oedipus, without the Titanic gift of defiance. But these modern and latter men may also become the last ones. Care, time and tragedy may not have been left behind in the march of progress. In the wastes of frantic activity the subject may find nothing but his own loss; the human, very human relations may be judged as soiled with too many mortal fears and aspirations, as not worth being; the cherished self may prove but a lonely shadow, with its solid reality in evil, with its movements and deeds coming out empty; the pre-Promethean dream shapes, images and ideas may revert to nothing while they are embraced as salvation. The human being, as felt by Stockmann, Loman, Orestes, may also be thought of ultimately in ab-solute ideas prevailing over trivial individuals, in historical determination amounting to just social warfare, in the last reality resting in the power of the sledge-hammer – as by Hegel, Marx, Nietzsche. Imagination which directed man-kind toward a Lord to discover that men will not serve him, now directs their images toward their servants the machines, and may discover that men will not master them. The technological gospel like the Christian one is far from tragic, bearing tidings of secular hope and conquest; yet like the other it may contribute to the tragic stream of history, if its hope changes to fear, its conquest to competition, if poetic making yields to social engineering and the lonely standing-out man is submerged in the mechanism of the crowd. This could be the end of tragedy, and of life: machines do not live.

The indications of a possible end do not mean that this radical history results in forecasting of doom. These dark observations on the present age are intended to counterbalance the modern man's naively smug assumption that he can gain infinity and pay nothing. The tragic descendants of Prometheus and of Faust do pay the price for the presumption of triumph over time in the human being. It shows in the rush of militant life, dis-regarding its proper horizon, de-testing the power of Care thus over-looking its expansion, trying to accelerate the thrust of centuries into days, toward escape – whence and whither? That which runs ever faster, must stop, slow down, or explode; but this lesson of the machine has not been learned by man. And the critical, the noon-time does not seem to be remote. If the human becoming tragic is taken for granted and "transcended," the end to the search of the human being can be in non-being. Yet no such end is here forecast; only out-lined as possible, as like-ly harmonizing with the pre-ceding ground of history, as within the power of self-making hence perhaps self-denying man. Not de-termining necessity is the vision pre-pared in this survey of tragic history, but the lonely, liberating voice in the wilderness – that of Orestes: "All must begin anew." While there is time, man becomes his future.

Has this history produced nations, moved their boundaries, given them rule or law? No. Has it provided wealth, established social classes, changed the distribution of work? No. Has it erected monuments, churches, museums? No. If it is history, it does not show in mass-produced entities, common experiences, sensational events – but perhaps more radically in their roots. It lives only in the words of protest. In them, the pervading quest of the human being is ex-pressed, externalized, recorded. In them, the speech out-lining human history shows not in mere answers but in questioning, thinking activity from which any answers must originate. Because they are not answers, they are neither positive not negative, yet on the other hand pre-pare and pre-cede both positions and negations in the ambivalence of hold and withdrawal, of protest for and against. Listen again to some words of the tragic men, listen for their quest ap-propriating both affirmation and rejection:

Oedipus – "It WOULD be sweet to live beyond the reach of sorrow." "My curse can rest on NO ONE but MYSELF." Hamlet – "WHETHER 'tis nobler in the mind to suffer ... OR to take arms?" "I COULD be bounded in a nutshell. and count myself a king of infinite space, WERE IT NOT that I have bad dreams." "What IS a man ...?" "If it BE NOT now, yet it WILL COME." Faust – "LET US CAST OURSELVES into the torrent of TIME." "The traces of my earthly days CAN NEVER SINK in the aeons unaware." "A curse on PATIENCE most of all!" "Hence is our soul upon the rack who feel, midst PLENTY, what we LACK." "One HANKERS for the brooks of life, ah, and for LIFE'S FOUNTAIN – HEAD." "TO BE, though but for a moment, is OUR TASK." Stockmann – "I SHALL HAVE done my duty." "A free man HAS NO RIGHT to soil HIMSELF with filth." "You WILL BRING ABOUT such a state of things that the whole country WILL DESERVE to be ruined." Loman – "What – what's the SECRET?" "A man CAN'T go out the way he came in ... a man has GOT TO ADD UP to something." Orestes – "I have one path only, and heaven knows WHERE it leads ... but it is MY PATH." "NEITHER slave NOR master ... I AM my freedom." "Give me your hand, and we will go – TOWARDS OURSELVES." "OUTSIDE nature, against nature, without excuse, beyond remedy, except what remedy I FIND WITHIN myself." And the "final form" of protesting wisdom, the dis-covery that out-lines the whole of this tragic history, the ap-propriation with its hold and withdrawal, with its subjectivity and subjection to being in time: "He only EARNS his freedom and HIS LIFE who takes them EVERY DAY by storm."

~

The being of man is not to be taken for granted, not in eternity, not in universality of nature, not in patient receptivity. Being is to be ap-propriated through time for everyone who would be a man in himself. For man, nothing is becoming, no right, no secret, no nature, aside from his human being. Yet for all this objectively unique urgency, for all either-or man con-ceives, for all his subjective subjection, it is being that makes the human tragic.

His tragic history dawns in a defiant encounter with time. Then it develops from the fear of Oedipus, not of a thing or happening, but of his possible self becoming through time. It is enriched in Hamlet's conscience withdrawing from the weeds of the world, holding on to the inner music of his heart made ready to be or not to be in time. It reaches for newer light when nightly Faust finds God and devil alien, patience of nature deadly Care-worn, and only the self-lit striving an unsinkable en-actment over time. In the ground-less acceleration of modern struggles, it contrasts for Stockmann the pure abstraction in his proper idea against the filthy hodge-podge of his communal every-day; it leads a more common individual, Loman, toward disoriented self-loss in the end-less quantification of crowd life; it challenges Orestes' liberation from nihilism in existence with the threat of an empty human time. So it reaches the noon balance between its necessary past and its only possible future, the questioning balance of position and negation for the human being; at noon, the shadow of tragedy may seem to have been left behind yet lie ahead and grow in time.

These are the roots of tragic protest. Nowhere do they emerge from particular entities in the world, from single peculiar experiences of men, from specific chains of events in time. The human subjects of tragic protest, existing as individuals, properly do manipulate entities, undergo experiences, partake in events; yet these are not what they protest, not what ap-propriates for them tragedy, not even what exclusively makes them human. The human roots of tragic protest rest in being.

To speak of being is to court the immediate danger of saying less or more than common understanding requests. Less, if the accusation should be that of easy, empty tautologies; more, if the criticism should complain against mystifying, untestable expressions; quite re-markably, both of these objections might even be made at the same time. But what logicians may regard as tautologies, such as "Man is a rational animal," need not be easy when first expressed but only when mechanically passed on through habit; also, far from empty, they can provide plenty of content for strife in thought. And what physical scientists may regard as untestable propositions, such as "If there is no God, then everything is permitted," need not be mystifying to those who at-test their truth in joy or despair. Perhaps this distinctive and doubtful status, thus assailed on two sides, pertains par excellence to meta-physical statements, if they have to speak of being. I therefore make this statement, claiming meta-physical status, in conscious danger of formal and technical opposition which may attack it as tautologous or mystifying or both: MAN'S TRAGIC PROTEST IS ROOTED ON THE GROUND OF HIS HUMAN BEING.

At the outset of this exploration my aim was declared to be no less than the tragic being of man. If any success attended my pursuit of it, this aim should now stand in some light; but not so that its present reflections should exterminate all night. No serious human aim can be so unreflectively visualized. Thus my last reflections, ap-proaching the ground of their light, must expose the dark remaining beyond this time.

If it is true that protest ex-presses the tragic being of man, this claim eliminates pre-occupation with entities, experiences, events encountered in the human world. But then, what is ex-pressed? Is anything still left to be spoken of ? No-thing, not a thing. Quite rightly: being is not a thing, yet genuine speech can concern itself with the ways man belongs to being. Perhaps some elucidation might be offered to those who shudder at the noun "being" but who neither could nor would avoid using the verb "to be." Consider some per-fectly ordinary examples of colloquial idiom: "This house is in the shade – is painted white – is a good example of colonial style – is replacing a previous home of the same family – is damaged beyond repair." Will you not grant that the word "is" has a different sense in each of these phrases? Of course, you may wish to reply that just on account of such variability this mere copula can be disregarded and the meaning contents examined without it. But perhaps this is rather begging the question; because even if the copula "is" should be left out – which easily happens in some languages like Russian – it is nevertheless implicit in the intention to speak. The question is, surely, how the various features of something can "be" grasped and spoken out, whether you say or omit the word "is." Not the word but its role in speaking is significant. And what about this variable role? In the examples cited, the various ways a house "is" were spoken out and per-vaded in varying depth. That for a few hours this house stands in the shade says something of interest to one wishing to avoid sun heat, but not much about the house; its white color is more enduring, still easily and indifferently changed; but the truth that it has been built in a definite style belongs to the house much more intimately, to alter it one would have to rebuild and the product would be other than "this house"; the statement of its antecedence and ownership yields, as it were, its "destiny": if a certain family had not wished to replace its previous home, this house would not have appeared at all; the last phrase again tells of its end, but mentions no purpose, only that the house faces annihilation beyond help. If you accept these explanations as reaching some point, perhaps now you might see this point in saying that speech can per-vade the being of some entity such as a house, with varying depth, import, concern, intimacy. Two comments should be added: one, that the intent of the preceding remarks does not coincide with the old terminological dualism, ascribing to entities either essence or accident, since of the statements cited none was in that sense essential while the accidents there described belonged to very different categories. Secondly, while the assumed pervasion of being in speech certainly has to do with time, this should not be mis-understood as simply concern with duration; the last reference to the unavoidable destruction should make this clear: while it strikes at the "heart" of the house, it may describe only a brief period in its being there.

Closer to the main trend of reflection, and more significant, is the question how human being is per-vaded in different approaches of speech, or if you prefer, how any man "is" anything – in so far as his ways of being can be characterized in words. Here also should be answered the difficulty you might have formulated already in the above references to a house: that while perhaps its being is approached through them in some sense, nevertheless that "being" appears reducible to and not divorceable from, the events or "experiences" proper to this entity: its coming into shade, its having been built and painted, its damage and destruction. The same objection has force against such statements as: "This man is an industrial executive – is the son of rich parents – is suffering from an incurable illness." What he "is" here reduces to what happens to him or possibly what he makes happen; the latter is not an insignificant distinction re-maining, however, within the sphere of happenings. But can you safely assert such a reduction with regard to the following statements? "This man is unfailingly just – is determined to succeed by any means – is a creative poet – is trying to find himself through these efforts – is at odds with the world he lives in." To be sure, in commenting on these phrases, you will be able to point to happenings or experiences implied, but for one thing it may be doubted whether these events will be of the same order as a house may undergo, and further, whether it is they that matter. Thus in speaking of someone's justice, you can have in mind incidents in his relations with other individuals, but these incidents and individuals as such do not exhaust your meaning; that is pertinent to his pursuing and preserving some balanced order among all incidents and individuals he can find in the world. In the second example, reliance on particular events is minimized in the man's determination to succeed by "any" means; you express only a dark allusion to some persistence, force or choice clinging through his life, without being able to tell whether he has been determined or determined himself that way. And when you call another man a "creative poet," you are not just selecting his occupation, to be contrasted with others; if you mean what you say, you bow here to the power of speech, intimately expressible in his emergent maker's hold – but not on pens, pencils or typewriters. Next, a man's "finding himself" you may regard as merely a metaphor, yet this metaphor is hardly applicable to any non-human entity; the reason for it is that the phrase attempts to grasp at this man's history in an appropriative sense in which other things, animate or inanimate, have no history, and thus their efforts, delights and defeats are not theirs, as a man's are his – although they all equally "happen." Last, whatever metaphorical flavor you may detect there, you can make sense by talking of a man's, and only a man's, antagonism with his whole world, just as you can talk of another's wholehearted acceptance of his; your sense will depend here on the sense he finds or seeks not in single entities, events, experiences, but among them, through the time of his existing into this available totality of which the isolated contents avail not enough – the world of human being.

Thus, if you even partly consent to such an understanding of simple fragments of colloquial language, you should now be able to see how in speaking one can attempt to follow some ways in which the human being "is." And that is to look for and bring into view not only incidents and individuals in his life but also their orderly or disorderly horizon, not only events as outcomes but the source of their eventuating, not only expressions but what presses them into speech, not just proper experiences but appropriating experienceability, not entities in sequence or consequence but their ground of the world. In brief, it is possible to approach not beings belonging to man but the being man belongs to in his time.

It is such an approach that has been pervading throughout this exploration and that is deemed appropriate to reflect tragic being expressed in protest. Once more let it be reiterated that everything said on these pages does not claim to outline the whole of human roots in being: only that wayward way of being rooted while uprooted and thus un-whole – which is known as tragic. How can be gathered the light reflected from this questionable source?

To define some images in the dark, it may be best to recall the earlier comparison of tragedy to an illness gripping a human individual. But immediately misconception should be averted by stressing that such a comparison does not provide for a physiological or psychological scope. Man is not in question here as an organism nor yet as a mind alone. And yet tragedy can be said to effect for the human being what illness does for the human organism: dis-organize it – or what insanity does for the human mentality: render it de-mented, un-mindful, in the sense of moving it outside the wholesome norms in security and accomplishment of man-kind. In a darker significance, tragedy is dis-ease. But perhaps indeed it is from this darker significance that men's understanding has developed in regard to the lighter phenomena of disease, physiological or psychological. Because the latter are not only variations in the organic or mental processes – plenty of these, while unusual, can be taken as sound and sane; they are such variations as bode ill or in a groping sense portend tragedy. In any case, what is missed and searched for is ease in living, acting, speaking, which is presumed for each individual to be available but not availing here, attainable but attained no more or not yet. This disposition of ease in the whole of existence, disrupted in cases of what is generally known as illness, is absent for man involved in tragedy. Common language gives some witness of this further depth: you strengthen the stress when speaking of a man's illness you also call it tragic, but when you have sincerely determined a man's lot as tragic, you will hardly say anything, mentioning also illness. This does not mean that tragic individuals must also suffer illness in the more ordinary sense of that word, but it does mean that while such illness affects in parts their relations with entities of the world in health: air, food, movement, communication – tragedy affects them more radically. The ground of ease, from which dis-ease can also eventuate and to which it is ever relatable, is man's well-being. The contrary ground or groundlessness in a man who is tragic, may be indicated as his ILL-BEING. From and to human well-being are given concepts and measures of health, sanity, order, propriety, value, inherent in sound men's ethos; and consequently they fail to harmonize with such ethos as may emerge from ill-being. That is why in exploring tragic existence one does not settle with, and must quest beyond, what is or is not good, or mad, or just, or improper. The insights may be admirable yet un-wholesome.

The ground on which tragedy grows in time and is ex-pressed into

protest, I call ill-being. How can I speak of it but protestingly, imaginatively, questionably? There can be no complete account, no
determination or evaluation, where terms and values do not belong,
where counters of entities are discounted, where not something whole
but un-whole no-thing is in question. There can be only felt images of
possible being. Such images I previously tried to elucidate; their dark
source of light I can still try to reflect.

To necessitate rejection of necessity; to be not at home at home; to
lose what has never been found; to hold wholly to what escapes; to
question without accepting any answer – these are some paradoxical
possibilities of ill-being, identifiable in men examined before. It might
be tempting to say simply that what obtains thus in a self-contradiction. And the word has been used in such a way; nevertheless it is
not an adequate word. As a basically logical term, it fits an abstract
relation in the idea, statically absolute in that it qualifies for dismissal.
So a square circle is dismissed as impossible. But what is reflected here
is not abstract, not static, calling not for dismissal but for attention
as vividly possible. The logical aspect of self-contradiction can be
paralleled by the physical aspect of self-canceling movement: the dog
choking on a leash, the fluid poured into a bottomless vessel, the up
and down of ocean waves, the disconnected racing engine. But again,
these images of things do no more than shape an aspect, since what is
questioned here is not a thing. Logic may claim: there is no being in a
clear self-contradiction; physics may claim: nothing is becoming in a
mere self-canceling movement. The rightness of these claims would
only indicate the alien scope of such approaches to man's tragic relation to being in ill-being. And even the feeling impression from the
preceding references, even the critical tones of the word "ill-being"
could be misleading. They would suggest some aura of frustration,
closure, emptiness; and while these suggestions should not be called
wrong, equally right would be suggestions of striving, openness,
power.

That which is thought here as ill-being, is being, not non-being; its
medium is possible time, not vacuously immutable impossibility; it
calls for conscientious awareness, not idle self-stultification. The root
word "ill" is not to provoke pity by implying an overwhelming assault
from without. It is precisely the question of tragedy to wonder about
the difference in being between "without" and "within," to ask if
anything is truly "within," to grasp at the substance of the "is." To
be human is to be faced with being. Its hold and withdrawal shape the
concern with finding and searching for the human self in time. The

human questioning time asks: Does it give or does it take away? Does one acquire it or does one consume it? In this possible multiplicity lies the single question whether there is a self within. Only man can ask this question: other live beings can become ill, but only man can be tragically faced with ill-being. And this possibility is tied to the wonder-full choice in understanding human existence: it is meta-physical.

But how, on this self-thought human horizon, does tragedy emerge? How does man enter ill-being, if he does not have to? This way of asking indicates a choice with its fundamental ambiguity between choosing and chosen. Every question presupposes a choice under-taking this or that answer, the right or the wrong one, the positive or the negative. Questioning is selecting, parting, loosening the ground questioned. The question-able human conscience thus responds to choice. And when it is the question of all questions, that of the human being as such, then in its under-taking, choosing or chosen, being for man becomes parted, shaken, sustains a rift, possibly a breach. Yet not all speech, not all questioning is tragic; even this meta-physical questioning of the ground need not enter tragedy, if it ever hovers on its brink. Tragedy opens when the questioning grasps the parting and not what is parted, when it further under-takes the rift and not its bridging, when it sustains the BREACH in its very self. Because this breach is not breached by one thing into another: the shaken question-ed being is the being of the questioner. The stronger loosening, singling out, pressing on, becomes the more loose, singular ex-pression. And the deeper rooted is the questionable search, the more uprooted the question-able searcher. The way down and the way up are one; what-ever is appropriatively en-closed yields further dis-closed openness; there is joy in powerful striving and there is despair in elusive failure but they belong together. Such is the un-grounded ground of tragic protest – such is ill-being.

Tragedy is not exhaustible in even the widest relations of entities with a human being, because it affects that to which any entities would have to be related, available, meaningful. In ill-being the self is parted from the ease of pursuing relations, establishing meanings, availing itself of anything – since itself is but pursued. The way in which the tragic human being is self-opening – or self-closing – is not open or close to anything or anyone else. Hence its unparalleled isolation: what there becomes all-one is thereby alone. Where available being is in question, what or who could be of any avail? Yet such ill-being need not yield to non-being: the void in view can be avoided, the outward impotence can bear inward potentials. Demand of being is not its negation. Thus the self-addressed pressure demands ex-pression, despite the lack of position or statement, despite the isolation from communicable speech. In such being alone ex-pression is self-pressed before passing into any shared world. The event of it is questionable silence or questioning protest; and only the latter provides for access to tragic being, though paradoxical, though posing as much as opposing. Therefore in the con-ceiving of protest will be found both self-conceit and self-contempt, abandoned projection and rejection, passion to own and action to disown. The tragic protest tests in speech the breach in being. Con-ceived in wonder, it becomes anxious questioning, inexorable parting, ruthless digging and biting – into the being of its self. And so with time it under-takes the whole of its world that is no longer whole. The breach into ill-being, earlier compared to self-contradiction or self-cancelation, can more adequately be imagined as SELF-VIOLENCE, compelling yet dispelling the unity of the violating and the violated. For the sake of violence, that to be defied, trans-cended, broken, must be; but through time of violence, dissecting, condemning, abandoning – how is it? This is the query of tragic ill-being.

I have tried to show that there is a difference for man between being he belongs to and entities belonging to him; but that difference, full of wonder for thought, is not determinate since its terms would have to be entities. In tragic relevance, the ground of ill-being has yielded the image of self-violence; yet tragedy can not define the being of an entity called "the self," nor on the other hand postulate some very untragic condition understood as "selflessness." And further, while I have repeatedly stressed that only a superficial approach will rest with an analysis of tragedy in terms of entities, events, experiences, in a tragic hero's existence, nevertheless it would be absurd to think of him as not involved with them as any human being in the world must be. This is indeed the issue of my whole exploration. The issue means an ex-pressive bridge between what issues and whence it issues. The elements of a tragic story do not determine the tragic being they issue from; but neither can they be undetermined or irrelevant to it, especially when in the protest ex-pressed by such existence they have to be taken as guiding clues for an imaginative approach. The image of self-violence also can be meaningful only if it bridges the dark truth of ill-being and what is more commonly accepted as tragic happenings. Yet its bridging is an issue and not wholly on the surface. On one side, in ordinary reference to someone's being ill, it would be superficial to imagine him as a calm, helpless patient at rest in a bed or a cell, neglecting the violence waged imperceptibly in the organism or the mind. On the other side, it would be superficial to decide that a story is tragic by reference to a number of ferocious fights, savage screams and bloody bodies. The true violence of a self's tragic protest need not be perceptible on the surface. It issues properly in violent speech which need not be shouting, violent attitudes which need not manifest overt brutality, violent thoughts which need not think of violence. To be sure, self-violence as imagined here can emerge into such drastic situations as mutilation of one's body, destructive ruin of what one loves best, persistent tendency to dispose of oneself; they belong to the same issue but are neither necessary nor exhaustive for it. While tragic men all belong to ill-being, there is a manifold in their ap-propriation of it or in their attempts at ap-propriation; any one's self, even in self-violence, is as much his own as his place in the world and time. Consequently, what issues through self-violence must in any event properly belong to the tragic being's choice, character and vision. The events come out of a breach and it would be vain to interpret them as placid, harmonious, constructive: they are breaking the path of an upheaval and a breakdown. But what is broken, how thoroughly, how perceptibly, that is contingent; it may be a hold on universal order and law, it may be human nature in some determinate sense, it may be the balance between future and past or between living and dying, or the man's tie of belonging to a God, to other men, to himself. In order to be imaginatively grasped as tragic, a man's story must be consentingly felt as serious; but to try determining its individual incidents serially, uniformly, quantitatively, would be to forget that his tragedy issues from his unique human being – even though it be ill-being.

And so once more should be reiterated the reason for the individual approaches expressively under-taken in this exploration, their ob-jective being bound to questioning protest of those individuals. The word "tragic" is understood in qualifying the human relation to or within being. That relation is one of becoming ap-propriation, thus it hinges on what can become proper to someone; its issue is referred to the dark notion of ill-being, thus it must not abstract from some being that can be so ill; it has been imagined as self-violence, thus it demands respect for at least the possibility of a self. Any human being, when seriously considered, constitutes an inimitably unique bond with being, whether in hold or withdrawal, whether of openness or closure, whether his or its. That bond with ill-being which issues in tragic protest can therefore be only imaginatively accessible for and through a unique individual involvement. From there alone derive tragedies of communities, centuries, cults or cultures; to deny it is to deny that these have historical significance only because historically men exist.

On the other hand, it would be wrong to think of tragedy as an unquestionable distinction or disaster for some few men only, like genius or beauty or congenital deformity. I have previously proposed the judgment: ALL MEN ARE POTENTIALLY TRAGIC. This of course is different from saying: all men are tragic. The latter judgment, ex-aggerated and inadequate, would have to interpret tragedy in refer-ence to such features as all men definitely share, like mortality or ignorance or relative unhappiness; but in doing so, it would have to overlook the uniqueness of every human being, and to obliterate the differences between Don Quixote and Sancho Panza, between Icarus and Monsieur Jourdain, between Peer Gynt and Walter Mitty. As a matter of fact, all men are not tragic; as a matter of imaginable possi-bility, all are. But this raises the question of men's partial partici-pation in these potentials, of their choice there, of the sense of pro-perty in possible being. You cannot become mortal, when you already are; you cannot become a genius, when you are not one. In both of these cases, the feature alluded to is an actual and not contingent determination of you as an entity; and in both cases time is irrelevant. Now when being tragic is thought of as possible for you, such narrow determinations open up into a horizon for temporal emergence, not just of things to come but of your self; within it, however, reverberates the echo of the question of time's taking or giving – the choice question. In present reference, this is not a simplified perspective of wish, license, desire, since you do not desire tragedy; nor is it any obvious forcing, constraint, compulsion, since you are not literally forced into tragedy. Yet, while the problem of choice is not so easy here, it belongs to the issue of ill-being, if all men are potentially tragic: do some make themselves or are they made tragic in time? It does not seem that one can adopt either one of these straightforward alternatives. On the one hand, the tragic man shows himself responding to choice and assuming responsibility for his self even through self-violence; indeed, without this, his tragic protest would loss its poignancy. Hence to understand him as passively overwhelmed would not render him justice. On the other hand, while courting danger of self-violence, while consciously striving after his elusive goal, he also encounters his own suffering and doom therein; and one finds it unthinkable that he should not avert it, if it were under his proper control. Hence to understand him as actively acquiring his destiny would again distort his situation. Wholly without choice, man's being could not be made tragic; with whole choice, it would not make itself tragic. Proper understanding must be pursued between or underneath these alternatives. Thus perhaps the necessity of the tragic hero can be characterized in saying that he chooses not to choose otherwise; the first part of this sentence would render his indeterminacy, the second his determination. If you ask how it is found that he chooses at all, my answer is that while no inferential process may reach it, his tragic ethos would not be itself without a conscious response to choice; and if you ask how it comes about that he does not choose otherwise, my answer is that while this does not clear the ground of choice for him, he conceives that no other choice could properly be his own. Tragic necessity thus revolves around the human question of what possible being can ever become one's own, particularly when it is ill-being.

The problem of the universal tragic potentiality of all men refers to a depth underlying some questionable ambiguities of speech. When one speaks of "the human being," one does not really set it in line with animate or inanimate beings, with factual or fictitious beings, and the like; even in the most objectively unbiased, scientifically minded discourse there is an in-dicative assumption in this expression – because, unlike the others, it is adopted and named, as it were, from the inside. It could never be spoken in any other way by any man; it suggests then: being as available to man, being there in midst a manifold of other beings but forever with the genuine horizon of human vision. In speaking of the human being, this in-dication lies unspoken – that anyone human must face being as such; and this means much more than just naming one being amongst various others. And further, in speaking of the human being, a certain indefiniteness is commonly permissible as to whether a particular individual is meant or what that individual must contain equally with all other humans. No doubt the context can clarify the intent; but the fact that both these intents are available suggests wonder whether, when and how anything proper is attributable to the human being. Proper, that is, to a particular human being, since nothing is proper to all humans alike – except their being human? These ambiguities are not merely linguistic; they are not restricted to the English idiom for similar remarks could be made concerning "l'etre humain," "menschliches Wesen," "istota ludzka." If not accidental, perhaps they are rather essential. The deep essence of the human being, so alluded to, is that man exists in the DIFFERENCE between one or many beings like and unlike – and being as such. The meta-physical wonder of this difference endows him with the question-able status ex-pressed in the words "I am"; this phrase is not at all synonymous with "being is" or "there is a being," and affects him much more intimately than those. But it affects him as a perplexity, a challenge, a quest – as a possibility emergent in time. The possibility sought in the difference is aimed between beings "without" – alien, not mine, in-different, and being "within" – there but unowned, not yet mine, differing from proper; it is aimed ap-propriatively toward my own being or being as my self. Yet it is but a possible quest, and at no time in human existence is being wholly owned.

What is the relevance of these meta-physical considerations to men's possible tragedy? It is this. Human pursuit of possible being has partial but indeterminate proprietary characteristics and thus yields the ambivalence of choice. It is false to say that tragedy is entirely created from "within" an individual self; and it is false to say that it is entirely adventitious from the world "without." How possible is ill-being for any man depends on the earlier suggested multiple factors in the sense of possibility. What is possible for you was analyzed to mean: what is becoming your power or control, what is like-ly and adaptable for your self, what is due to the hap-pening or mishap-pening of time. As you dis-cover being for your self you may or may not under-take the outward power of its coming into question, into decisive parting, into a breach; your inward order may persist or desist in the shattering of self-violence when the violent quest for being proves less or more like-ly than your self proper thus far. As your whole being is queried, more precisely: what being is yours – it should not be strange that the query also embraces what choice is yours in so entering ill-being. But this ambivalence of choice is most aggravated in the last of the factors of possible being, the temporal hap or mishap.

Aristotle was neither naive nor wrong when he described tragedy as misfortune; only the sense of "fortune" and "misfortune," arising from the present reflections, is not to be simply found in his words. Understanding tragedy as not determinable in or by events does not permit any such easy correlation as: when all happens well to a man. it is his fortune; when bad things happen, it is his mis-fortune and so tragedy. As one point, happenings need be neither good nor bad, since it is thinking that can make them so; as another, what is considered someone's good fortune, can ruin him; in contrast, whatever merely happens, in-differently, without being intimately chosen, is hardly tragic. The superficial identification of some sequence of events with fortune or misfortune, applied to a tragic story, cuts its hero away from any proper participation in it, changes him unheroically into a pathetic sheep-victim, and makes his striving for responsibility even in pain and danger apparently fanciful and absurd. Tragedy as understood here, is due to ill-being; but ill-being explodes the sane and sound norms of good and evil. Therefore what sane and sound observers may judge as good or evil events, as fortune or misfortune, need not be chosen as such in tragic protest. This does not mean that temporal hap-pening is quite irrelevant to the human being in becoming tragic. But it does mean that temporal hap or mishap encloses and discloses more than a scattered passage of events; it enfolds the tragic man's assimilation and appropriation of them, his vision, character and his choice of them for his ill-being. What hap-pens possibly to you is due to what you properly are, to what becomes your self, to what you choose to be in time: your possibility is the being you can own. Yet as long as you exist, you do not own it now, not at any now-moment; and you can not claim that you-already make happen the yet-coming. In the hap, it becomes your own, it becomes you; but not aside from the hap. Your being yields no substitute for time. Mis-hap is no less happening, events turning ill are wholly themselves as events; it matters not whether they are praised or blamed by others, whether you appear admirable or shocking in having them happen to you. What matters is whether and how they become your being, how they experience your fragile self, how you choose to appropriate them, how you are still there to own them. Because ill-being comes by violence, dis-order, im-property, and for the choice sought in it there may no longer be a choosing self. The possible range between the might of tragic greatness and the frailty of tragic mediocrity is indefinite; you and every other man belong to that range of human questionable ill-being.

MIS-FORTUNE in the stricter sense suggested here is not identifiable in any events just on account of their being criticizable as unpleasant, bad, disturbing or evil, by an in-different though sympathetic crowd of observers. Mis-fortune is determinable only by the man undertaking or under-going such events, and even by him in no ultimate terms: because mis-fortune is understood as such fortune, hap, or destiny, as can bring him to miss his own being – thus he could never determine it a posteriori. Such tragic destiny is possible for all men. But how possible it is for any particular man, what choice would be his in appropriating it, how much of tragic hap-pening must be made by him and how much for him – these questions cannot be decided here. They cannot, for various reasons. One is that tragedy is not a proper ground for blanket generalizations. Another reason is that the "amount" of choice in any human subject is hardly measurable; if it were, it would not belong to each man's unique horizon of possible being, a horizon vaster and deeper than the objective reality of entities surrounding him. And still another reason is that the question of possible or chosen destiny is submerged in the mysterious flow of thought about how being hap-pens to man in time. The exquisitely human possibilities of destiny, arising from the awareness of choice in being, can and need be reflected on by each man; but they cannot be determined in-differently for the human being as such. Ill-being can hap-pen to you, and your self can enter it ap-propriating; yet these two statements refer to one and the same existential possibility of your own. The hap of time is not exclusively yours, yet you belong to it with the whole choice that is yours. Thus there will never be a precise answer deciding how a man's tragedy might be "produced" all on his own or how it might be "induced" upon him by his fate, his devil or his god, Because tragedy, like all other possible destinies, issues from man's manifold ways of coming toward being in time.

The dark source of human tragic possibilities has been referred to as ill-being, in contrast to well-being. I have attempted this for the sake of suggesting to your imagination the radical distance and question-able distinction of men to whom tragedy hap-pens, compared to the norms natural, logical, moral, religious, aesthetic, prevailing amongst those who exist in well-being. This should by no means be conceived as an attempted bifurcation or exhaustive classification of being available to men. Being as the ground of what there is bears no number and under-lies all classes. All conceptual frameworks of human meta-physics are empty without it; but this does not imply that being provides determinate contents for meta-physical theories. So it is also with the imaginative suggestions of the preceding pages. The paradoxically ill-expressible ill-being issues in tragic protest, this has been claimed; but it has in no wise been claimed that it can have no other issue. The more so with regard to the "normal" well-being; aside from saying that it is not tragic, nothing has been said about it, and surely much could be. All the more open, orthodox and organized conquests of men rest on the ground of their quest for well-being. Reason and justice and happiness could never come to birth without some ap-propriation of order in the hap of time. The finality of death itself cannot abolish men's image of perfection, since it extends the finite perspective for perfecting life. But in their more or less happy striving, men's awareness of well-being need not and must not be uniform: their uniqueness provides the wealth of humanity. Therefore the notion of well-being is but a pale receptacle for the multiplicity of thoughts, feelings, and actions which all belong to it. In the context of my exploration it is not offered as a well-founded category but only as an indispensable brighter reflection surrounding the dark well for the tragic issues of ill-being. And to go further, the contradistinction of ill-being and well-being is in no sense ultimate or exclusive. Even in these approaches to tragic protest, allusions had to be made to being possible and real, being proper and improper, being human and superhuman or subhuman. Needless to say, the history of meta-physics could supply uncounted other instances of expressive grasp; and if one considers that all of them are fruits of con-ception of but a few thinkers in but a few centuries in flower, the manifold of future approaches defies the imagination. None of these terminological attempts must therefore be regarded as final determinations of being as such. Being is in them and equally beyond them: it is not de-terminable, manipulable, conquerable, as beings are. Individual finite men are thus in their human being subject to it: not as servants to a lord but not as lords of being, either, even if they should master all beings there are. Men's hold and belonging to being can be expressed by saying that all human concepts, images, enactments, records, discoveries, yield nothing but a differentiation of ways to be – of WAYS TO BEING. Not in the terminus but in the way is being faced by men. And since despite their dreams of rest, of position and safety, all men's ways to come toward being are temporal, therefore the question-able risk of being on the way is understood as becoming. One very human, dark and dangerous way to be in time has been pursued here through the ex-pression of tragic protest.

The tragic protest speaks of men in their being. If I have had any success in my efforts to elucidate the darker shades of this view, then therein you will find the justification of this existential exploration, undertaken imaginatively to bridge the superficial disconnection be-tween tragic fictions and tragic facts. I claim no definitive accomplish-ment yet I hope I have communicated to you some of my conviction that nothing less will do for the understanding of what is tragic but to explore the tragic human being as such.

The tragic protest speaks in words. This can make it for you questionable, ineffective, derivative – merely poetic. Yet words are not without real power, unless everything human is. Because whatever you think of as essentially human is not available without speech. If words are in one sense less than entities, in another sense they are more. Speech names, symbolizes, reflects entities, events, experiences, and it is naturally no substitute for them. Regarded as only a mirror of the objective contents of the world, speech can show various inadequacies. But speech belongs to its human subject – and how is the world available without him who avails himself of it through the power of words? Speech is not the human being; but it is its expression. In his own way of weaving, construing, adapting, correlating, selecting words, every man secures the horizon for his vision of truth, the appropriation of his character for what becomes his in existence, the making of his choice subject to the question of his being. No man could exist without some claim to truth, without striving for something of his own, without some question-ability. As this applies equally to every tragic human being, the speech of protest expressively collects and reflects their vision, character and choice. Their protest is what they genuinely have to say, being what they are; it is poetic in making their history be there in words; it is not their tragedy but it is its expression opening access to others. Only in a consenting approach to it you can come to know tragic being also possible for you.

The tragic protest speaks for and against. In its violence, in its dark ambiguity, in its rejection of so many entities, events, experiences, it does attest the being of the witness. Not happily, not serenely, not even rationally perhaps. He is, though, not quite as you are. The vision of the tragic hero you may never happen to see; the character in his making himself alone you may detest as alien; the choice he demands as freely his own you may renounce as determined. Yet these are what being puts in question for him; thus he exists in his protest, for his time. Happily, you may never enter his tragedy. But you may not deny him the property of his protest. Because like him, you are human and have to face being, for your time. And for every human existent, being is questionably at stake. For some, it happens – tragically.

Subject Index

Action 45–48, 55, 60, 65–67, 72, 77, 91–94, 112–115, 141, 184, 206, 252, 253, 258
Aesthetic 2–3, 12–13, 19, 83, 122, 172, 229, 230, 233, 274
Aloneness 40, 75, 139, 152, 157, 160, 180, 218, 267
Anxiety 62, 126–127, 214, 218
Appropriation 11, 13, 58, 94, 116, 136, 174, 184, 206, 207, 208, 212, 217, 223, 229, 232, 249, 254, 255, 257, 258, 260, 264, 267, 269, 272, 273, 274, 276
Being 22, 32, 85, 89, 118–119, 135, 171, 191, 216, 230, 231, 233, 235, 236, 242, 246, 247, 251, 252, 260–261, 261–276
Care 59, 103, 117, 126–129, 131–132, 137, 141, 182, 184, 186, 187, 188, 191, 258, 259, 261
Character 8, 12, 16, 232, 269, 273, 276; in Prometheus 36–40, Oedipus 54–58, Hamlet 73–79, Faust 108–115, Stockmann 145–150, 162–164, Loman 183–188, Orestes 203–212
Choice 14–16, 93, 110, 156, 195, 199, 216, 233, 264, 267, 269, 270, 271, 272, 273, 274, 276; in Prometheus 40–41, Oedipus 44–45, 56, 57, 60, Hamlet 88–96, Faust 118, 135–139, Stockmann 164, 169–170, Loman 175, 188, 191–192, Orestes 206, 212, 216–217, 220
Christianity 73, 74, 86, 100, 113, 119, 124, 130, 194, 198, 201, 246, 247, 248, 257, 258, 259
Comic 25, 47, 61, 84, 254
Conscience 64, 67, 72, 73, 75, 80, 85, 89–96, 158, 200, 203, 204, 211, 222, 232, 257, 261, 267
Contradiction 144, 169, 171, 266
Crowd 52–53, 77, 152–161, 173, 180, 189, 200, 201, 203, 219, 224, 228, 256, 259
Daring 30, 40, 85, 111, 117–118, 127, 141, 159, 204, 219
Death 25, 73, 80, 85–88, 117–118, 173, 190, 196, 197, 201, 213, 214, 215, 222, 224, 274
Defect 24, 36, 48, 56, 82, 90, 136, 170, 183, 205
Defiance 29–30, 33, 42, 119, 128, 196, 203, 257, 258, 260
Dramatic 4–10
Ethos 16, 90, 163, 178, 231, 237, 251, 265, 271
Events 6–9, 61, 113, 162, 228, 234, 245, 261, 263, 264, 269, 272, 273
Evil 37, 49, 78, 80, 84, 101, 103, 107, 130, 139, 141, 142, 161, 177, 188, 197–199, 205, 210, 217, 218, 222, 223, 224, 258, 273
Existence 18–19, 61, 80, 85, 92, 95, 106–107, 150, 163, 171, 176, 207, 208, 212, 215, 223, 225, 228, 252, 274, 275, 276
Fate 13, 29, 45, 51, 52, 60, 72, 101, 182, 195, 216, 274

Name Index

Achilles 73
Adam 37, 245, 247
Aeneas 240
Aeschylus 21, 28, 227
Alexander of Macedonia 240
Anaximander 37
Aristotle 22–27, 62, 108, 145, 204, 228, 244, 272
Bacon Francis 228
Baudelaire 255
Beauvoir Simone 177
Brutus 71, 240
Caesar 21, 240, 245, 256
Camus Albert 219
Cervantes 255
Charlemagne 240
Cicero 45
Conrad Joseph 60
Darwin Charles 247
Democritus 228
Descartes 121, 228, 241, 245, 257
Don Quixote 270
Dostoyevsky 22, 137
Dulcinea 21
Faust 21, 42, 59, 74, 83, 86, 97–142, 144, 145, 162, 164, 170, 175, 177, 179, 194, 197, 204, 207, 211, 212, 214, 219, 222, 229, 231, 232, 236, 237, 244, 245, 252, 258, 259, 261
Galileo 228
Goethe 21, 97
Greene Graham 22
Hamlet 19, 20, 49, 64–96, 104, 109, 112, 113, 116, 118, 122, 133, 135, 156, 158, 161, 183, 196, 204, 209, 212, 215, 219, 231, 232, 237, 243, 244, 252, 256, 257, 258, 261
Hegel 144, 247, 259
Heine 255
Hemingway Ernest 22
Heracles 240
Heraclitus 257

NAME INDEX

Socrates 19, 20, 51
Sophocles 44
Stockmann 143–171, 183, 203, 215, 219, 224, 231, 232, 236, 243, 252, 258, 261
Swift Jonathan 255
Tamerlaine 21
Tasso 255
Tiresias 47, 48, 50–52, 53, 54, 57
Tristan 240
Ulysses 19, 20
Vercors 33
Wagner Richard 107
Walter Mitty 270
Wotan 107
Zarathustra 201, 222
Zeus 27, 30–34, 42, 52, 101, 180, 194, 195–200, 203, 206, 208, 210, 211, 215, 216, 217, 218, 220, 221, 222

DATE DUE